The New
Urban Reality

PAUL E. PETERSON
Editor

The New
Urban Reality

THE BROOKINGS INSTITUTION
Washington, D.C.

11-15-87 sam

THE BROOKINGS INSTITUTION is an independent organization devoted to nonpartisan research, education, and publication in economics, government, foreign policy, and the social sciences generally. Its principal purposes are to aid in the development of sound public policies and to promote public understanding of issues of national importance.

The Institution was founded on December 8, 1927, to merge the activities of the Institute for Government Research, founded in 1916, the Institute of Economics, founded in 1922, and the Robert Brookings Graduate School of Economics and Government, founded in 1924.

The Board of Trustees is responsible for the general administration of the Institution, while the immediate direction of the policies, program, and staff is vested in the President, assisted by an advisory committee of the officers and staff. The by-laws of the Institution state: "It is the function of the Trustees to make possible the conduct of scientific research, and publication, under the most favorable conditions, and to safeguard the independence of the research staff in the pursuit of their studies and in the publication of the results of such studies. It is not a part of their function to determine, control, or influence the conduct of particular investigations or the conclusions reached."

The President bears final responsibility for the decision to publish a manuscript as a Brookings book. In reaching his judgment on the competence, accuracy, and objectivity of each study, the President is advised by the director of the appropriate research program and weighs the views of a panel of expert outside readers who report to him in confidence on the quality of the work. Publication of a work signifies that it is deemed a competent treatment worthy of public consideration but does not imply endorsement of conclusions or recommendations.

The Institution maintains its position of neutrality on issues of public policy in order to safeguard the intellectual freedom of the staff. Hence interpretations or conclusions in Brookings publications should be understood to be solely those of the authors and should not be attributed to the Institution, to its trustees, officers, or other staff members, or to the organizations that support its research.

Foreword

TWO TYPES of urban change have left America's older industrial cities in severe decline: technological innovations in transportation, communication, and manufacturing have made their infrastructure and land use patterns obsolete, and accelerating racial change has made inner cities the primary home for minority groups, particularly those with low incomes and poor job skills. The essays in this volume delineate those changes and consider which, if any, public policies can retard or reverse the cities' decline. The papers show the futility of federal actions designed to slow the technological changes that are contributing to a more decentralized pattern. Instead, the editor argues in his introduction that the most successful urban policies may not be specifically urban at all, but policies designed to encourage racial dispersion by increasing the choices available to minorities.

These papers were originally presented at a conference on "The Future of Our City" held at the University of Chicago under the joint auspices of the university's Committee on Public Policy Studies and the Law School. The conference was organized by Paul E. Peterson, the editor of this volume, who at the time was chairman of the Committee on Public Policy Studies and is now director of the Governmental Studies program at Brookings. The conference was sponsored by a grant from the law firm of Mayer, Brown and Platt in honor of the centennial of its founding. Explaining his firm's decision to commemorate its founding in this way, Leo Herzel, a partner, noted that "law firms—whose future is closely tied to that of large cities—must try to understand and improve the urban reality in which they find themselves."

Because of the location of the conference in Chicago, special attention was given to specific conditions in that city, but the authors did so in a context that examined the future of industrial cities more generally. The contributors to the volume differ in the weight they place on the significance of technological as distinct from racial change, and they do not all subscribe to the same policy prescriptions. But together the essays illuminate how these changes have combined to produce a new urban reality not clearly foreseen even two decades ago.

The editor wishes to thank the many people who contributed to the conference at which these papers were presented. In particular, he wishes to thank William C. Apgar, Walter Blum, Willard L. Boyd, Gerhard Casper, William Cousins, Jr., J. David Greenstone, Ronald E. Grieson, Daryl F. Grisham, Donald H. Haider, Deborah L. Haines, Leo Herzel, James H. Hodge, John F. Kain, Martin Kilson, Edmund W. Kitch, Ronald Krumm, Robert L. Lineberry, Louis H. Masotti, David J. Olson, John H. Perkins, Frances Fox Piven, Milton Rakove, David Segal, Richard P. Taub, J. W. Henry Watson, Bernard Weissbourd, and Franklin E. Zimring. Adele Pardee assisted in organizing the conference.

Research assistance at Brookings was provided by Alice G. Keck, James E. McKee, Todd A. Patterson, Felicia M. Widmann, and Nancy E. Withers, and secretarial assistance was provided by Pamela D. Harris, Janet Hathaway, Robert L. Londis, and Judith H. Newman. Nancy Davidson edited the papers, giving valuable assistance on both style and content. Thomas M. Guterbock and Gerald D. Suttles offered constructive comments on the papers as prepared for publication. Diana Regenthal prepared the index, and Nancy Snyder proofread the book.

The titles and affiliations of the authors of the essays included in the volume are as follows: Elijah Anderson, associate professor of sociology, University of Pennsylvania; Brian J. L. Berry, dean, School of Urban and Public Affairs, Carnegie-Mellon University; Terry Nichols Clark, professor of sociology, University of Chicago; Anthony Downs, senior fellow in Economic Studies, Brookings Institution; Herbert Jacob, Hawkins Distinguished Professor of Political Science and professor of law, University of Wisconsin at Madison; John D. Kasarda, professor and chairman of the Department of Sociology, University of North Carolina at Chapel Hill; Gary Orfield, professor of political science and public policy, University of Chicago; Kenneth A. Small, associate professor of economics, University of California at Irvine; and William Julius Wilson, Lucy Flower Distinguished Service Professor and chairman of the Department of Sociology, University of Chicago.

As in all Brookings publications, the interpretations, conclusions, and recommendations presented here are those of the authors and should not be ascribed to Mayer, Brown and Platt, to any other agency or foundation that funded research reported herein, or to the trustees, officers, or other staff members of the Brookings Institution.

BRUCE K. MACLAURY
President

February 1985
Washington, D.C.

Contents

Tables

Figures

PAUL E. PETERSON

Introduction: Technology, Race, and Urban Policy

THE industrial city has become an institutional anachronism. If the great manufacturing centers of Europe and the American Snow Belt developed as by-products of the industrial revolution, their decline is no less ancillary to contemporary technological change. The United States needs ever-fewer workers to produce the physical products it consumes but expects more service from workers as diverse as medics, therapists, short-order cooks, and security guards. Two to three decades ago urbanists sought to save the industrial city by redeveloping central business districts, or creating model cities that would transform poverty-stricken neighborhoods, or "energizing" citizens to participate in planning their community's future.[1] Few would venture to propose such schemes today. Quite apart from political changes that have occurred in Washington, economic and social changes have moved so far that reversing their direction no longer seems feasible or even desirable. Industrial cities must simply accept a less exalted place in American political and social life than they once enjoyed. Policies must adapt to this new urban reality.

But to say that the industrial city must adapt to late twentieth century realities is only the beginning, not the end, of the conversation. The essays included in this volume pursue this topic by examining the ways in which technological change and social relationships interact to generate a distinctively American set of urban problems. Although each essay has its own topic, together they ask the following questions: Is the industrial city declining because technological innovation has rendered its infrastructure

1. The word comes from an unpublished version of a poverty manual drafted by the Chicago Commission on Urban Opportunity, as cited in J. David Greenstone and Paul E. Peterson, *Race and Authority in Urban Politics* (University of Chicago Press, 1976), p. 20.

1

and land use patterns out of date and inappropriate for the late twentieth century economy? Or has the severity of racial distrust contributed to the decline of industrial cities by accelerating rates of change in both residential choice and employment opportunities? Can any set of public policies retard or reverse the decline of the industrial city? Are any of these policies the responsibility of the federal government?

The essays in this volume do not provide any single set of answers to these questions. The first two essays emphasize the underlying techno-logical, economic, and social processes that place definite limits to urban futures. John Kasarda portrays the dramatic population and employment shifts that have occurred and calls for smaller, livelier cities built around a service economy. Brian Berry then shows how marginal has been the gentrification countermovement that has restored historic neighborhoods in some cities to a new prominence. Islands of renewal they may have been, but they have occurred in seas of decay.

Elijah Anderson turns the discussion in a quite different direction with his finely tuned analysis of black-white relations in one of these gentrifying neighborhoods. His ethnographic analysis is given special meaning and poignancy by William Wilson's forceful reexamination of black family life, which argues that the very trends Patrick Moynihan lamented in 1965 have only accelerated in the two decades that have passed since that work was published. The segregated social and political context within which black families find themselves is then presented in bleak detail in Gary Orfield's case study of Chicago.

The final set of essays examines some of the policy responses that have been proposed. Kenneth Small concludes that changes in transportation policy can have only the most limited effects on the urban economy; Herbert Jacob casts doubt on the efficiency of increasing police expenditures as a way of reducing urban crime; Terry Clark provides an optimistic note by showing that cities can in fact keep their fiscal house in order, even if they must adapt to population loss and economic decline; and Anthony Downs concludes with a retrospective review of all the papers that at once despairs of the current racial dilemma and points with hope to developments within the black community.

As one can see from even this highly synoptic overview, the essays do not agree perfectly either on the nature of the problem or on the appropriate solution. But even though the information in these essays can be used to substantiate a range of policy positions, together they provide a distinctive perspective on the new urban reality of the 1980s. In this interpretive introduction I seek to show the interconnections among the essays and develop certain implications not specifically stated in any of them. My argument can be stated simply: Even though technological change is profoundly reshaping urban life in ways beyond the control of policymakers in a pluralist democracy, the deleterious side effects of technological change are exacerbated in perverse ways by continuing racial tension and conflict, a social fact that cannot be altered apart from decisive intervention by the federal government.

The Impact of Technology

More than any other factor, the pace and shape of technological innovation has given urban development its rate and direction. Cities of the Northeast and Midwest were formed along harbors, near river conjunctions, and along canal routes because water transport was so much more efficient and less expensive than movement over land. Convenient access to the fixed transportation grid that waterways provide came at a premium, and as a result dense configurations of commerce, industrial activity, and workingmen's neighborhoods huddled against the waterfront. When railroads were built, they typically complemented and enhanced transport by water. In many cities the railway ran along the lakeshore, seacoast, or riverfront. Consequently, rail routes typically reinforced the settlement patterns originally formed by rivers and harbors.

So potent were the joint effects of fixed rail and water transportation routes on the life and location of American cities that sociologists and economists developed theories of urban growth and land use that assumed (for purposes of analytic simplification) that the energy animating a city came from a single point at its core, much as the sun gives energy and direction to the planets and their moons orbiting around it.

The Solar Thesis

In sociology this solar understanding of urban processes was known as the concentric circle thesis (see figure 1), developed in the 1920s by what was known as the "Chicago school."[2] At the core of these circles was the

2. Ernest W. Burgess, "The Determinants of Gradients in the Growth of the City," *Publications of the American Sociological Society*, vol. 21 (1927); Robert E. Park, Ernest W. Burgess, and Roderick D. McKenzie, *The City* (University of Chicago Press, 1967); and Harvey W. Zorbaugh, *The Gold Coast and the Slum* (University of Chicago Press, 1929).

Figure 1. *Solar Diagram of Urban Form and Growth*

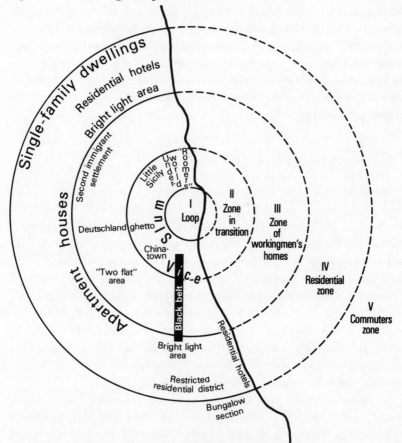

Source: Harvey W. Zorbaugh, *The Gold Coast and the Slum.* © University of Chicago Press, 1929.

central business district, located at the nexus of key transportation routes. Adjacent to the core, one typically found a transition zone consisting of specialty shops, skid rows, rooming houses for singles, and cheap housing for immigrants. These households and businesses were willing to tolerate the noise and pollution of the inner city either because they could not afford the transportation costs of a more distant location or because they wanted easy access to central-city services. Workingmen's apartments gravitated to the third ring; within the fourth lived middle-income people, leaving the outer circle to well-to-do managers and professionals. The latter enjoyed the space and greenery of suburbia because they could afford the time and money it took to commute long distances to the city core. The

Chicago school reached the conclusion that this outer ring could not be much more than forty-five minutes to an hour distant from the central business district because commuters were unwilling to spend much more than two hours a day traveling back and forth between work and residence.

The solar model of the city not only provided a map of its shape at a single moment, but it also provided a frame within which one could understand growth induced by technological change. As technology allowed greater density at the core and as the distance that commuters could travel within an hour greatly increased, the city exploded outward from the center at an astounding rate.

Even by 1920, when this model was first developed, it was apparent that the central business district itself expanded outward and upward, both because portions of the transition zone were converted to office space and industrial use and because skyscrapers were built as tall as technology and land values permitted. As the central core expanded, the density of residential land in outer circles typically decreased because innovations in transport enabled one-hour commuting from distances once thought to be beyond the influence of the central business district.[3] Streetcars and trolleys gave way to railroads and highways, which eventually were supplemented by expressways, bridges, and tunnels. People living not far from Philadelphia could suddenly contemplate commuting to New York; suburban neighbors in Maryland could be found working in either Baltimore or Washington; and Gary, Indiana, became a constituent component of the Chicago metropolitan area. The outer ring of the five concentric circles, which at the turn of the century was no more than ten miles from downtown, is today easily sixty miles from the center of big central cities.

As the central-city core expanded and the outer ring removed itself from the suburbs to the "exurbs," all other circles moved outward accordingly, producing patterns of change and transition that have often been the bane—and sometimes the hope—of urban neighborhoods. Apartments that once housed working-class families now house the poor and the transient. What was once regarded as professional housing became occupied by clerks and salesmen. The Poles and Italians, who once replaced the Irish and Germans, gave way to blacks, Hispanics, and Asians. Some inner-city neighborhoods have been abandoned altogether.

3. Edwin S. Mills, *Studies in the Structure of the Urban Economy* (Johns Hopkins University Press, 1972), pp. 48–49; and Barry Edmonston and Thomas M. Guterbock, "Is Suburbanization Slowing Down? Recent Trends in Population Deconcentration in U.S. Metropolitan Areas," *Social Forces*, vol. 62 (June 1984), pp. 905–25.

Although this solar model of urban form and development was first conceptualized by sociologists, urban economists writing in the 1950s and 1960s gave the model mathematical precision by positing that in a competitive market each parcel of land would be put to the use that yields the greatest return on investment.[4] Land at the center is especially valuable because many economic activities benefit from close access to the core of the transportation grid. As one moves outward from the center and the cost of transport increases, land falls in value. Activities less dependent on close proximity to the core migrate to these lower-rent neighborhoods. Economists tested this solar model by showing that land values fell, other things being equal, as one moved further from the core of the metropolitan area.[5] Not surprisingly, one also finds sharp, even exponential, declines in population density as one moves outward from the central business district. Where land is less expensive, it is used less intensively by both households and firms.[6]

The solar theory of the city was so attractive to its adherents that sociologists thought they were observing natural processes of human adaptation to their environment. Urban growth, invasion of neighborhoods by newcomers, and ethnic succession were said to be ecological processes, as a community gives up one set of inhabitants and activities for another. The study of human ecology was a discipline not fundamentally different from that of the ecologist of the forest, who observes the way in which changes in habitation alter the composition of the animal population. What happened in individual communities, solar theorists claimed, was only a gravitational response by residents to broader economic and social forces occurring in places far removed from the neighborhood.

This solar view of the city was qualified in various respects, of course. For one thing, many cities abut large bodies of water—oceans, the Great Lakes, expansive rivers—that break the circle or ring abruptly at a particular point (see figure 1). A seascape also enhances the attractiveness of residential

    4. Edwin S. Mills, *Urban Economics* (Scott, Foresman, 1972).
    5. Richard Muth, *Cities and Housing* (University of Chicago Press, 1969); Wallace E. Oates, "The Effects of Property Taxes and Local Public Spending on Property Values: An Empirical Study of Tax Capitalization and the Tiebout Hypothesis," *Journal of Political Economy*, vol. 77 (November–December 1969), pp. 957–71; and Harvey S. Rosen and David J. Fullerton, "A Note on Local Tax Rates, Public Benefit Levels and Property Values," *Journal of Political Economy*, vol. 85 (June 1977), pp. 433–40.
    6. Mills, *Urban Economics*, chap. 6; Thomas M. Guterbock, "The Push Hypothesis: Minority Presence, Crime, and Urban Deconcentration," in Barry Schwartz, ed., *The Changing Face of the Suburbs* (University of Chicago Press, 1976), pp. 137–61.

land immediately adjacent to it, and early sociologists were quick to observe that "coasts" in urban areas seemed almost to turn to "gold," as the very rich found select places that offered the opportunity of combining residential luxury with close proximity to work.[7] Finally, smaller nodes of economic activity, unusual land formations, and specific transport facilities could also bend or otherwise alter the shape of what were normally concentric circles.

The Sectoral Thesis

Less easily treated as a minor exception to the overall solar pattern was the tendency, noted even by early sociologists, for manufacturing activity to locate itself along transportation corridors rather than simply at the very center of the city. Although manufacturers needed large blocks of land in close proximity to the transportation grid, they had less demand for the high-priced land within the central business district than did those engaged in commerce and administration. As a result, many cities have always had industrial belts that connected to the water, rail, or highway network at some convenient point outside the city core. In quite another sector of the city, the highest-income communities tended to congregate together, extending across several, if not all, the concentric rings. Indeed, some analysts claimed cities were organized along sectoral lines that were structured by the overall transportation grid, not simply by the city center. Instead of appearing as a series of circles revolving around a central point, cities were best conceptualized as a series of bands or sectors differentiated by the specialized activity taking place within them.[8]

The sectoral model had many advantages. It accurately identified exceptions to the solar pattern; it showed the multiplicity of forces shaping urban growth and decline; it recognized that outcomes were the result of the voluntary decisions people had made;[9] and it allowed room for political

7. Zorbaugh, *The Gold Coast and the Slum.*

8. See Homer Hoyt, "The Pattern of Movement of Residential Rental Neighborhoods," in Harold M. Mayer and Clyde F. Kohn, eds., *Readings in Urban Geography* (University of Chicago Press, 1959), pp. 501 ff.; Walter I. Firey, *Land Use in Central Boston* (Harvard University Press, 1947); William H. Michelson, *Man and His Urban Environment: A Sociological Approach* (Addison-Wesley, 1970), pp. 3–32. See also the synthetic statement by Leo F. Schnore, "On the Spatial Structure of Cities in the Two Americas," in Philip M. Hauser and Leo F. Schnore, eds., *The Study of Urbanization* (Wiley, 1965), pp. 347–98.

9. Christen T. Jonassen, as quoted in William H. Michelson, "What Human Ecology Left Behind in the Dust," in Paul Meadows and Ephraim H. Mizruchi, eds., *Urbanism, Urbanization, and Change*, 2d ed. (Addison-Wesley, 1976), p. 68.

intervention to alter the shape of the city. Yet these virtues were also its limitations. Unlike the solar model, which identified fundamental forces at work—a growing central business district, technological change, and neighborhood succession—the sectoral model was unable to distinguish the pervasive from the idiosyncratic, the characteristic from the atypical, the rule from the exception. For these reasons, the solar thesis proved for decades to be too potent an explanatory model to be dislodged from its predominant intellectual position. But in the last quarter of a century technological developments have moved forward so swiftly that the solar system once created by the central business district "sun" has exploded into a mosaic of smaller constellations. The very technological development that seemed to have concretized the concentric circle model—the beltway or outer-ring expressway—greatly weakened the capacity of the center. The beltway did confirm the fact that cities had taken a circular form and that, given a specific distance from the center, particular transportation needs arose. But as the circular expressway was built, it created its own belt of industrial and commercial activity, which had a capacity for exchange completely bypassing the center. As Kenneth Small demonstrates, the more improved the beltway system became, the less need people had for the central city.

The beltway itself is just the surface manifestation of much deeper, more complex technological processes. The airport, the expressway, the air conditioner, the telephone, the computer, and a host of other innovations each contributed to the deconcentration of economic activity that has marked the past quarter of a century. In crucial respects all the United States is urban. Nearly every part is well connected to the nation's transportation and communication grid. Few places lack electrification, television, telephones, hospitals, or schools. Except for those desperate for high culture or haute cuisine, any region, town, or city can meet wants and needs as well as any other. Places are now so similar in all other respects that minor variations in climate can suddenly emerge as major determinants of economic activity.

Given these changes, one is tempted to restate the sectoral thesis by making an assumption exactly opposite to the one that ordinarily undergirds the solar model. Instead of assuming (for analytical purposes) that all economic activity takes place in the central business district, one might assume that economic activity is evenly (or randomly) distributed across a metropolitan area. Every point in the metropolitan area is equally proximate to the same number of equally desirable job opportunities. No location

has exceptional market value (as distinct from particular value to a specific
individual) because of its proximity to a node of economic activity. If this
model approximates reality, one would find no relationship between the
value of land and its distance from what used to be called the central
business district.[10] At least one study of western metropolitan land values
has shown that distance from the center no longer affects the value of
suburban housing. Instead, this and other studies show that housing values
are more a function of residential amenities—the level of air pollution, the
quality of local schools, the social standing of one's neighbors, and the
relationship between taxes paid and benefits received from one's local
government.[11]

The model still assumes that people want to live near their jobs. Yet
jobs have no effect on land values, because jobs are distributed evenly
throughout the metropolis. Under such circumstances the differential
availability of neighborhood amenities dominates the value of residential
land.

From a Solar to a Sectoral System

How fast is this country moving toward complete deconcentration of
economic activity within metropolitan areas? The answer to this question
requires a distinction among various kinds of activities. Retail trade is now
almost entirely decentralized. Shopping centers are splashed more or less
randomly across metropolitan areas; in most cities, downtown department
stores are no longer even the flagship stores of the firm. To the extent that
the central business district remains a center of retail trade, it is the specialty

10. From this assumption one moves easily to the conclusion that the distinction between
city and countryside breaks down and inhabitants disperse themselves evenly across the
nation. One can avoid such a conclusion by making the assumption that artificial or natural
barriers preclude job or residential location in a band of space surrounding the metropolitan
area, a not infrequent cause of metropolitan boundedness.

11. Henry O. Pollakowski, "Effects of Property Taxes and Local Public Spending on
Property Values," *Journal of Political Economy*, vol. 81 (July–August 1973), pp. 994–1003.
See also Oates, "The Effects of Property Taxes and Local Public Spending on Property
Values"; Rosen and Fullerton, "A Note on Local Tax Rates"; and Robert S. Bednarz, *The
Effects of Air Pollution on Property Values in Chicago* (University of Chicago Press, 1974).
Ridker and Henning found inconsistent relationships between housing values and distance
from the St. Louis central business district in 1960. The expected decline in value occurred
from the central business district to the city line, but after that the further away the community,
the more valuable was the property. Ronald G. Ridker and John A. Henning, "The Determinants of Residential Property Values with Special Reference to Air Pollution," *Review of
Economics and Statistics*, vol. 49 (May 1967), pp. 246–57.

shops that predominate, almost as if Ghirardelli Square has replaced Macy's. The trends in industrial activity are much the same. One does not need the central city to manufacture cars or clothes, bolts or belts, fans or furniture. On the contrary, labor costs, crime, inadequate parking, high taxes, poor schools, and cramped quarters induce many an industrialist to abandon the city for more hospitable quarters elsewhere. Over the next decade industrial employment as a percentage of the United States work force will undoubtedly continue to fall; more likely than not, central cities will bear more than their proportionate share of that decline.

Many believe that central business districts still have a comparative advantage as sites for banking, administration, and the exchange of professional services. As evidenced by the 1970s office boom in New York, Los Angeles, San Francisco, Chicago, and other regional centers, many corporate heads still believe that a central-city location facilitates effective administration of their firms. Kasarda maintains that face-to-face communication is essential for establishing the mutual trust necessary for complex negotiations among business and professional elites. Others argue that corporations are reluctant to forgo the prestige of a Fifth Avenue, La Salle Street, or Union Square address. Kasarda also points out that only big cities provide the restaurants, cultural activity, and night life that traveling executives expect as part of their business routine.

In an age where all locations are intrinsically of roughly equal value, prestige and extracurricular perquisites may count for much. Nonetheless, one also notes the growth of hotels, conference centers, and office buildings near airports and in the other outlying areas far from the city center. Many firms are also finding it possible to split the clerical and routine administrative tasks of their operations from the executive functions that may be more dependent on a central location. Although demand for central-city office space continues, the next office boom may be scattered far more widely than that of the 1970s. And even if a few cities like San Francisco, Boston, and New Orleans can build their economies around entertainment centers for executives and tourists, it is hardly a model that can be sustained on a massive scale.

The Policy Response

The decline of the older industrial city can thus be seen as little other than an unfortunate by-product of technological advance and economic success in a land-rich society. Americans now have the wealth and resources to live in less congested, cleaner, warmer, greener, and seemingly happier places. If the leaders of central cities lament the change, that is hardly sufficient grounds for active action to retard an otherwise desirable transformation. The cry for urban aid may simply be a plea from special interests—governments from declining regions and groups concentrated in particular areas. If the government responds to such demands of the League of Cities, it may simply perpetuate a pattern of resource allocation that individual Americans have said with their feet that they no longer wish to continue.

Terry Clark's work on fiscal strain lends credence to this line of argument. In his sophisticated analyses of the fiscal policies of a representative sample of American cities, Clark shows that local political factors are as much responsible for the fiscal well-being of cities as are any set of economic factors. His study demonstrates that local fiscal health consists of the ability to live within one's means and the capacity to keep short-term debt from becoming an escalating part of the city's budget. He shows that no specific level of per capita spending is necessitated by the governmental responsibilities of a particular locality. Above a certain threshold, there is no level of expenditure utterly required. Instead, as Jacob's work on police activity demonstrates, the amount of public services provided and the cost of delivering those services vary widely among American cities. Clark also shows that as cities lose their population, they can take steps to reduce their expenditures proportionately. While the processes of change may be conflictual and unpleasant for many of those directly engaged, there is now little doubt that cities can adjust their budgets to fiscal realities, just as households and firms find it necessary to take severe measures to avoid bankruptcy. Recent events seem to bear out Clark's analysis. Even in the face of major cuts in federal aid and shrinking tax revenues from recession-weakened local economies, cities have managed to keep their fiscal houses in order. "A couple of years ago, people were hysterical about local governments dropping like flies," commented one observer in late 1983. But, he continued, "that's just not the nature of the beast. They are going through tough political battles and cutbacks in services. But massive defaults and bankruptcies? No."[12]

A city's fiscal situation can be quite independent of its underlying economic well-being. Federal aid to cities may be welcomed by mayors

12. John E. Petersen, as quoted in Rochelle L. Stanfield, "America's Largest, Oldest Cities Seem to Have Found a Formula for Survival," *National Journal*, November 12, 1983, p. 2357.

eager to avoid tax increases and pressed by a multiplicity of demands for additional services. It is more difficult to show that federal aid to urban governments helps them forestall the exodus of people and firms. If technology is the only force shaping urban change, fiscal bailouts may be a helpful short-term transition measure, but they can hardly be the basis for a long-term federal policy. To justify governmental intervention one needs to examine other dimensions of the urban problem.

The Question of Race

Although technological innovation has shaped the course of American cities, it hardly seems to account for all the permutations that have occurred. Why is some land adjacent to the city center virtually desolate while other land, not far distant, is densely packed and overcrowded? Why do some neighborhoods deteriorate rapidly while others with similar housing stock and infrastructure maintain their solidity? Why do some cities lose population and firms at much more rapid rates than other cities no better placed in the nation's transportation system? Are cities declining because of social factors that operate independently of underlying technology? Specifically, has America's "peculiar" problem, the question of race, affected land use decisions in major metropolitan areas?

The Size and Shape of Racial Change

At least at the surface level it seems difficult to deny the importance of race for the pace and direction of urban change. In the past thirty years many American cities have dramatically changed their racial coloring. In the twenty largest cities of the Northeast and Middle West (hereinafter referred to as the Snow Belt cities) the white population fell by over 2.5 million, or 13 percent, between 1960 and 1970 and by another 4 million, or 24.3 percent, by 1980.[13] The black population in the same cities grew by 1.75 million (35.8 percent) in the first of these decades and by over

13. The cities are New York, Chicago, Philadelphia, Detroit, Baltimore, Indianapolis, Washington, Milwaukee, Cleveland, Columbus, Boston, St. Louis, Kansas City, Pittsburgh, Cincinnati, Minneapolis, Buffalo, Toledo, Newark, and St. Paul; data are taken from U.S. Department of Commerce, Bureau of the Census, *Census of Population*, 1960, vol. 1; 1970, vol. 1, pts. A and B; advance reports, 1970, series PC, sec. 1, pp. 1, 2, and PC, vol. 2, sec. 2, p. 51; 1980 supplemental reports, series PC, vol. 80, sec. 1, p. 5; and advance reports PHC, vol. 80-v.

Table 1. *Measures of Economic and Social Well-Being of Blacks and Whites in the Five Largest Metropolitan Areas of the Snow Belt, 1980*[a]

Percent unless otherwise indicated

Measure	White	Black	White-black difference
Median family income (dollars)	24,194	13,299	10,895
Income below poverty line	8.0	29.6	21.6
Adult population employed	58.3	46.4	11.9
Unemployment rate	6.4	15.4	9.0
Female-headed households with children under 18	13.9	51.7	37.8
Completed high school	70.2	56.3	13.9
Living in owner-occupied housing	60.8	36.3	24.5

Source: Chicago Urban League, "A Perspective on the Socio-economic Status of Chicago-area Blacks," November 1983.
a. New York, Chicago, Detroit, Philadelphia, and Boston.

200,000 (3 percent) in the most recent one. Reliable data on the size of the Hispanic population are more difficult to obtain, but Kasarda, using the best data available, reports that in the four largest cities of these regions the Hispanic population grew by nearly 400,000, or 26 percent. As a result of these changes, Snow Belt cities have become homes for racial minorities; in the twenty largest the white population in 1980 was only 53.8 percent. Clearly, the processes of urban decline have been accompanied by an equally profound process of racial succession.

That cities have become homes for blacks means that they have also become the residence for many of society's most unfortunate. Although differences in the social and economic well-being of urban whites and blacks are well known, their magnitude deserves emphasis. In the five largest metropolitan areas of the Snow Belt— New York, Chicago, Detroit, Philadelphia, and Boston—blacks consistently found themselves to be at a great disadvantage in 1980 (table 1). On the average, their median family income was little more than $13,000, while white income was over $24,000. The percentage of blacks living below the poverty line was 30 percent; for whites, only 8 percent. The percentage of adult blacks employed was 12 percentage points less than the percentage of adult whites employed. Nearly 52 percent of all black female-headed households have children under the age of 18, while fewer than 14 percent of comparable white households do. Urban blacks' households are less likely to include an adult male, and they are more likely to live in rented quarters.

William Wilson forthrightly delineates the magnitude of these and other racial differences in one of those rare essays that uses quantitative data to chilling effect. He details the problems of black unemployment, poverty, family disintegration, welfare dependency, and crime. Two decades ago one could optimistically believe that these problems would recede with the enactment of civil rights legislation, increased educational opportunities, affirmative action programs, and increased black political participation. In fact exactly the opposite has happened. Even though many of the better-educated black Americans have in the past quarter century become respected members of middle-class America, the well-being of black Americans as a whole has in many respects deteriorated.

It is this poor black population that has replaced a white population that has increasingly chosen to move to suburbs, small towns, and the Sun Belt. In 1980, 58 percent of all blacks in the United States lived in central cities of metropolitan areas, compared with 25 percent of all whites.[14] In the metropolitan areas of the Snow Belt, 77 percent of the blacks live in the central city, but only 28 percent of the whites do.

Solar and Sectoral Explanations of Racial Change

To explain disproportionate black concentration in central cities, economists have offered two distinct theories. The first explanation applies the solar theory to the question of residential location by race. People with higher incomes typically spend a higher percentage of the portion of their budget allocated for transportation and housing on housing expenditures than do those with lower incomes. In order to maximize the utility they receive from their transportation and housing budget, they accept the somewhat greater costs of transportation that come from distant commuting in order to obtain more housing on less expensive land (per square yard) on the periphery of the city. Low-income people crowd together in three-story walk-up apartments or in small bungalows behind steel fences on narrow lots nearer to the central business district because they must pay the cost of living on land that is more expensive per unit in order to keep their transportation costs relatively low. Because blacks have much lower incomes than whites, it is not surprising that they have concentrated themselves in the central city.

That explanation is particularly persuasive for historic residential settlement patterns. But in the past two decades job dispersion has occurred

---

14. Katharine L. Bradbury, Anthony Downs, and Kenneth A. Small, *Urban Decline and the Future of American Cities* (Brookings, 1982), p. 75.

at such a rate that it is no longer evident that an inner-city location reduces transportation costs. Indeed, Kasarda argues the opposite thesis: that blacks in the central city are increasingly isolated from new employment opportunities that are disproportionately to be found on the periphery.

Downs's alternative theory of residential location is a far more persuasive explanation for contemporary practice.[15] He notes that laws prohibit the construction of housing for low-income residents on the periphery of American cities (in contrast to many of the world's other cities, which are often surrounded by shanty towns or publicly subsidized worker housing). Zoning laws, building standards, sanitation requirements, and sheer racial discrimination preclude the construction of substantial amounts of housing for low-income minorities in outlying areas. Subsidies for low-income housing are seldom, if ever, provided by state or local governments, and federal efforts to construct decentralized subsidized housing are sporadic, token, and generally ineffectual. Also, the multitude of suburban governments, each responsible for their particular community but insensitive to the welfare of the metropolitan area as a whole, creates a powerful institutional barrier to such action.

With access to the periphery foreclosed to low-income blacks, they secure housing in urban areas in the one place it is available: the older housing stock of central cities. Building codes are less rigorously enforced for existing housing stock than for new housing. Older homes can be allowed to deteriorate slowly until their quality makes them attractive only to those with low incomes. As low-income blacks move into such neighborhoods, their presence causes the value of property in the surrounding area to fall even further. It is thus the restrictions on the construction of low-income housing on the periphery of the metropolitan area that encourage concentrations of minorities at the center.

Downs's explanation of racial concentration has much in common with the sectoral explanation of urban development, because it argues that the location of the black poverty sector is a function of political decisions, not a product of anything inherent in urban growth. The sectoral view is especially persuasive when applied specifically to the allocation of land use between black and white Americans. As Orfield's case study of segregation in Chicago graphically demonstrates, blacks and whites usually concentrate separately in large bands or sectors of the city, producing vast territories of segregated living. I have already mentioned the fact that metropolitan

15. Anthony Downs, *Neighborhoods and Urban Development* (Brookings, 1981), chap. 7.

blacks in the Snow Belt are nearly three times as likely to live within the central city as are urban whites. Within the central city, too, blacks and whites live in separate areas. Even after the passage of numerous civil rights acts, central-city housing was nearly as segregated in 1970 as it had been in 1960.[16] A more recent study of Chicago that used 1980 census information found that over 85 percent of the black population of the city lived in precincts (areas that typically include three to four city blocks) that were racially homogeneous (90 percent or more black).[17] Neighborhoods containing both blacks and whites are usually communities undergoing processes of racial transition.

Ethnic transition, to be sure, has been the norm in urban areas since the late nineteenth century, as the solar theorists clearly recognized. Each period of transition was marked by a sense of loss on the part of established residents, perceptions of invaders as morally and intellectually inferior, and overall gloom about processes of decay and deterioration. But even when the similarities of racial change today to ethnic change in the past are recognized, certain poignant differences remain. Except in unusual circumstances, racial change is more rapid, more dramatic, and more conflictual than other ethnic successions. The newcomers are more visible, suffer from more severe stigmatization, are perceived as culturally more different, and are regarded as more threatening.

Even under the best of circumstances the intergroup tension between urban blacks and whites is intense. Elijah Anderson's ethnographic analysis brilliantly captures the suspicious interracial mood that prevails even when one could hardly expect more harmonious conditions: the whites, not the blacks, are the invaders; their arrival portends rising, not falling, property values; the whites are young, upwardly mobile, liberal, avant-garde, and tolerant to the point of avoiding race-specific language when referring to unpleasant incidents ("kids" and "toughs"; not blacks, Negroes, or much worse); and middle-class blacks work cooperatively with whites in community organizations. Even under these circumstances, as Anderson relates, there are fears and uncertainties that govern relations on the neighborhood's streets, playgrounds, and other public places. Streets are crossed at the sight of strangers; eyes are raised and lowered circumspectly; parking places are selected with care; and particular times of the day are regarded

16. Annemette Sorensen, Karl E. Taeuber, and Leslie J. Hollingsworth, Jr., "Indexes of Racial Segregation for 109 Cities in the United States, 1940 to 1970," *Sociological Focus*, vol. 8 (April 1975), pp. 125–42.

17. Election Data Services, "Analysis of Redistricting Plan" (Washington, D.C., 1981).

as dangerous. As Anderson shows, these street relations spill over into other neighborhood conversations and practices.

In the more usual circumstances of neighborhood transition, the prospects for intergroup relations are much worse: older, conservative, working-class whites suffer the loss of their community's streets and institutions to young black families of moderate to low income; property values fall; segregation of neighborhood associations and informal meeting places is virtually complete; and one hears frequent, if semiprivate, expression of racial slurs. Under these circumstances, streets are abandoned after daylight hours, steel fences are erected, watchdogs bark viciously, organized gangs patrol school grounds, large real estate signs proclaim the fears of others, bankers withdraw financial support, reports of rapid increases in crime circulate through the neighborhood, and closeout sales are held by local businesses.

Too often the explanations for these processes of racial change take the form of blaming one racial group or another. Whites are said to be intolerant, or blacks are called intolerable. If one or both of these claims were correct, then the problem could be left to churches, schools, and other civilizing institutions, as, indeed, some political leaders would do. But, unfortunately, the reality is so much more complex that it leaves individuals— both white and black—entrapped by a social phenomenon that cannot be addressed apart from political leadership and coordinated effort.[18]

Consider first the question of white intolerance. Some whites think that blacks are less able, less ambitious, and undesirable neighbors and playmates for their children. Yet most whites also make distinctions among blacks, recognizing the obvious fact that these characterizations cannot be universally applied. And most whites accept that black people, like themselves, have the constitutional right to enjoy educational opportunities, employment, and access to housing without regard to their racial background. The vast majority of whites say they do not object to a limited number of black families living nearby, especially if they are law-abiding, respectable ones, but, on the other hand, a majority of whites admit they would move from a neighborhood that is predominantly black, if only because they believe that in such a case they could not avoid those blacks whose behavior they deplore.[19]

The arrival of a few blacks in a neighborhood is generally thought to

18. Thomas C. Schelling, *Micromotives and Macrobehavior* (Norton, 1978), chap. 4.

19. "A Question of Race," *Gallup Opinion Index*, report no. 160 (Princeton, N.J., November 1978), p. 25.

portend the appearance of more. In the first stages of transition the emigration of whites from the area may be due to nothing more unusual than the normal turnover of housing.[20] But with the winds of racial transition in the air, it becomes difficult to get newcomers to purchase homes in a community whose future has become suspect. It may be harder to get a loan, and real estate brokers may propose alternative neighborhoods with a more promising future. Buying a home is the single largest investment most Americans make, and they are well advised to do so prudently. The family that avoids a neighborhood showing the earmarks of racial transition may do so for reasons that have little to do with their own racial beliefs.

Yet it does not take long for a pattern of such decisions to develop a momentum of its own. What began quite innocently turns into a panic. As young black families replace older white ones, the racial composition of the neighborhood school changes rapidly (even when neighborhood change itself is quite incremental). Homeowners watch property values drop as their neighbors try to sell their houses to the few white prospects still willing to take a chance. As more of the sales involve racial transition, people begin to wonder whether they will be the last to move. Just as people sell in a bear market so as to avoid still further losses, so homeowners sell their homes just to get out of the neighborhood. As Orfield points out, too much has probably been made of the power of those nefarious real estate brokers who "bust blocks" by selling homes to one or two black families, buying out the remaining white homeowners, and then turning a handsome profit on the exchange. Where the conditions for panic exist, entrepreneurs capitalize on them. Without those conditions, panic peddlers either lose money or pursue another trade.

This pattern of costly racial succession can occur even when each and every white participant is acceptant of at least some black neighbors. Even liberals can believe that their neighbors are intolerant or that bankers are discriminating or that real estate brokers are panic peddlers. If they think any or all of these things, they may feel that it is only heroic and utopian to oppose broad forces over which they have no control. Indeed, inner-city residents have often heard anecdotes about activists who aggressively preached the virtues of integrated neighborhoods one week only to announce the next that "circumstances" forced them to sell their home. Usually the tales are told as exposés of hypocrisy; in fact they are testimony

---

20. Harvey L. Molotch, *Managed Integration* (University of California Press, 1972), chap. 8.

to the helplessness of individuals in a social context not of their making—
nor, conceivably, of anyone's.

If the problem cannot be simply laid on the white person's doorstep,
can it be attributed to black people instead? As William Wilson shows,
blacks are far more likely to be arrested and convicted for crimes against
person and property. But ironically, the very black families seeking housing
in white neighborhoods are least likely to warrant such concern. It is the
intact, middle-class, upwardly mobile, two-income black family that has
the resources to rent or purchase property in a predominantly white
neighborhood.[21] The search by these blacks for integrated housing is often
motivated by a desire to move into a safer, quieter, more attractive community. Middle-class blacks select transition areas not only because they
find many suburban areas all but excluded to them, but also because they
prefer living in integrated neighborhoods rather than overwhelmingly
white ones. In the twenty metropolitan areas of the Snow Belt, 70 percent
of blacks who purchased a single-family home in 1980 chose a central-city
location (for whites, the comparable figure was only 20 percent). The black
middle-class families moving into previously all-white neighborhoods are
typically as eager to maintain neighborhood standards as the property
owners who preceded them.

Community problems arise from the secondary consequences of racial
transition. As whites avoid neighborhoods that have attracted black residents, community institutions weaken and property values fall. As black
residents participate routinely in neighborhood activities, other blacks,
not necessarily neighborhood residents, use the facilities of the integrated
neighborhood, which are often of better quality than those within the black
ghetto. Under the cover of quite ordinary and acceptable social practice,
an underground economy may arise. The very outcome everyone wishes
to avoid becomes increasingly probable in spite of the residents' intentions.
While the only thing to fear is fear itself, its presence casts a frightening
shadow indeed.[22]

Impact of Race on Urban Decline

I have discussed neighborhoods and communities, but what can be
closely observed one block at a time has repercussions for entire cities and

21. Downs, *Neighborhoods and Urban Development*, chap. 7.
22. Schelling, *Micromotives and Macrobehavior*, chap. 4.

counties as well. As blacks left a depressed rural South, they moved to particular cities either because their growing economies needed semiskilled and unskilled workers (Detroit, Oakland, Newark, and Gary), or because they were located on convenient transportation routes (Philadelphia and Chicago), or because they bordered the rural areas where blacks had always been concentrated (Baltimore, St. Louis, and Atlanta).

In the face of substantial black in-migration, whites left cities at a disproportionately rapid rate. In a major study, Bradbury, Downs, and Small analyzed economic and racial factors affecting central-city decline. They discovered that both between 1960 and 1970 and again between 1970 and 1975 the higher the percentage of blacks in a city, the greater its population loss to its suburban hinterland. They also found that the greater the number of suburban governments, the greater the exodus from the city. In addition, whenever suburban areas were served by one or more school systems different from the central-city school system, the city's population loss was greater.[23] What makes these findings especially striking is that they show the independent effect of race on urban decline, even after the effect of a wide variety of economic factors, such as transportation facilities, housing stock, and per capita income, has already been taken into account.

A few statistics displayed in table 2 emphasize the significance of the racial factor. Growing cities in expanding metropolitan areas experienced an actual decline of 0.4 percent of their black population between 1960 and 1970, to 14.5 percent. But the declining cities in declining metropolitan areas witnessed a 7.8 percent increase in their black population over the same period; by 1970 the percentage had reached 27.4 percent. This pattern has continued through 1980. In the twenty Snow Belt cities, the thirteen with a black population of 20 percent or more in 1970 lost an average of 16.6 percent of their total population in the ensuing decade. The seven cities with a black population of less than 20 percent suffered a total population loss of only 8.6 percent.

23. Bradbury, Downs, and Small, *Urban Decline*, chap. 5. In another attempt to compare the relative effects of racial factors affecting the rate of suburbanization (as distinct from technological ones), Marshall finds the percentage of blacks, the frequency and intensity of racial conflict, and crime rates to be positively associated with white suburbanization. The author regards those factors to be relatively unimportant compared with what he regards as the "pull" of new housing and new jobs in the suburbs. But these "pull" variables are endogenous factors as much affected by suburban migration as the cause of it. Harvey Marshall, "White Movement to the Suburbs: A Comparison of Explanations," *American Sociological Review*, vol. 44 (December 1979), pp. 975–94. Also see Guterbock, "The Push Hypothesis."

Table 2. *Racial and Ethnic Characteristics of Central Cities, 1960–70*

City description	Number of cities	Percentage of population black, 1970	Change in percentage of population black, 1960–70	Percentage of population Hispanic, 1970
All cities in sample	121	18.7	2.8	6.1
Growing city in growing SMSA	44	14.5	−0.4	11.0
Stagnant city in growing SMSA	32	18.0	2.1	2.7
Severely declining city in growing SMSA	19	24.0	6.2	3.4
Stagnant city in declining SMSA	11	16.1	4.8	5.5
Severely declining city in declining SMSA	15	27.4	7.8	2.7

Source: Katharine L. Bradbury, Anthony Downs, and Kenneth A. Small, *Urban Decline and the Future of American Cities* (Brookings, 1982), p. 75.

Future Trends in Racial Change

Some believe that the racial problem in central cities is likely to recede even without vigorous policy intervention. As Wilson points out, immigrant groups have generally encountered the greatest resistance whenever in-migration was continuing at a rapid rate. As newcomers sought a niche in the urban economy, they were overwhelmed by the waves of compatriots coming after them. In the case of blacks, the toeholds they had carved out between the wars were hardly adequate to bear the traffic that cities experienced in the postwar period. But in recent years, the rate of black in-migration has declined sharply. In the twenty Snow Belt cities the black population, which had increased by 35.8 percent in the 1960s, grew by only 3 percent in the 1970s. Actual declines can be expected in the 1980s. Perhaps the flow has peaked; perhaps Hispanics are now the group of greatest concern.

The flow of Hispanics to urban America is certainly among the most significant changes occurring in the 1980s. But it is just as possible that Hispanics will overtake blacks in the struggle for place and position in American society as that they will replace them at the bottom rung of the ladder. Hispanics do not carry the stigma of slavery; they subdivide into a multiplicity of nationality groups, each with its own heritage and identity; like immigrants in the past, they are likely to be among the most ambitious and industrious of their people; and they are varied in skin color and national identity and can physically blend into the hues of European immigrant groups relatively easily. Already it is clear that Hispanics are residentially less segregated than blacks. One study of thirty-five cities in the Southwest found that Mexican-Americans were less segregated from whites than blacks were.[24] Similarly, an analysis of 1980 census data for Chicago found that only 3.4 percent of the city's Hispanics lived in precincts that were ethnically homogeneous (compared with 85.2 percent for blacks), and 50 percent of the Hispanics lived in precincts in which they were less than half the precinct's population.[25] Hispanics also live in growing cities in prosperous parts of the United States. There is no evidence that their presence adversely affects the urban economy; on the contrary, according to one statistical analysis, they have a stimulative effect.[26] Also, compared with blacks, Hispanic families are more likely to have both a male and female parent in the home; childbirth comes at a later age for a Hispanic woman; and their rate of intermarriage with whites is higher.[27] Perhaps the economic and social position of Hispanics will deteriorate as immigration rates accelerate, but it is equally plausible that the language barrier will prove less severe than the color barrier.

One might also hope that as black in-migration to urban areas slows or even reverses itself, the pressure on transition zones will disappear. Even if segregation cannot be moderated, the uncertainties and conflicts experienced in border areas may subside. But a continuing black demand for additional housing in new areas is to be expected, in large part because blacks will seek to upgrade the quality of their housing. Berry estimates

24. Leo Grebler, Joan W. Moore, and Ralph C. Guzman, *The Mexican-American People: The Nation's Second Largest Minority* (Free Press, 1970), pp. 286–87.

25. Election Data Services, "Analysis of Redistricting Plan."

26. Bradbury, Downs, and Small, *Urban Decline and the Future of American Cities*, chap. 5.

27. Robert Michael and Nancy Tuma, "Entry into Marriage and Parenthood by Young Men and Women: The Influence of Family Background" (University of Chicago, National Opinion Research Center, August 1984).

that urban housing stock has a half-life of fifty years. Since much of the housing stock occupied by blacks is older than that, it is the housing in black neighborhoods that is most likely to be vacated, demolished, or abandoned. As this housing is removed from the housing stock, blacks search for better homes, whites move away in anticipation of black encroachment, and the cycle of urban succession continues. It is unlikely that the slowdown in black migration to urban areas can alone resolve the racial dimensions of the urban problem.

Berry's insightful analysis of the processes of gentrification also casts doubt on any expectation that market forces alone can reverse the processes of urban decay. He shows first how limited and isolated the urban pioneer movement has been. Young, childless professionals who prefer downtown socializing to backyard barbecuing will continue to seek homes in selected neighborhoods that contain prime-quality older housing stock (which when remodeled can be said to be "restored"), especially if these neighborhoods are adjacent to central business districts enjoying a growth in administrative and professional services. Yet these islands of renewal, as Berry rightly describes them, occur within seas of decay. Indeed, it is the rampant collapse of many neighborhoods throughout the central city that seems to allow one or two to revive. Once decay has spread so rapidly and widely, desirable homes are so distant from the core and so expensive to acquire that middle-class households less dependent on schools, parks, and child-oriented recreation centers find it worthwhile to invest in selected inner-city neighborhoods. The urban pioneers are to be congratulated for their shrewdness, hard work, perspicacity, and racial toleration, but they can hardly be heralded as redeemers that will allow the city to be reborn.

Nor can one assume that overall economic growth will automatically have secondary consequences beneficial to urban areas. As desirable as growth otherwise may be, technological innovation and economic prosperity only accelerate processes of urban change. As people are able to earn more, they have the resources to move. Because land is relatively inexpensive, people can buy new housing elsewhere and firms can construct new plants in different locations. Because the country is large, its citizens can run from one another, and they can (for a time) escape their racial dilemma instead of addressing it.[28]

28. The United States is one of the most sparsely populated industrialized countries of the world. In comparison with an average density per square mile of 256 in Europe and 825 in Japan, the 225.2 million people in the continental United States in 1980 were spread across 2,964,000 square miles, yielding an average of only 76 inhabitants per square mile. To be

A Nonurban Policy for Urban America

Addressing the urban race problem does not mean Band-Aids should be devised to help out particular declining cities. Revenue sharing merely lightens the local fiscal burden; it does not touch underlying social processes. Community development programs may be of help to particular cities or neighborhoods, especially if they capture the lion's share of available federal funds. Urban enterprise zones may resuscitate individual neighborhoods by relieving businesses of a variety of regulatory and tax burdens and by subsidizing their operations in other indirect ways. But these kinds of policies only shift problems from one neighborhood to another or from one city to the next. Also, programs designed to help communities may help the property owners living in them but not necessarily other residents of those areas.[29] To the extent that a community is renewed, rehabilitated, or gentrified, its land increases in value. While landlords are delighted, tenants—whether they be firms or individuals—only pay more rent, and current residents give way to more prosperous ones able to afford the benefits the renewed community can offer.

I do not wish to discourage cities and neighborhoods from using their own resources to improve the quality of life in their community. Urban redevelopment projects, tax incentives for firms, improved police protection, cleaner and more attractive parks, and better schools can all be ways of reviving the central city. Yet such advice is more well-meaning than helpful. Often when cities are not effectively pursuing such goals, it is because their market position is too weak or their internal political conflicts too intense to permit leaders to pursue an appropriate strategy. Or, equally likely, the capacity for effective action may be beyond available knowledge. As Jacob shows in his study, greatly increased police expenditures have hardly improved the ability to reduce crime.

But I do wish to discourage the federal government from attempting to

---

sure, many of these miles are available only for low-density use. But even if one considers population densities within the heavily urbanized coastal regions of the United States (thereby excluding not only mountains and deserts but also some of the richest agricultural land in the world), the density is still less than that of all Europe and less than half that of Germany, Belgium, and the United Kingdom. Such a low density means that land in the United States is relatively inexpensive.

29. See Edwin S. Mills and Wallace E. Oates, "The Theory of Local Public Service and Finance," in Edwin S. Mills and Wallace E. Oates, eds., *Fiscal Zoning and Land Use Controls* (D.C. Heath, 1975), pp. 1–12.

give aid to cities for programs they can best do themselves. Each city has to decide for itself how best to attract residents and firms. Since the correct strategy varies from place to place, it is best developed at the local level where people have intimate knowledge of the factors most likely to affect success. Federal mandates are likely to be inappropriate to many of the contexts in which they are applied. If it is a matter of local political leadership, federal subsidies can hardly supply that; indeed, they may simply be used to entrench incompetents already in office.

Instead of developing remedies on behalf of urban areas, the federal government should concentrate its attention on policies that have no specifically urban component to them at all. In doing so, it would continue a well-established tradition of shaping urban futures largely through programs whose ostensible purpose was utterly different. Consider, for example, the role the federal government has played in establishing an intercontinental highway system, an integrated system of airways, a national banking system protected by the Federal Reserve Board, a rural electrification system, inexpensive water for arid areas through a system of dams and canals, housing for veterans and other homeowners, a national higher educational system, and a national system of medical care, disability insurance, and social security. Amenities once available only to urban Americans are now to be found almost everywhere—in large measure because the federal government required, financed, or otherwise encouraged a relatively uniform set of national standards and services.

Many of these uniformities helped to create the conditions under which urban deconcentration could occur. Without these programs, the movement of jobs and people to suburbs and exurbs, and to small towns and sunnier places, is simply inconceivable. One need not condemn these programs to observe that they have for decades influenced and shaped the course of population movements in the United States.

Yet there is one arena—welfare provision for the neediest segments of the population—in which the federal government has hesitated to establish a uniform set of guidelines and policies. At a time when the federal government, through the programs just listed, was enabling most American firms and workers to choose from an ever-wider array of locales the site best suited to their tastes and needs, one segment of the population—those dependent on welfare—was refused the same degree of flexibility and choice. Instead, the government has permitted and financed a system that encourages the neediest groups in the population to remain isolated in racially segregated areas within the nation's central cities.

The best urban policy, and the one most in keeping with American traditions, would thus not focus on the special needs of particular cities at all. Instead, it would be directed toward dispersing racial concentrations by increasing the choices available to racial minorities. The most direct method, of course, is that offered by Gary Orfield: a coherent, metropolitan plan for housing and school integration that would eliminate race as a factor in neighborhood selection. The advantages of such a policy are legion. It accords with the constitutional requirement forbidding discrimination on the basis of race. Metropolitan plans, compared with desegregation plans carried out solely within central cities, leave fewer opportunities for white flight from integrated settings. Also, the racial proportions within schools can be more balanced if the white population from the entire metropolitan area is included in the plan. In many cities the distances students need to be bused can be reduced, because many parts of black communities are closer to white suburbs than to white portions of the central city. Integrated neighborhoods can be excepted from a busing plan, thereby enhancing their attractiveness and stability. Communities might also accept modest amounts of low-income, racially integrated housing as the price for minimizing involvement in busing programs. Over time, one might begin to realize what now seems only utopian: an integrated neighborhood school.

But, as Downs points out in his concluding essay, this plan, though noble, is hardly practicable. Although some progress has been made since the Brown decision in 1954, most central cities and their schools are as segregated thirty years later as they were the day the Supreme Court declared such practice unconstitutional. A national urban policy based primarily on a campaign for comprehensive desegregation seems as doomed today as it has been in decades past.

The difficulties stem in part from the massive array of institutions through which a desegregation policy must be promulgated. Federal efforts to desegregate metropolitan areas require the support of the courts; the coordinated efforts of numerous branches of the federal government; the cooperation of central cities, suburbs, and states; and the participation of a plethora of other groups and agencies. Opportunities for delay, obstruction, and a mobilized opposition are numerous. The tendency to compromise leads to token, incremental change, which is often counterproductive.[30]

Centralized administration of the nation's welfare system provides an

30. Jennifer L. Hochschild, *The New American Dilemma* (Yale University Press, 1984).

alternative mechanism for grappling with the urban problem. Currently, welfare provision for low-income families is closely connected to residence in a particular locale. Even though the federal government pays for nearly 70 percent of the costs of public assistance, almost half of all health and medical costs, and 55.5 percent of other social welfare expenditures, many, if not most, of the regulations determining eligibility requirements and benefit levels are written by state and local governments.[31] Federal money is given to states, counties, and localities to be distributed according to locally defined criteria and principles. As a result, the country permits national resources to be allocated according to the political whims of specific states and communities.

At one time local communities were more or less separate from one another, and each state and community needed to design health, welfare, and social service policies that fit their distinctive economic practices and social mores. But today the very technological changes in transportation and communication that contributed to the urban problem have also integrated local and regional economies to the point where welfare policy can no longer be adequately designed and financed locally. The Reagan administration argued in 1982 that at least in the case of medicaid it is inappropriate for the federal government to bear program cost without also assuming responsibility for program administration as well. In my view, the case for federal assumption of both costs and program responsibilities is no less strong in the welfare policy arena.

It is said that federal assumption of welfare and medical costs would either raise benefits in southern and rural areas or reduce benefits in northern urban areas. It is further claimed that a single national policy could not take into account differential costs of living or wage levels in urban and rural areas and in different regions of the country. However, current interstate variations in the level of welfare benefits range as widely as 490 percent, even though wages for unskilled workers vary by no more than 220 percent from the highest to the lowest wage area of the country. Stated in less extreme terms, 90 percent of the wage areas of the United States sampled by the Bureau of Labor Statistics pay unskilled workers an amount within 30 percent of the national average, but only 58 percent of the states sustain welfare families at a level within 30 percent of the national average payment.[32]

---

31. Alma W. McMillan and Ann K. Bixby, "Social Welfare Expenditures, Fiscal Year 1978," *Social Security Bulletin*, vol. 43 (May 1980), p. 11.

32. Thomas R. Dye, "Party and Policy in the States" (Florida State University, Policy Studies Program, February 1984), table 1.

A measure of the variation in per capita income among the fifty states declined from 24.4 in 1950 to 14.1 in 1980, but the same measure showed an increase from 29.3 to 34.1 in the variation in monthly welfare benefits to families with dependent children over this same period.[33] Clearly, state and local control of welfare has had effects well beyond a mere regional adjustment for differential economic conditions. If regional cost-of-living considerations are of great concern in conjunction with this program (though treated as irrelevant by social security), they could be taken into account by a federal program that explicitly allows benefits to vary with local variations in the cost of living or with wage levels for unskilled workers.

Under current arrangements welfare recipients and others in need of medical and social services have strong incentives to locate or remain in urban areas where benefit levels are higher. As Terry Clark has shown, a 10 percent increase in welfare benefits increases net black in-migration into cities by about 1 percent.[34] A uniform set of welfare and medical policies would remove these incentives. Of course, one would not expect their promulgation to result in an overnight exodus of poor people from central cities, but just as the elderly (who no longer need to locate in any particular place to receive governmental help) have shown a preference for smaller, less densely populated communities, one might expect to see a similar trend among other individuals lacking an economic incentive for an urban location.

33. Data on 1977 wage differentials are for seventy-three metropolitan areas and ninety-three service contract areas, which include rural and semiurban locations outside major metropolitan areas. U.S. Department of Labor, Bureau of Labor Statistics, *Area Wage Surveys: Metropolitan Areas, United States and Regional Summaries, 1977*, bulletin 1950–77 (Government Printing Office, 1980), pp. 94–97.

Data on welfare assistance represent the average monthly amount of aid a family receiving aid for dependent children received in 1980, by state, for the fifty states, as reported in the *Social Security Bulletin*, vol. 45 (April 1982), p. 35. The average payment in California is $431 per month, 4.9 times as much as the average payment of $87.80 in Mississippi. The coefficient of variation for wages is 0.20; for welfare it is 0.38. Within states there can be considerable variation in assistance levels by county, and the number of observations of welfare policies is less (50) than the number of observations of wage levels (166). As a result, I have underestimated the extent to which welfare policies range more widely than wage differentials. Location makes even more of a difference in the amount of welfare benefits one receives than these figures imply.

34. Terry N. Clark and Lorna C. Ferguson, *City Money: Political Processes, Fiscal Strain, and Retrenchment* (Columbia University Press, 1983), pp. 214–16. Also see Richard J. Cebula, "Local Government Policies and Migration," *Public Choice*, vol. 19 (Fall 1974), pp. 85–93; Gordon F. DeJong and William L. Donnelly, "Public Welfare and Migration," *Social Science Quarterly*, vol. 54 (September 1973), pp. 329–44; and Janet R. Pack, "Determinants of Migration to Central Cities," *Journal of Regional Science*, vol. 13 (August 1973), pp. 249–60.

Such a policy will do more than merely shift the racial problem from cities to small towns and the countryside. In part the intractable nature of black poverty in the United States comes from its excessive concentration. Dispersion and diffusion can have multiple benefits. The poor and the dependent would have greater choice and need not constantly reconnect themselves to bureaucracies with every move. To the extent that many would move away from the central city, the poor would suffer less crime and enjoy greater family stability. A consolidated system of administration would allow for greater centralization of information and improved ability to minimize fraudulent activity. Inasmuch as central cities would be relieved of their special responsibility for the plight of the poor, they could concentrate on those matters of urban development that fall more appropriately within their scope of competence.

Centralized financing and administration of the welfare state is no panacea for the urban problem. Insofar as technological change will continue to work to the benefit of some cities and regions at the expense of others, urban decline will remain an inevitable counterpoint to national economic growth. But such a policy will at the very least relieve those governments least equipped to care for the disadvantaged from disproportionate responsibilities. At the very least welfare policy should not contribute to the concentration of poverty and deprivation, thereby perpetuating a cycle of dependency, instability, and crime.

Admittedly, the time for institutionalizing a centralized welfare system has yet to arrive. The shibboleths and slogans of states' rights and grassroots democracy continue to have great political currency, even though many of the country's most popular social policies—social security, medicare and food stamps—are almost entirely the fiscal responsibility of the federal government. It will take time before the United States accepts what is commonly understood to be the case in Europe: state and local governments are not the proper financial and administrative locus for programs of social redistribution. Yet the underlying rationale for a national welfare policy is so compelling that each effort to rethink federal arrangements in the United States returns to this question. Nixon had his welfare reform plan, Carter had his own welfare initiative, and Reagan called for a nationalized medicaid program. While an artificially created federal fiscal crisis currently postpones attention to this question, it can hardly be kept from the national political agenda for another decade. The cities' needs, the needs of blacks, and the capacity of the country are simply too great.

PART ONE

The Processes of Urban Growth and Decline

JOHN D. KASARDA

Urban Change
and Minority Opportunities

Two fundamental yet conflicting transformations pervade the recent history and near-term prospects of older, larger U.S. cities. The first is *functional,* as these cities change from centers of production and distribution of material goods to centers of administration, information exchange, and higher-order service provision. The second transformation is *demographic,* as their resident populations change from a predominantly white European heritage to predominantly black, Hispanic, and other minorities.

Accompanying the functional transformation of these cities have been changes in both the composition and sizes of their overall employment bases. During the past two decades most older, larger cities have experienced substantial job growth in occupations associated with knowledge-intensive service-sector industries. However, selective job growth in these high-skill, predominantly white-collar industries has not nearly compensated for employment declines in manufacturing and other predominantly blue-collar industries that had once constituted the economic backbone of these cities. As a result, the total number of jobs available in most older, larger cities has shrunk considerably over the past two decades.

Likewise, concurrent with the demographic transformation of these cities, there have been substantial changes in the socioeconomic composition and total size of their residential populations. As predominantly white middle-income groups have dispersed from the cities (initially to the suburbs and now increasingly to the exurbs and nonmetropolitan areas), they have been only partially replaced by predominantly lower-income

The analysis presented in this chapter was supported by the Office of Policy Development and Research, U.S. Department of Housing and Urban Development, and the National Science Foundation.

33

minority groups and a relative trickle of returning urban professionals. The outcome has been dramatic declines in both the total size and aggregate personal income level of the cities' resident populations, while concentrations of their economically disadvantaged continue to expand.

The simultaneous transformation and selective decline of the employment and residential bases of the cities have contributed to a number of serious problems, including a widening gap between urban job opportunity structures and skill levels of disadvantaged residents (with corresponding high rates of structural unemployment), spatial isolation of low-income minorities, and rising levels of urban poverty and welfare dependency. Associated with these problems have been a plethora of social and institutional ills further aggravating the predicament of people and places in distress, such as high crime rates, poor public schools, deteriorating public infrastructures, and the decay of once-vibrant residential and commercial areas of the cities.

The federal government responded to the hardships confronting cities and their inhabitants by introducing a variety of urban programs over the past two decades. Unfortunately, these programs have had little effect in stemming overall urban decline or improving long-term employment prospects for underprivileged city residents. Indeed, mounting evidence suggests that the plight of economically distressed cities and their underprivileged residents is worse today than before the urban programs began.[1]

The inability of federal programs to stem urban decline results primarily from the overarching technological and economic dynamics influencing the locational choices of various industries and the changing roles of major cities in advanced service economies. This chapter will elaborate on these dynamics and changes, especially as they have altered the capacity of America's older cities to offer entry-level jobs and socially upgrade disadvantaged resident groups.

The guiding thesis is that cities always have and always will perform valuable economic and social functions, but changing technological and industrial conditions (both nationally and internationally) alter these functions over time. In this regard, it must be remembered that blue-collar job opportunities expanded most rapidly in the largest and oldest cities during a transportation and industrial era that no longer exists. During

1. Katharine L. Bradbury, Anthony Downs, and Kenneth A. Small, *Urban Decline and the Future of American Cities* (Brookings, 1982); and James W. Fossett and Richard P. Nathan, "The Prospects for Urban Revival," in Roy Bahl, ed., *Urban Government Finances* (Sage, 1981).

this era, cities had comparative advantages over other locations that substantially reduced the costs and raised the efficiency of firms concentrating in these cities. These advantages included superior long-distance transportation and terminal storage facilities; an abundance of immigrant labor willing to work for extremely low wages; many nearby complementary businesses; and availability of private and public municipal services such as police and fire protection, sewage systems, and running water.

Modern advances in transportation and communication technologies, the spread of population and public services, and changing modes of production organization have virtually wiped out the comparative advantages of major metropolitan cities as locations for large-scale manufacturing and warehousing facilities. The precipitous decline of blue-collar jobs in the cities during recent decades reflects, in part, their loss of comparative locational advantages in these industrial sectors.

Nevertheless, just as older, larger cities have lost their competitive strength to hold or attract jobs in their traditional blue-collar industries, many are exhibiting new competitive strengths as locations for a variety of postindustrial growth industries. These emerging strengths are in the administrative office, communication, financial, professional, and business service sectors and in cultural, leisure, and tourist industries. I will argue that the exploitation of these competitive strengths and a reversal of the buildup of growing concentrations of disadvantaged persons in the cities are essential to urban economic revitalization and renewed minority opportunity. This is so because no policy that would be either politically or economically feasible could overcome the cost disadvantages of central-city locations for manufacturing and most other blue-collar industries that once served both to support and socially upgrade massive numbers of low-skill residents.

To explicate the latter contention and provide an interpretive foundation for analyzing contemporary urban problems, the following section provides a broadbrush sweep of the spatial-economic development of the nation's oldest cities. Next, recent changes in the employment bases and demographic compositions of these cities will be documented, with illustration of the widening mismatches between the educational requirements of new urban growth industries and the educational attainment of urban minorities. The implications of these mismatches for post-1970 rises in rates of urban minority unemployment will then be examined, as will government programs focused on these problems. Special attention will be given to the possibility that place-targeted public assistance programs are anchoring and isolating disadvantaged persons in localities of limited opportunity. The chapter concludes with policy suggestions to revitalize cities and facilitate the mobility of economically displaced minorities from distressed urban areas to reduce their growing rates of isolation, unemployment, and welfare dependency.

The Evolving Structure and Functions of America's Cities

This country's oldest cities originated during the colonial era as mercantile centers of commerce and shipping. Since their chief function was that of funneling raw materials from their immediate hinterlands to the nascent metropolitan economy of eighteenth century Europe, these cities evolved at deep-water sites on long-distance riverine and oceanic routes.[2] By today's urban standards, the cities of colonial America were minuscule— not a single place would have met the current metropolitan criterion of 50,000 residents.

As America entered the nineteenth century, it remained a rural-agrarian nation. Fewer than 4 percent of the U.S. population resided in places of 8,000 or more. Urban expansion during the first two decades of the nineteenth century progressed at a sluggish rate, as externally oriented commerce and shipping continued to dominate the economic bases of fledgling cities. Regional and national markets were constrained by limited transportation systems, while the bulk of urban manufacturing and goods production was of a cottage industry and handicraft form.

The next fifty years witnessed a dramatic development of railroad, highway, and canal systems that substantially broadened urban access to the country's rich raw material resources, spun off new inland towns and cities, and created a nationally integrated exchange network among cities, smaller trade centers, and hinterland villages. At the same time, a revolution was occurring in food production technology and organization that both generated the agricultural surplus that supported a growing nonagricultural population and displaced large numbers of subsistence farmers. Steam-powered machinery and mass production technologies were introduced that, together with entrepreneurial innovations in credit, banking, and finance capitalism, gave rise to large corporate business organizations and their primary units of production—factories. With high domestic fertility

2. Brian J. L. Berry and John D. Kasarda, *Contemporary Urban Ecology* (Macmillan, 1977), pp. 272–74.

rates and increased immigration from abroad providing both an expanded domestic market for manufactured goods and abundant, cheap labor to staff the factories, all the requisites for the rise of America's industrial cities were in place.

Viewed spatially, the industrial cities developed as highly concentrated forms around rail and waterway terminal points within access of northern coal fields. The reasons for such concentration rested in transportation costs and the mechanized application of steam power. Because steam cools quickly and dissipates easily, it must be used where it is produced.[3] Since coal—the fuel used to produce steam—had high transportation and terminal costs, business expenses could be minimized by factories clustering around the terminal and sharing bulk carriage costs. Because the terminal was also the point where other raw materials utilized in the production process were received and finished products distributed, factories concentrating there accrued further cost advantages.

Moreover, during the latter half of the nineteenth century raw materials used in the manufacturing process and finished products tended to be far heavier and bulkier than they are today, and short-distance transportation technologies were, at best, primitive. Under such conditions, agglomeration became cumulative and mutually reinforcing. Complementary units that serviced the factories or utilized their by-products located as close to the factories as possible, as did storage warehouses and wholesalers distributing finished products. Workers employed by the factories, service shops, and warehouses, constrained by pedestrian movement, clustered tightly within walking distance of their place of employment. As late as 1899, the average commuting distance of workers in New York City from their home to their place of employment was roughly two blocks.[4]

Thus the industrial cities that evolved in the late nineteenth century were compact agglomerations of production and distribution facilities, centers of corporate capital accumulation, and both the residence and workplace of millions of unskilled and semiskilled migrants. Industrial expansion and concentrative migration converged in space, generating explosive city growth. Chicago, for example, which was incorporated in 1833 with a population of 4,100, grew to over 2 million residents by 1910, the vast majority of whom resided and worked within a three-mile radius of the city's center.

Spurring the dramatic growth of the industrial cities were a rapidly ad-

3. Amos H. Hawley, *Urban Society*, 2d ed. (Rutgers University Press, 1981), pp. 71–72.
4. John J. Palen, *The Urban World* (McGraw-Hill, 1975), p. 53.

vancing western resource frontier and strengthening commercial markets interacting with a powerful entrepreneurial spirit which held that individualism, competition, the pursuit of profit, and economic growth were uniformly positive and beneficial. In this political-economic climate, urbanization and industrialization surged together, catapulting the entire country into a period of enormous economic expansion. By the end of the nineteenth century, the output of America's industrial cities surpassed the combined total industrial output of Britain, France, and Germany, the world's leaders in 1860.[5]

A point that merits emphasis is that the employment bases of the country's early industrial cities were characterized by entry-level job *abundance*, compared with their current entry-level job *scarcity*.[6] It was this job abundance, with few requisites for entry, that attracted the waves of migrants and offered them a foothold in the urban economy. The rapidly expanding job base accompanying national economic growth in turn provided ladders of opportunity and social mobility for the migrants, most of whom were fleeing nations or regions of substantial labor surplus.[7]

Migration thus served an important equilibrating function, bringing into better balance local population numbers with local labor needs, while also improving the life chances of the immigrants. The latter was particularly true for the millions who were economically disadvantaged—initially arriving from Europe, followed by southern whites and southern blacks (as well as rural northerners) who were displaced by technological and organizational transformations in twentieth century American agriculture.[8]

5. Raymond A. Mohl, "The Industrial City," *Environment*, vol. 18, no. 5 (1976), pp. 28–38.

6. Anthony Downs, *Opening Up the Suburbs: An Urban Strategy for America* (Yale University Press, 1973); Theodore P. Kovaleff, "Industrialization and the American City," in Frank J. Coppa and Philip C. Dolce, eds., *Cities in Transition: From the Ancient World to Urban America* (Chicago: Nelson-Hall, 1974); and Hawley, *Urban Society*.

7. John Bodner, Roger Simon, and Michael P. Weber, *Lives of Their Own: Blacks, Italians, and Poles in Pittsburgh, 1900–1960* (University of Illinois Press, 1982); Reynolds Farley, "The Urbanization of Negroes in the United States," *Journal of Social History*, vol. 1 (Spring 1968), pp. 241–58; Stanley Lieberson, *A Piece of the Pie: Blacks and White Immigrants Since 1880* (University of California Press, 1980); JoEllen Vinyard, *The Irish on the Urban Frontier: Nineteenth Century Detroit, 1850–1880* (Arno Press, 1976); and Oliver Zunz, *The Changing Face of Inequality: Urbanization, Industrial Development and Immigrants in Detroit, 1880–1920* (University of Chicago Press, 1982).

8. Neil Fleigstein, *Going North: Migration of Blacks and Whites from the South, 1900–1950* (Academic Press, 1981); and Michael J. Greenwood, *Migration and Economic Growth in the United States: National, Regional and Metropolitan Perspectives* (Academic Press, 1982).

The access to opportunity and social mobility that America's industrial cities provided the migrants was obtained at significant human cost, however. Migrants frequently had to pull up deep community roots, permanently leave close friends and relatives behind, and adjust to a totally different way of life. Upon arriving at their urban destinations, they were usually greeted with scorn and prejudice by other groups who had preceded them to the city.[9] Lacking financial resources, unaccustomed to city ways, and often without English language skills, immigrants were ascribed the lowest status and were residentially segregated in overcrowded ghettos in the least desirable sections of the city. A polluted, unsanitary physical environment contributed to high morbidity and mortality rates, as did the hazardous working conditions found in the factories. Political corruption and human exploitation were common, working hours were long, and there was no such thing as a minimum wage. By today's dual labor market theory classification scheme, virtually all immigrants held "dead end" jobs.[10]

Nonetheless, there was an abundance of these jobs for which the only requisites were a person's willingness and physical ability to work. This surplus of low-skill jobs and overall economic growth provided the older industrial cities with a unique role in the nation's history as developers of manpower and springboards for social mobility.[11]

Technological Advance and Blue-Collar Job Deconcentration

During the first half of the twentieth century, a number of innovations occurred in transportation, communication, and production technologies that markedly reduced the locational advantages the older, compactly structured cities had previously held for manufacturing and distributing activities. Manufacturers and wholesalers soon found that older urban street patterns were not conducive to automobile and truck movement. Traffic congestion, lack of employee parking space, and problems of freight transfer greatly increased direct and indirect costs, particularly for those manufacturers and wholesalers located in the old, densely settled sections of the cities. On the other hand, the development of suburban highway systems, widespread automobile ownership, and increased dependence by manufacturers and wholesalers on trucking for receiving and shipping made uncongested suburban sites more attractive. Manufacturers and

9. Phillip M. Hauser, *Population Perspectives* (Rutgers University Press, 1960).
10. See Ivar Berg, *Sociological Perspectives on Labor Markets* (Academic Press, 1981).
11. R. D. Norton, *City Life-Cycles and American Urban Policy* (Academic Press, 1979).

wholesalers recognized that by locating on or near the suburban expressway they could reduce their transportation costs, tap an adequate automobile-owning labor supply, and solve problems of employee parking and freight transfer.

The changing mode of manufacturing technology from unit processing to mass production and assembly line methods also hastened the urban exodus of blue-collar industries. Early central-city manufacturing facilities had been constructed as multistory loft-type structures that are not adaptable to much of today's mass production technology. The assembly line, in particular, has large horizontal space requirements that are more difficult and costly to obtain in the central city than in the suburban rings. Likewise, large-scale wholesalers shifting to automated freight-transfer systems found it more practical and less costly to build newly designed facilities on relatively inexpensive suburban ring land (that was often more accessible to regional and national markets) than to convert their obsolete inner-city structures. Owners of newer manufacturing and warehousing facilities that had large space requirements would rarely even consider a central-city site, most locating their facilities in the suburban rings and beyond.

A third, yet no less important, factor stimulating the deconcentration of blue-collar industry was the widespread development of suburban public services and external economies that had previously been restricted to the central cities and their immediate built-up areas. The spread of electric and gas power lines, running water, sanitary waste systems, police and fire protection, and highway services throughout the suburban rings released manufacturing and related industries from their previous dependency on central cities. Moreover, rapid suburban development after World War II brought housing, local suppliers, subcontractors, and other complementary services to nearby areas.

By 1960 further advances in transportation and communication technologies and growing industrial competition from nonmetropolitan areas and abroad made the larger, older cities almost obsolete as locations for manufacturing and warehousing facilities.[12] A massive exodus of blue-collar jobs from the cities commenced, and it has accelerated ever since.

12. John D. Kasarda, "The Implications of Contemporary Redistribution Trends for National Urban Policy," *Social Science Quarterly*, vol. 61 (December 1980), pp. 373–400; George Sternlieb and James W. Hughes, eds., *Post-Industrial America: Metropolitan Decline and Inter-Regional Job Shifts* (Rutgers University, Center for Urban Policy Research, 1975); and Gerald Suttles, "Changing Priorities for the Urban Heartland," in David Street and associates, eds., *Handbook of Contemporary Urban Life* (Jossey-Bass, 1978).

Retail and Service-Sector Shifts

Retail trade and consumer services followed their traditional middle- and upper-income patrons to the suburbs, exacerbating blue-collar job declines in the cities. Between 1954 and 1978 more than 15,000 shopping centers and malls were constructed to serve expanding suburban and exurban populations. By 1975 these shopping centers and malls were the locus of over one-half of the annual retail sales in the United States.[13]

For the current generation of suburbanites, enclosed regional malls have become their Main Street, Fifth Avenue, and community social and entertainment center—all wrapped up into one. The malls not only contain retail establishments of every size, price range and variety, but they also offer professional offices, restaurants, movie theaters, public service outlets, and common space utilized for inexpensive patron attractions. The broad spectrum of goods and services offered by the malls along with special customer amenities (such as controlled climate; pedestrian arcades insulated from automobile traffic, noise, and polluted air; good security and lighting for safer and more relaxed nighttime shopping; free parking) and their accessibility to the automobile-oriented suburban population have combined to give the regional malls a distinct competitive edge in capturing the metropolitan retail dollar. Indeed, large enclosed malls have become so successful that many major cities are now trying to simulate them in their downtowns in an attempt to recoup some of their lost share of metropolitan retail sales and employment.

Urban Growth Industries

There are, nonetheless, significant counter trends occurring in certain retail and service sectors as businesses and institutions offering highly specialized goods and services continue to be attracted to downtown areas. The specialized and complementary nature of these establishments still makes it advantageous for many to choose central locations that maximize their accessibility to certain consumers and businesses. Such establishments as advertising agencies, brokerage houses, consulting firms, financial institutions, small luxury goods shops, and legal, accounting, and professional complexes have been accumulating in the central business districts,

13. Peter O. Muller, "The Outer City," Resource Paper no. 75-2 (Washington, D.C.: Association of American Geographers, 1976).

replacing traditional department stores and many other standardized retail goods and consumer services establishments that were unable to compete effectively or afford the rents at a central location.

The past two decades have also witnessed a remarkable growth of high-rise administrative office buildings in the largest cities' central business districts. Even with major advances in telecommunications technology, many administrative headquarters rely on a complement of legal, financial, public relations, and other specialized business services that are most readily available at the cities' cores. Moreover, unlike manufacturing, whole-sale trade, and retail trade—which typically have large space requirements and whose products cannot be efficiently moved in a vertical direction— most managerial, clerical, professional, and business service functions are highly space intensive and their basic product (information) can be trans-ferred as efficiently vertically as horizontally. Thus people who process information can be stacked, layer after layer, in downtown high-rise office buildings with no loss in productivity. Indeed, such stacking and the resulting proximity often enhance the productivity of those who require extensive, nonroutine personal interaction. The outcome has been an office building boom in central business districts.

There are two other growth industries in major cities that have been increasingly important to downtown vitality. The first is convention and tourism business, fostered by an increasing number of professional and trade associations and rising incomes of a sizable, mobile segment of the national and international population. The second is industry associated with entertainment, cultural, and leisure services, catering to the above groups and to increasing numbers of city dwellers who are single profes-sionals or childless dual-income couples.

The convention-tourism and cultural-entertainment industries may be referred to as "gathering-service" industries because both operate via the convergence of large numbers of individuals from widely dispersed loca-tions to a single site where the service is provided. Gathering-service industries typically have high agglomeration and mutual-scale economies; concentrating together enhances their functional complementarity, am-biance, and market appeal. Many large cities are recognizing that their dense clusters of hotels, restaurants, nightclubs, sport arenas, museums, and theaters, if situated in clean, pedestrian-safe areas, are effective mag-nets for attracting round-the-clock growth industry resources back to their cores. In addition, these clusters serve as important social and aesthetic complements to the increasing number of nine-to-five high-rise office towers beginning to dominate their downtowns.

Effects on Job Opportunities

The transformation of older cities from centers of production and distribution of material goods to centers of information exchange and service consumption has profoundly altered the capacity of these cities to offer employment opportunities for disadvantaged residents. The increments in urban blue-collar jobs spun off by newer service industries employing or catering primarily to higher-income persons have been overwhelmed by central-city job losses in more traditional goods-producing and -distributing industries. Aggravating these blue-collar job losses has been the exodus of middle-income population and general retail trade and service establishments from much of the city beyond the central business districts. These movements have combined to further weaken secondary labor markets and isolate disadvantaged groups in economically distressed areas where opportunities for employment are minimal.

Major cities in the northern industrial belt have been particularly hard hit by changes in their economic base and the loss of blue-collar jobs. Unfortunately, it is many of these same cities that experienced the largest post–World War II migration flows of people whose educational backgrounds do not equip them for employment in new urban growth industries. As a result, their inner-city unemployment rates are well above the national average and inordinately high among educationally disadvantaged urban minorities caught in the web of change.

The next section illustrates the scope of the problem by documenting the spatially conflicting industrial and demographic transformations that have occurred in the largest northern cities since World War II, first in terms of the changing compositions and educational requisites of their employment bases and then in terms of the changing demographic composition and educational attainment of their residents. An examination of the consequences of these transformations for minority unemployment and welfare dependency will follow.

Changing Urban Employment Bases

An overview of changes in the number of private-sector jobs in twelve of the country's largest northern cities between 1948 and 1977 is provided in table 1. The most dramatic employment declines have been in central-city manufacturing; all twelve cities experienced major and accelerating

Table 1. Central-City Employment Changes in Twelve U.S. Cities, by Sector, 1948–77 and 1967–77

Thousands

Central city and period	Sector				
	Manu-facturing[a]	Wholesale[b]	Retail[b]	Selected services[b]	Total
New York					
1948–77	−331	−122	−209	153	−508
1967–77	−286	−83	−94	31	−432
Chicago					
1948–77	−301	−52	−101	58	−396
1967–77	−181	−41	−50	45	−227
Philadelphia					
1948–77	−171	−27	−63	15	−246
1967–77	−106	−19	−24	2	−147
Detroit					
1948–77	−185	−22	−79	−4	−290
1967–77	−56	−21	−33	−11	−120
Cleveland					
1948–77	−103	−11	−41	10	−144
1967–77	−51	−6	−14	2	−68
Boston					
1948–77	−51	−28	−32	28	−83
1967–77	−29	−13	−12	14	−40
St. Louis					
1948–77	−80	−23	−45	1	−148
1967–77	−39	−13	−15	−3	−69
Milwaukee					
1948–77	−42	−5	−7	10	−43
1967–77	−27	−5	−3	12	−23
Baltimore					
1948–77	−48	−8	−35	10	−82
1967–77	−34	−7	−16	4	−53
Pittsburgh					
1948–77	−26	−14	−34	10	−64
1967–77	−30	−8	−11	6	−43
Newark					
1948–77	−54	−11	−24	*	−89
1967–77	−30	−7	−11	−3	−51
Minneapolis-St. Paul					
1948–77	−14	−9	−22	24	−20
1967–77	−35	−9	−8	12	−40
Total					
1948–77	−1,405	−331	−691	316	−2,112
1967–77	−904	−231	−290	112	−1,312

Sources: U.S. Bureau of the Census, *Census of Manufacturing* and *Census of Business*, selected years (Government Printing Office, 1950, 1971, 1981). Figures are rounded.

* Less than 1,000.

a. Covers 1947–77 rather than 1948–77.

b. Includes proprietors and partners.

employment contractions. New York City and Chicago each lost more than 300,000 manufacturing jobs between 1948 and 1977, with the most pronounced employment losses occurring in both cities after 1967.

Wholesale and retail trade employment in all cities likewise deteriorated considerably. However, there are temporal differences. Whereas the majority of central-city retail employment losses occurred before 1967, two-thirds of the wholesale employment losses (like those in manufacturing) occurred after 1967. The accelerating pace of central-city job losses in the manufacturing and wholesale sectors reflects the growing diseconomies of central-city locations for production and warehousing activities.

The selective nature of job declines in most large cities is indicated by the data for their service industries. Only Detroit exhibited a net loss in service-sector jobs between 1948 and 1977, and this is entirely accounted for by losses since 1967. St. Louis and Newark joined Detroit in experiencing net job declines in service industries between 1967 and 1977.

On the other hand, Chicago and New York City have shown substantial vitality in their service industries since World War II. Even in these cities, though, service job growth was overwhelmed by employment declines in manufacturing, wholesale trade, and retail trade. Thus between 1948 and 1977 Chicago lost a total of nearly 400,000 jobs and New York City lost more than 500,000. In each case, the vast majority of overall job losses resulted from blue-collar employment declines.

The twelve cities listed in table 1 experienced a combined loss of more than 2 million jobs between 1948 and 1977. The majority of the decline occurred after 1967, with most of it attributed to job losses in manufacturing. Conversely, analysis of employment change in the suburban rings of these same twelve cities, using the same data sources, shows remarkable job expansion between 1948 and 1977. As a whole, the twelve rings added a net of almost 4 million private-sector jobs between 1948 and 1977, nearly double the total number of jobs lost by their central cities during that period. Of this combined suburban ring job growth, 1.4 million jobs were in manufacturing, 536,000 in wholesale trade, 1.2 million in retail trade, and 800,000 in selected services.

For broader comparative purposes, table 2 presents a summary of employment changes between 1967 and 1977 in the four industrial sectors for all metropolitan central cities categorized by metropolitan age, 1970 population size, and region. Striking gradients of employment change are immediately apparent in the manufacturing, wholesale, and retail sectors. The older and larger the city, the greater the absolute number of job losses

Table 2. *Change in Number of Central-City Jobs, by Sector*
and by Metropolitan Age, Size, and Region, 1967–77
Thousands

Metropolitan characteristic	Number of cities	Sector				
		Manu-facturing	Wholesale[a]	Retail[a]	Selected services[a]	Total
Age[b]						
Before 1900	49	−1,228	−271	−265	410	−1,354
1900–20	63	−35	30	224	352	571
1930–50	53	67	51	198	177	492
After 1950	82	118	54	253	148	573
Population[c]						
Under 250,000	115	46	56	247	166	514
250,000–500,000	63	−2	42	187	193	420
500,000–1,000,000	36	−197	26	102	198	128
Over 1,000,000	33	−925	−259	−126	530	−280
Region						
Northeast	42	−745	−161	−189	99	−995
South	99	137	55	389	468	1,049
North central	68	−555	−74	−1	224	−407
West	38	85	44	210	296	635

Source: U.S. Bureau of the Census, *Census of Manufacturing* and *Census of Business*, selected years. Figures are rounded.
a. Includes proprietors and partners.
b. Decade at which central-city population first exceeded 50,000.
c. As of 1970 census.

in each of these three industrial sectors. The most severe job losses by far were experienced by cities that achieved metropolitan status before 1900 and were in metropolitan areas with 1970 populations exceeding 1 million. Conversely, younger, smaller central cities experienced aggregate growth in manufacturing, retail, and wholesale employment.

Regional differences are also striking with regard to more recent central-city changes in manufacturing, retail, and wholesale employment. Central cities in the northeast and north central regions experienced aggregate employment losses in manufacturing, wholesale, and retail employment, while central cities in the South and West registered aggregate employment gains in all three industrial sectors.

By contrast, in the selected services category there were aggregate central-city employment gains in all census regions. More interestingly, selected service employment gains were greatest in the largest and oldest central-city classifications—exactly opposite the patterns found in manufacturing, retail, and wholesale employment. Because of the growing importance of service-sector employment in structurally changing cities, more detailed and more current analysis of this sector is in order.

The Rise of Information-processing Industries

Examination of the three-digit and four-digit standard industrial classifications (SICs) within the service sector shows that selected service employment encompasses a wide variety of tasks and skill requisites (the category includes bootblacks, parking lot attendants, financial analysts, and medical doctors).[14] Such diversity in aggregated employment statistics clouds more than it clarifies significant transformations taking place in the employment bases of cities.[15]

The appraisal of transforming city economies requires decomposition of selected service employment into at least the three-digit classification detail. This can be done using the U.S. Census Bureau's *County Business Patterns* data for selected cities whose city and county boundaries correspond. Three large northern cities—New York City, Philadelphia, and Boston—meet this criterion. Table 3 provides a breakdown of selected services employment into information processing and other services in these cities.

New York City gained more than 650,000 jobs in its information-processing industries between 1953 and 1980 while losing more than 525,000 jobs in its manufacturing and construction industries. Notice further the selective nature of service employment expansion, especially during the past decade. From 1970 to 1980, employment in information-processing industries continued to mushroom in New York, Philadelphia, and Boston, whereas employment in other, predominantly blue-collar, service industries (such as barbershops, car washes, and domestic services) declined considerably in each city. In just ten years, New York City lost more than 100,000 jobs in its predominantly blue-collar service industries, Philadelphia nearly 30,000 such jobs, and Boston nearly 10,000. All three cities experienced even larger absolute employment declines in their traditional retail and wholesale industries.

The extent of transformation of older, larger cities from centers of material

14. U.S. Department of Commerce, *Standard Industrial Classification Manual, 1972* (Government Printing Office, 1972).

15. Thomas M. Stanback, Jr., and Thierry J. Noyelle, *Metropolitan Labor Markets in Transition: A Study of Seven SMSAs*, Final Report, Contract USDL 21-36-78-33 (U.S. Department of Commerce, 1981).

Table 3. *Central-City Employment in Three U.S. Cities, by Sector, 1953, 1970, and 1980*
Figures in thousands

Central city and sector	Number of jobs			Percent of total		
	1953	1970	1980	1953	1970	1980
New York						
Total employment[a]	2,977	3,350	2,866	100	100	100
Agriculture and mining	5	5	5	*	*	*
Manufacturing and construction	1,176	971	650	40	29	23
Retail and wholesale	805	779	596	27	23	20
Selected services						
Information processing[b]	646	1,172	1,302	22	35	45
Other services	344	424	314	12	13	11
Philadelphia						
Total employment[a]	788	772	628	100	100	100
Agriculture and mining	0.7	0.7	0.5	*	*	*
Manufacturing and construction	398	291	171	50	38	27
Retail and wholesale	206	180	134	26	23	22
Selected services						
Information processing[b]	98	220	271	12	28	43
Other services	85	81	52	12	10	8
Boston (Suffolk County)						
Total employment[a]	402	465	437	100	100	100
Agriculture and mining	2	0.9	0.5	*	*	*
Manufacturing and construction	130	105	77	32	22	17
Retail and wholesale	132	111	82	32	24	19
Selected services						
Information processing[b]	87	194	232	22	42	53
Other services	51	55	46	13	12	10

Source: U.S. Bureau of the Census, *County Business Patterns*, selected years, and 1970 *Occupation by Industry* statistics. Figures are rounded.
* Less than 1.
a. Total classified employment and industry subcategories, excluding government employees and sole proprietors.
b. Service industries (excluding government, retail, and wholesale) in which more than one-half the employees hold executive, managerial, professional, or clerical positions.

goods production to centers of information processing is highlighted by proportional changes in their industrial employment bases between 1953 and 1980. During that period, employment in manufacturing and construction industries as a share of total private-sector employment dropped from 40 to 23 percent in New York City, from 50 to 27 percent in Philadelphia, and from 32 to 17 percent in Boston. During the same period, employment in information-processing industries as a proportion of total private-sector employment expanded from 22 to 45 percent in New York City, from 12 to 43 percent in Philadelphia, and from 22 to 53 percent in Boston. By 1980 New York City and Boston each had more employees in information-processing industries than in the manufacturing, construction, retail, and wholesale industries combined. This represents a dramatic metamorphosis since 1953, when employment in these more traditional urban industries outnumbered employment in information-processing industries in each city by at least a three-to-one margin.

Educational Requirements for Urban Employment

To determine the extent to which inner-city unemployment is structural in nature requires going beyond describing industrial-sector job changes in cities. One must assess educational prerequisites for employment in the cities' transforming economies. Although much has been said about declines in entry-level jobs in cities and the growth of knowledge-intensive industries, there has been little actual measurement of the phenomenon. The following analysis documents changes in entry-level and knowledge-intensive jobs in cities during the past ten years in terms of average educational levels of employees. In this analysis, entry-level industries are those whose jobholders' average educational levels are less than high school completion, whereas knowledge-intensive industries employ persons whose average educational levels exceed two years of college.[16]

Table 4 presents entry-level and knowledge-intensive industry employment changes between 1970 and 1980 for nine major cities—the three

16. Industry employment changes in cities by average educational level of jobholders were estimated by synthesizing individual-level data on the schooling completed by jobholders in detailed classified industries with data on aggregate job changes that have occurred within each industry in each city. To measure average educational levels of employees in detailed urban industries, the March 1982 *Current Population Survey* was used to compute the mean years of schooling completed by all central-city residents who were employed in two-, three-, and four-digit SIC-coded industries. Computed mean educational levels were then assigned to each detailed industry classified in *County Business Patterns*. Industries were designated as entry-level or knowledge-intensive as described in the text. Aggregate job changes within each educationally classified industry were then traced between 1970 and 1980 for nine major cities whose boundaries are either identical to or closely approximate those for which place-specific industrial employment data are available in *County Business Patterns*. For additional details, see John D. Kasarda, "Urban Structural Transformation and Minority Opportunity," report prepared for the Office of Policy Development and Research, U.S. Department of Housing and Urban Development, 1982; and John D. Kasarda, "Entry-Level Jobs, Mobility, and Urban Minority Unemployment," *Urban Affairs Quarterly*, vol. 19 (September 1983), pp. 21–40.

Table 4. *Employment Changes, by Industry's Average Educational Requirements, for Nine U.S. Cities, 1970–80*

Figures in thousands

City and industrial categorization[a]	Number of jobs, 1980	Change, 1970–80	
		Number	Percent
New York			
Entry-level	763	−472	−38.2
Knowledge-intensive	462	92	24.9
Philadelphia			
Entry-level	208	−102	−32.9
Knowledge-intensive	91	25	37.8
Baltimore			
Entry-level	108	−52	−32.4
Knowledge-intensive	32	5	20.6
Boston (Suffolk County)			
Entry-level	115	−34	−22.6
Knowledge-intensive	75	19	33.3
St. Louis			
Entry-level	103	−23	−18.2
Knowledge-intensive	21	−8	−26.3
Atlanta (Fulton County)			
Entry-level	136	−19	−12.1
Knowledge-intensive	41	11	35.6
Houston (Harris County)			
Entry-level	457	194	73.8
Knowledge-intensive	152	83	119.4
Denver			
Entry-level	110	14	14.5
Knowledge-intensive	44	21	91.4
San Francisco			
Entry-level	142	13	−10.2
Knowledge-intensive	65	21	46.8

Sources: U.S. Bureau of the Census, *Current Population Survey* tape, March 1982, and *County Business Patterns*, 1970, 1980. Figures are rounded.

a. Entry-level industries are those where mean schooling completed by employees is less than twelve years; knowledge-intensive industries are those where mean schooling completed is more than fourteen years.

cities shown in table 3 plus Baltimore, St. Louis, Atlanta, Houston, Denver, and San Francisco. These cities were added to provide regional representation as well as to enable comparison of declining urban job bases versus expanding ones.

Changing educational requisites for urban employment are strikingly apparent in the four large northeastern cities. Between 1970 and 1980 New

York City lost nearly 500,000 jobs in entry-level industries, whereas Philadelphia lost over 100,000, Baltimore over 50,000, and Boston over 33,000. Conversely, employment in knowledge-intensive industries expanded by at least 20 percent in each of the four cities during the decade.

St. Louis, like a number of other declining industrial cities in the Midwest, experienced employment contraction in both its knowledge-intensive and entry-level industries. In aggregate terms, however, its entry-level industry employment declined substantially more than its knowledge-intensive industries.

As an older, larger southern city, Atlanta's experience is consistent with that of major cities in the Northeast. Rather substantial employment declines occurred in its entry-level industries while employment growth took place in its knowledge-intensive industries. However, Atlanta's entry-level employment declines have not been quite as severe as those of the four northeastern cities, in either absolute or percentage terms.

Houston, Denver, and San Francisco depart rather sharply from the patterns of the other cities shown in table 4. All three exhibit employment growth in their entry-level industries as well as in their knowledge-intensive industries. Houston (Harris County) is particularly striking: entry-level industries expanded by nearly 200,000 jobs there between 1970 and 1980. Individual-city analysis of changing minority unemployment rates and rates of minority labor force participation during the decade revealed that minorities residing in Houston fared much better than those in other central cities.[17]

Changing Demographic Compositions

A rather clear picture emerges from the above analysis. There have been precipitous declines in employment in northern central-city industries that traditionally sustained large numbers of less-educated persons. The job losses have been only partially replaced by growth in white-collar service industries with substantially higher educational requisites. This has implications for the expansion in large northern cities of population groups whose typical educational backgrounds place them at a serious disadvantage as the economies of these cities transform.

Table 5 summarizes the racial and ethnic compositional changes between

17. Kasarda, "Urban Structural Transformation."

Table 5. *Population Changes in Four U.S. Cities,*
by Race and Ethnicity, 1970–80
Figures in thousands

Central city	Total population	Non-Hispanic Whites	Blacks	Others	Hispanic	Percent minority
New York						
1970	7,895	5,062	1,518	113	1,202	36
1980	7,072	3,669	1,694	303	1,406	48
Change, 1970–80	− 823	− 1,393	176	190	204	. . .
Chicago						
1970	3,363	1,999	1,076	40	248	41
1980	3,005	1,300	1,188	96	422	57
Change, 1970–80	− 358	− 699	111	56	174	. . .
Philadelphia						
1970	1,949	1,247	646	11	45	36
1980	1,688	963	633	28	64	43
Change, 1970–80	− 260	− 283	− 13	17	19	. . .
Detroit						
1970	1,511	820	652	9	30	46
1980	1,203	402	754	18	29	67
Change, 1970–80	− 308	− 418	102	9	− 1	. . .
Total change, 1970–80	1,749	− 2,794	377	271	396	. . .

Source: U.S. Bureau of the Census, *Census of Population* summary tapes, 1970, 1980. Figures are rounded.

1970 and 1980 within the four largest northern cities (New York City, Chicago, Philadelphia, and Detroit). New York City, which experienced an overall population decline of over 823,000 during the decade, actually lost 1,393,000 non-Hispanic whites. Thus, in just ten years, New York's non-Hispanic white population (that is, its nonminority population) dropped by an amount larger than the total population of any other U.S. city except Los Angeles, Chicago, Philadelphia, and Houston. Approximately 40 percent of the loss of non-Hispanic whites in New York City was replaced by an infusion of over 570,000 Hispanics, blacks, and other minorities during the 1970s. By 1983 New York City's minority population had climbed to 52 percent of the city's total.[18]

Chicago's demographic experience during the 1970s was similar to New York City's. More than 50 percent of Chicago's minority population increase during the decade consisted of Hispanics. However, it is important to point

18. John D. Kasarda, "Hispanics and City Change," *American Demographics* (November 1984), pp. 24–29.

out that Chicago also experienced the third largest absolute increase of non-Hispanic blacks of any U.S. city. By 1980, 57 percent of Chicago's resident population was composed of minorities, with projections showing the minority proportion climbing to nearly 70 percent during the 1990s.[19]

Philadelphia had the smallest aggregate population decline of the four cities. The number of both non-Hispanic whites and non-Hispanic blacks declined in Philadelphia between 1970 and 1980, while Hispanics and non-Hispanic and other minorities increased. Philadelphia's substantial decline in non-Hispanic whites, together with its net increase of 23,000 minority residents during the 1970s, raised its minority percentage to 43 percent in 1980.

Detroit experienced the highest rate of non-Hispanic white residential decline of any major city in the country. Between 1970 and 1980 Detroit lost more than one-half of its non-Hispanic white residents. Concurrently, Detroit had the fourth largest absolute increase of non-Hispanic blacks of any city in the country, falling just behind Chicago in black population increase. Combined with modest increases in both Hispanics and other minorities, Detroit's large increase in black residents and sharp drop in non-Hispanic white residents transformed the city's residential base from 46 percent minority in 1970 to 67 percent minority in 1980.

The bottom row of table 5 provides a summary of demographic transformation and residential decline in the four cities. Between 1970 and 1980 they experienced an aggregate loss of 2,794,000 non-Hispanic whites, while their Hispanic residential bases increased by nearly 400,000. Added to the Hispanic increase during 1970 were substantial cumulative increases of non-Hispanic blacks and other non-Hispanic minorities, resulting in a total increase of more than 1,040,000 minority residents in the four cities during the decade.

Educational Distribution of Blacks and Whites

Racial minorities are at a serious structural disadvantage in central cities that are losing entry-level industry jobs because substantially larger proportions of city minority residents lack the formal schooling to take advantage of information-processing jobs that are expanding in the cities. To illustrate this structural disadvantage, table 6 presents data on years of schooling completed by white and black central-city residents.

19. Ibid.

Table 6. *Years of School Completed by Central-City Residents Aged 16–64, by Race, Sex, and Region, 1982*
Thousands

	Region			
Race, sex, and schooling	Northeast	North central	South	West
White males				
Did not complete high school	1,042	816	1,008	613
Completed high school only	1,137	1,109	1,160	916
Attended college one year or more	1,138	1,187	1,761	1,626
White females				
Did not complete high school	1,117	766	1,108	712
Completed high school only	1,405	1,455	1,592	1,109
Attended college one year or more	976	1,118	1,590	1,320
Black males				
Did not complete high school	399	425	618	143
Completed high school only	322	417	493	132
Attended college one year or more	226	247	350	160
Black females				
Did not complete high school	534	516	714	146
Completed high school only	518	494	651	172
Attended college one year or more	283	279	383	190

Source: U.S. Bureau of the Census, *Current Population Survey* tape, March 1982. Figures are rounded.

The data show that the modal education category for central-city black males and black females in the Northeast, the north central region, and the South is "did not complete high school." Conversely, for white male central-city residents in these three regions, the modal education category is "attended college for one year or more." For white females in cities in these three regions, high school completion is the modal category. The statistics of note, however, relate to the much smaller proportion of black central-city residents with schooling levels appropriate to the expanding industries in northern cities and the higher proportions with education levels appropriate primarily to the declining industries.

Black residents in western cities, however, have more favorable educational levels to take advantage of new urban growth industries. In 1982 the number of blacks in western central cities who attended college for at least one year was greater than the number who did not complete high school. The educational distribution for whites shows western cities to have, by far, the highest share of educated nonminority populations of the four regions. Nearly one-half of the white male and female central-city residents aged 16–64 in the West have attended college for at least one year.

In sum, it is apparent that large proportions of black central-city residents still do not possess the education to participate in information-processing industries beginning to dominate urban employment bases. This is particularly the case for blacks residing in larger cities in the northeast and north central regions. With entry-level jobs rapidly disappearing from these cities, their less-educated minority populations are especially disadvantaged.

Transportation and the Isolation of Urban Minorities

An additional structural impediment inner-city minorities face is their increased distance from current sources of blue-collar and other entry-level jobs. As industries providing these jobs have dispersed to the suburbs, exurbs, and nonmetropolitan peripheries, racial discrimination and inadequate incomes of inner-city minorities have prevented many from moving with their traditional sources of employment. Moreover, the dispersed nature of job growth sites makes public transportation from inner-city neighborhoods impractical, requiring virtually all city residents who work in peripheral areas to commute by personally owned automobiles.

The combined costs of maintaining, operating, and insuring an automobile in major cities are substantially higher than elsewhere. This is particularly the case in older, larger, densely settled cities. In fact, automobile ownership in the core areas of these cities is so expensive relative to the actual or potential incomes of their disadvantaged residents that most cannot afford this increasingly essential means of securing and maintaining blue-collar employment.

The severity of the problem of access to deconcentrating blue-collar job opportunities is documented in table 7. This table presents the proportions of black and Hispanic households in New York City, Philadelphia, and Boston who do not have an automobile or truck available. More than one-half of the minority households in Philadelphia and Boston are without a means of personal transportation. New York City's proportions are even higher, with only three out of ten black or Hispanic households having a vehicle available. More detailed breakdowns of data show that in New York City's core boroughs (Brooklyn, Bronx, and Manhattan) fewer than three out of ten black or Hispanic households had an automobile or truck available in 1980.

Table 7. *Central-City Minority Households with No Automobile or Truck Available, 1980*
Percent

	Central city	Black households	Hispanic households
	Philadelphia	50.9	50.8
	Boston	51.3	54.9
	New York	69.3	71.3
	Bronx	71.1	72.9
	Brooklyn	72.2	73.9
	Manhattan	84.7	83.5
	Queens	43.4	49.4
	Staten Island	54.2	38.6

Source: U.S. Bureau of the Census, *Census of Housing, 1980, Detailed Housing Characteristics*.

It should be pointed out that the figures in table 7 refer to *all* black and Hispanic households in each city or borough. It stands to reason that black and Hispanic households whose members have lower income and educational attainment have even less access to personal means of transportation. Thus, with automobile or truck ownership becoming increasingly necessary for blue-collar job access by poorly educated inner-city minorities, many find themselves confined to areas of declining opportunity.

Consequences of Minority Confinement

Confinement of minorities to inner-city areas of blue-collar job decline has had three serious outcomes: rising unemployment, increased labor force dropout rates, and growing welfare dependency.

Rising Central-City Unemployment

Table 8 presents central-city unemployment rates for black and white males by region and years of schooling completed. For all regions, central-city unemployment rates rose steadily for both races, with the exception of better-educated white males. The importance of education for urban employment can be observed by reading down the columns from "did not complete high school" to "attended college for one year or more." Within racial groups, those who did not complete high school had substantially higher unemployment rates, with the absolute gap in unemployment rates between the lowest and highest educational categories widening between 1969 and 1982. The disproportionate concentration of central-city black

Table 8. *Unemployment Rates of Central-City Males Aged 16–64,*
by Race, Region, and Years of School Completed, 1969, 1977, and 1982

Region and schooling	White			Black		
	1969	1977	1982	1969	1977	1982
All regions						
Did not complete high school	4.3	12.2	17.7	6.6	19.8	29.7
Completed high school only	1.7	8.0	11.0	4.1	16.2	23.5
Attended college one year or more	1.6	4.7	4.4	3.7	10.7	16.1
All education levels	2.6	7.7	9.5	5.4	16.5	23.4
Northeast						
Did not complete high school	3.7	13.9	17.2	7.6	20.9	26.2
Completed high school only	1.7	9.4	10.3	3.4	18.2	21.9
Attended college one year or more	1.4	6.0	4.8	7.1	13.9	18.6
All education levels	2.4	9.6	10.2	6.1	18.6	22.6
North central						
Did not complete high school	4.9	12.8	24.3	8.3	26.2	34.8
Completed high school only	1.1	8.0	14.5	3.3	18.0	35.8
Attended college one year or more	1.3	3.5	3.8	1.4	12.3	22.2
All education levels	2.6	7.6	12.2	6.0	20.6	32.0
South						
Did not complete high school	3.4	9.9	13.2	3.8	14.5	28.2
Completed high school only	0.8	5.9	6.8	3.6	13.5	16.6
Attended college one year or more	1.7	3.1	2.9	3.6	6.2	13.6
All education levels	2.0	5.7	6.4	3.7	12.6	19.9
West						
Did not complete high school	6.4	12.0	17.3	11.6	22.2	32.9
Completed high school only	4.2	8.6	13.4	9.6	17.7	15.9
Attended college one year or more	1.9	6.4	6.0	2.9	13.2	9.9
All education levels	3.9	8.2	10.1	8.3	17.0	16.5

Source: Computed from U.S. Bureau of the Census, *Current Population Survey* tapes, 1969, 1977, and 1982.

males in the lowest category of completed schooling in every region but
the West (shown in table 6) no doubt contributes to the widening gap over
time between overall white and black urban unemployment rates (table
8). For white male central-city residents at all educational levels unemployment rates rose from 2.6 percent in 1969 to 9.5 percent in 1982,
whereas the same rates for black males rose from 5.4 to 23.4 percent during
this period.

It is important to note, however, that substantial racial differences in
central-city unemployment rates remain even when controlled for schooling
completed. Indeed, black male central-city residents in the northeast and
southern regions who attended college had higher rates of unemployment
in 1982 than did white central-city residents in these same regions who

did not complete high school. Putting aside possible racial differences in the quality of schooling, such discrepancies do suggest that problems of racial discrimination may be compounding the structural disadvantage central-city blacks face given their overall educational distributions.

Discouraged Workers and Other Labor Force Dropouts

Rising central-city unemployment rates for minorities illustrate only a portion of the problem of urban economic displacement, because these rates cover only persons who have actively sought employment during the four weeks before being surveyed. Excluded entirely from the labor force and unemployment statistics are disabled persons, those who have simply given up looking for work because they believe no jobs are available (discouraged workers), and those who want to work but cannot hold employment for a variety of physical or personal reasons.

To tap changing labor force nonparticipation rates among central-city blacks and whites, I computed a statistic measuring the proportion of each city's males aged 16–64 who are not in school and not in the labor force. The numerator of this statistic is the number of males classified as being neither employed, unemployed, nor in school. The denominator is the total number of males classified as employed, unemployed, and not in the labor force (excluding those in school). In other words, the "in school" population has been simultaneously subtracted from the numerator ("not in labor force") and from the denominator ("labor force" plus "not in labor force").

Table 9 provides the labor force nonparticipation rates by race, age, and region for black and white males in 1969 and 1982. These rates clearly show that unemployment figures do not fully reveal the extent of racial differences in formal participation in central-city economies. For every region and age group, black males have markedly higher rates of labor force nonparticipation than white males. Moreover, whereas central-city white male nonparticipation rates increased modestly between 1969 and 1982, the rates for black males climbed substantially. Just as the central-city racial gap in unemployment rates is widening, so is the racial gap in urban labor force nonparticipation.

Urban Employment Decline and Subsistence Surrogates

At the same time that blue-collar jobs have disappeared from larger northern cities, with corresponding rises in minority unemployment and

Table 9. *Proportion of Male Central-City Residents Not in School and Not in the Labor Force, by Region, Race, and Age, 1969 and 1982*

Region and age	1969		1982	
	White	Black	White	Black
All regions				
16–24	4.5	8.2	5.4	16.5
25–64	5.8	10.3	9.2	17.1
Northeast				
16–24	6.9	12.2	6.8	20.1
25–64	6.9	10.7	10.8	18.4
North central				
16–24	3.2	7.2	6.1	12.4
25–64	5.1	9.9	9.3	19.3
South				
16–24	4.0	6.9	4.2	17.0
25–64	5.0	10.6	8.2	14.5
West				
16–24	4.5	6.0	4.6	16.1
25–64	6.0	9.3	8.7	18.1

Source: U.S. Bureau of the Census, *Current Population Survey* tapes, 1969, 1982.

labor force nonparticipation rates, the minority populations in many of these cities have continued to expand. This seemingly dysfunctional demographic expansion, which contrasts sharply with that predicted by market equilibrium models, raises some fundamental questions: What continues to attract or hold minority and other disadvantaged persons in central cities undergoing severe blue-collar employment decline? How are economically displaced inner-city residents able to survive? What, in brief, is the economic substitute for traditional blue-collar jobs?

Answers to the above are provided, in part, by the data presented in table 10, which displays the absolute numbers of central-city household heads in each labor force category along with the respective proportion who receive assistance from at least one of three major welfare programs: public or subsidized housing, aid to families with dependent children and other cash assistance, and food stamps. The differentially high rates of welfare recipiency of minority householders who are unemployed or not in the labor force is clearly revealed. This is especially so for black female household heads.

Moreover, consistent with the analysis presented in tables 8 and 9, table 10 shows that black householders of both sexes have far greater proportions

Table 10. *Welfare Recipiency Rates of Central-City Heads
of Households Aged 16–64, by Region, Race, Sex,
and Labor Force Status, 1982*

Figures in thousands

	Number of heads of households			Percent receiving welfare[a]		
Region, race, and sex	Employed	Unem- ployed	Not in labor force	Employed	Unem- ployed	Not in labor force
All regions						
White males	7,969	536	901	4	21	16
White females	2,834	190	1,015	8	28	46
Black males	1,434	229	306	9	39	40
Black females	1,121	228	900	28	73	82
Northeast						
White males	1,781	133	250	5	19	21
White females	661	47	373	9	23	58
Black males	321	48	72	12	41	39
Black females	290	53	313	29	75	84
North central						
White males	1,845	174	205	4	27	15
White females	677	55	219	8	42	48
Black males	330	99	98	9	52	35
Black females	255	90	241	27	72	82
South						
White males	2,502	92	240	4	16	16
White females	843	44	215	7	26	35
Black males	605	63	90	8	19	50
Black females	452	58	268	30	76	79
West						
White males	1,842	136	207	3	20	11
White females	653	43	208	8	20	35
Black males	178	20	46	4	32	38
Black females	124	26	79	18	63	86

Source: U.S. Bureau of the Census, *Current Population Survey* tape, March 1982. Figures are rounded.
a. Welfare recipiency defined as receiving assistance from at least one of three programs: public or subsidized housing, aid to families with dependent children, or food stamps.

who are unemployed and not in the labor force than their white counterparts. Indeed, cities in the northeast and north central regions have more
black female household heads who are unemployed or not in the labor
force than who are employed. Conversely, among white female heads of
households in cities in the same regions, those employed outnumber the
combined total of those unemployed and those not in the labor force by a
substantial margin.

Regional differences in proportions of male household heads employed are also striking. For example, table 10 shows that only 63 percent of black male household heads in cities in the north central region were employed in 1982, compared with 80 percent of black male household heads in cities in the South. To understand better how large portions of black male unemployed householders are surviving in economically changing northern cities, contrast the welfare recipiency rates of the unemployed residing in the northeast and north central regions with those residing in the South. In the north central region, for example, more than 50 percent of unemployed black male householders were receiving welfare assistance, compared with less than 20 percent of those in southern central cities. These public assistance rates, along with the much larger proportions of central-city black male householders who are unemployed in northern cities, illustrate the differential scope of welfare economies in northern cities, which serve as partial subsistence surrogates for their declining production economies.

Targeting, Anchoring, and Demographic Disequilibria

From a policy perspective it is important to realize that while the expanding urban production economies of the past offered large numbers of disadvantaged residents entry into the mainstream economy and opportunities for mobility, today's urban welfare economies often have the opposite effects—limiting mobility and reinforcing the concentration and isolation of those without access to the economic mainstream. Many well-intentioned public assistance programs, for example, have been specifically aimed at inner-city areas of greatest economic distress, thereby providing the subsistence infrastructure that keeps disadvantaged people there. By relying increasingly on place-oriented public housing, nutritional, health care, income maintenance, and other assistance programs, a large minority underclass has become anchored in localities where additional welfare aid is directed because of severe employment loss and other indicators of distress.

Serious problems of racial discrimination, inadequate transportation, and insufficient low-cost housing in areas of employment growth further obstruct mobility and job acquisition by this underclass, as do their frequent deficiencies in technical and interpersonal skills so necessary to obtain and hold jobs. The outcome is that growing numbers of potentially productive minorities find themselves confined to segregated areas of urban decline where they subsist, without job opportunities, on a combination of government handouts and their own informal economies. Such isolation, dependency, and blocked mobility breed hopelessness, despair, and alienation, which in turn foster drug abuse, family dissolution, and other social ills that disproportionately afflict the urban disadvantaged.

This is certainly not meant to imply that targeted government aid to people and places in distress is unnecessary or without solid merit. Most urban welfare programs have had imperative palliative effects, temporarily relieving some very painful symptoms associated with the departure of blue-collar jobs (such as the inability of the unemployed to afford housing payments or adequate nutritional and health care). However, while some success has been achieved in relieving such pains, the disequilibrium in distressed cities between low-skill labor availability and low-skill labor needs grows worse.

Spatial Inequities and Equality of Opportunity

This demographic disequilibrium, sustained in part by government subsidies, may work against the long-term economic health of distressed cities and their structurally unemployed residents. Imagine, for instance, what would have happened in the first half of this century if the great numbers of structurally displaced southerners who migrated to economically expanding northern cities in search of jobs and a better life had been sustained in their distressed localities by public assistance. It is possible that many would never have moved and that the significant advances in income levels and living standards that both the South and their out-migrants experienced would not have occurred.

Circumstances today are analogous, but regionally the reverse. Many economically changing northern cities are now characterized by excesses of structurally displaced workers as their blue-collar job bases wither. For example, the March 1984 unemployment rates in Gary, Indiana, and Pontiac, Michigan, were both over 20 percent, whereas in the Raleigh-Durham-Chapel Hill area and in Austin, Texas, they were under 4 percent.[20]

A more equal and, it may be contended, socially equitable territorial

20. Bureau of Labor Statistics, *Employment and Unemployment in States and Local Areas*, March 1984.

distribution of unemployment (say, no place continuously carrying more than 12 percent unemployment) could prevent the downward economic spiral that persists in some distressed cities. It is possible that this downward spiral continues because the social overhead burdens and problems associated with exceptionally high unemployment rates create negative externalities that dissuade new businesses from locating in such cities. If this is so, then under conditions of national economic growth a locality with excessively high unemployment has much poorer prospects of attracting new employers and economically rebounding than a locality with a moderate unemployment rate.[21]

The conclusion to be drawn is that greater spatial equity in sharing the nation's unemployment burden may be essential to greater equality of opportunity for distressed cities and their disadvantaged residents. As long as disproportionately large numbers of unemployed persons remain concentrated in these cities, the economic future of both will be bleak.

New Urban Policies for New Urban Realities

To address the problem of inequities resulting from insufficient private-sector investment in areas of severe blue-collar employment decline, some have suggested a national development bank, a reconstruction finance corporation, enterprise zones, or government-business-labor partnerships, which might "reindustrialize" these areas or otherwise rebuild their historic employment bases. Such suggestions are as unrealistic as they are nostalgic. Government subsidies, tax incentives, and regulatory relief contained in existing and proposed urban policies are not nearly sufficient to overcome technological and market-driven forces redistributing blue-collar jobs and shaping the economies of the major cities. Nor would reversing these redistributional trends and inhibiting urban economic transformation necessarily be in the longer-term interest of either the cities or the national economy.

On the contrary, encouraging the return of older blue-collar industries to urban core areas may additionally saddle urban economies with stagnating or declining industries and further weaken the cities' competitive economic position. Indeed, efforts to assist distressed urban areas through policies

21. See David Birch, *Job Creation in Cities* (Massachusetts Institute of Technology, MIT Program on Neighborhood and Regional Change, 1980), on the importance of new firm development for job creation in cities.

that direct older industries to the inner cities where these industries could experience greater costs or lower productivity may well conflict with efforts to strengthen the national economy upon which the health of the cities is inextricably dependent. Economic advancement of cities and maximum job creation can best be accomplished through government programs and private-sector initiatives that promote urban service industries whose functions are consistent with the roles computer-age cities most effectively perform. The most promising new growth industries for cities include headquarter offices, marketing, finance, research, communication, and other information-processing activities.

This new urban reality calls for fresh thinking and more future-oriented public policies regarding infrastructure development. Just as canals, railways, paved streets, running water, and electric power lines once provided cities with comparative advantages for processing and transporting goods, successful cities of the future will develop computer-age infrastructures that will provide them with comparative advantages for processing and transmitting information. As a start, concerted efforts must be made to "wire" cities so that businesses locating in them can quickly and efficiently receive, process, store, and transmit immense amounts of data and information. Cities should also take advantage of their economies of scale and provide municipally owned supercomputer facilities to service their growing information-processing industries on a cost-sharing basis. Those cities that take the lead in providing advanced information-processing infrastructures will hold a competitive edge over others whose infrastructure development remains geared to an older industrial age.

The competitive edge of major cities in providing cultural and leisure services offers additional opportunities for urban economic and demographic revitalization. Although the outflow of middle-income residents from cities still surpasses the number returning, research indicates that important demographic selection mechanisms based on consumer tastes and household composition are operating. Middle- and upper-income people who are moving back to large cities or choosing to remain in the cities are predominantly single professionals, childless couples with dual incomes, older families whose last child has left the household, those leading unconventional life-styles, and others who cherish and can afford the rich cultural amenities, specialized services, and myriad stimuli that downtown living offers.[22] These groups no doubt will serve as the primary demographic

22. See Shirley B. Laska and Daphne Spain, eds., *Back to the City: Issues in Neighborhood Renovation* (Pergamon, 1980); and Kasarda, "The Implications of Contemporary Redistribution Trends."

component of inner-city residential revitalization in the years ahead. For them, the emerging consumption-oriented city is more attractive than dispersed, low-density, home-centered communities.

A related issue new urban policies must address is the growing importance people and businesses are placing on "quality of life" in making decisions about residential and commercial location. In the earlier industrial age, technological and product constraints provided cities with a near monopoly in capturing national economic and demographic growth. Today, most of those constraints are gone. People and businesses are increasingly free to locate where they perceive the social and physical environment as more desirable. If large cities are to compete effectively for higher-income residents and better jobs, they must improve their image to be perceived as safe, clean, and well managed. Those cities that continue to be viewed as crime-ridden, dirty, and politically prolifigate will consistently lose out, regardless of other comparative advantages they offer.

Helping Those Caught in the Web of Change

Cities that improve their social and physical environments and adapt to their emerging service-sector roles should experience renewed demographic and economic vitality. However, many urban residents who lack appropriate skills for advanced service-sector industries are likely to remain on the bottom rungs of the socioeconomic ladder. Indeed, their economic plight could further deteriorate. For example, New York City, capitalizing on its strength as an international financial and administrative center, experienced a net increase of 167,000 jobs between 1977 and 1981.[23] Yet, while the city's total employment base was expanding, its overall minority unemployment rates continued to climb. This is because virtually all of New York's employment expansion was concentrated in white-collar service industries, whereas manufacturing employment dropped by 55,000 jobs and wholesale and retail trade employment declined by an additional 9,000 jobs during the four-year period. These figures, together with the demographic and employment data presented for New York City earlier in this chapter, testify that the mismatch between the urban residential composition and job opportunities can worsen even under conditions of overall central-city employment gains.

23. Bureau of Labor Statistics, selected reports, 1977 and 1982; and *Washington Post*, October 21, 1982.

The stark reality of rising urban minority unemployment under transforming (and possibly even growing) city economies, together with the improbability that government programs can stimulate sufficient numbers of blue-collar jobs in these cities, calls for a shift in policy emphasis. Politically popular (but ineffective) jobs-to-people strategies and essential urban welfare programs must be better balanced with serious efforts to upgrade the education and skills of disadvantaged city residents *and* with people-to-jobs strategies that would facilitate the migration of the structurally unemployed to places where job opportunities appropriate to their skills are still expanding. Contrary to conventional wisdom, there have been massive increases in entry-level jobs nationwide during the past decade. Nearly 1.8 million nonadministrative jobs were added in the food and drink industry alone between 1974 and 1984. This employment growth, the vast majority at the entry level in fast food and drink establishments, is more than twice the total number of production jobs that exist in America's automobile manufacturing and iron and steel industries combined.[24] Unfortunately, entry-level job expansion in such rapidly multiplying service establishments has occurred almost exclusively in the suburbs, exurbs, and nonmetropolitan areas, far removed from concentrations of low-skill urban minorities.

The inability of most inner-city minorities to follow decentralizing entry-level jobs (either because of racial discrimination, inadequate knowledge and resources, or subsidized anchoring) is among the chief reasons for the widening gap in black-white rates of unemployment and labor force nonparticipation. It is also a major contributor to rising demographic disequilibria in the transforming cities and their correspondingly high social overhead burdens. In this regard, smaller central cities, populated largely by those who actually desire to live in them (minorities as well as whites) and by those who have appropriate employment opportunities available, would create far more vibrant cities than those of today, in which millions of disadvantaged persons are confined without jobs and without much hope for jobs.

To increase the mobility options of the urban disadvantaged, revised policies should be considered that would partially underwrite their more distant job searches and relocation expenses. Additional policies must be aimed at further reducing housing and employment discrimination and other institutional impediments to the mobility of minorities who wish to

24. Bureau of Labor Statistics, *Employment and Earnings*, May 1974 and May 1984.

leave distressed urban areas. Finally, existing public assistance programs should be reviewed to ensure that they are not inadvertently attracting or bonding large numbers of disadvantaged persons to inner-city areas that offer limited opportunities for employment.

All of the above, of course, must be complemented by broader economic development policies fostering sustained private-sector job generation. Programs assisting the retraining or mobility of disadvantaged urban minorities will prove fruitless unless new and enduring jobs are available at the end of the training programs or moves.

The vexing dilemma of the urban underclass will certainly not be entirely solved by these and other strategies proposed here. However, without an expanding national economy, improved education and technical training programs for the urban disadvantaged, stricter enforcement of civil rights legislation, and the mobility of the underclass from economically distressed ghettos, the permanence *and* growth of the underclass will be assured.

BRIAN J. L. BERRY

Islands of Renewal
in Seas of Decay

I RECALL the incredulity with which some of my urban studies colleagues at the University of Chicago greeted the first draft of my paper, "The Geography of the United States in the Year 2000," when I circulated it in 1969. I had suggested that there were clear signs that the century-long trend of population concentration was coming to an end. The society had, I thought, concocted solvents that were dissolving the glue of centrality. Urbanization, a process marked by increasing size, increasing density, and increasing heterogeneity of immigrant population clusters, was being succeeded by "counter-urbanization," a process of population deconcentration marked by decreasing size, decreasing density, and increasing homogeneity of the population selectively left behind by emigration.

The statistics that have emerged from the 1980 census bear witness to my speculations in ways that 1960–70 trends reported in the 1970 census did not: at the regional level, the more densely populated northeastern industrial heartland has declined and the Sun Belt and mountain state rimlands have grown; smaller towns and nonmetropolitan areas have expanded at the expense of metropolitan areas; and within metropolitan regions, suburbanization and exurbanization have increased and both central cities and older suburbs and industrial satellites have declined. These shifts have been facilitated by a housing industry that, despite cyclical perturbations, has consistently constructed many more housing units than the growth in numbers of households appeared to warrant, generally in new locations on the periphery of existing built-up areas, resulting in rounds of relocations that have emptied older neighborhoods.

The support of the National Science Foundation under contract SES-7909370 is gratefully acknowledged, as is the assistance of William Collins, Govind Singh, and Milagros Maldonado.

The housing stock can be viewed as a set of gross substitutes organized into a commodity chain system.[1] Layers of new housing are attractive substitutes that draw upwardly mobile households from older housing types that, in turn, attract households from the units they occupy further down the chain. Any excess of new construction over household growth (and involuntary withdrawals from the stock caused by natural disasters, fires, redevelopment, highway programs, and the like) thus is transferred down the housing chain; "filtering" takes place as households climb the commodity chain and as older housing moves down the social scale. The final resting place of any excess supply is in the least attractive locations. If excess supplies are large, removal of the unwanted units can empty these locations of their structures, creating both a problem and an opportunity— reuse of the vacant land.

Two examples of the magnitudes involved should illustrate. In the Chicago metropolitan area, household growth between 1970 and 1980 was about 302,000, but 484,000 new housing units were built. During the decade vacancies increased by 48,000 units; however, about 135,000 housing units were withdrawn from the stock. In the Pittsburgh metropolitan area, comparable 1970–80 figures are: household growth, 69,000; new construction, 100,000; vacancy increase, 17,000; and withdrawals from stock, 14,000.[2]

In metropolitan areas as a whole, just over 6 million excess housing units were removed from the nation's housing inventory between 1960 and 1970 and some 7 million between 1970 and 1980. The rate of removal each decade was approximately 10 percent of the initial stock. Since successive waves of new housing have been added ringlike around existing built-up areas, the filtering process has always been from periphery to inner city. The excess supplies of the past two decades therefore have become all too evident in boarded-up buildings, vandalized hulks, and vacant lots in central-city neighborhoods. and as the older housing of the inner rings has been removed, the phenomenon has spread outward, producing widening seas of decay.

1. Lawrence D. Schall, "Commodity Chain Systems and the Housing Market," *Journal of Urban Economics*, vol. 10 (September 1981), pp. 141–63; and John B. Lansing, Charles Wade Clifton, and James N. Morgan, *New Homes and Poor People* (University of Michigan, Institute for Social Research, 1969).

2. The figures for new construction and withdrawals from stock are estimated. Comparable figures for 1960–70 in Chicago are: household growth, 285,000; new construction, 481,000; vacancy increase, 7,000; and withdrawals from stock, 189,000. For Pittsburgh, the figures are 49,000; 115,000; −2,000; and 68,000. U.S. Bureau of the Census, *Census of Population and Housing*, 1960, 1970, and 1980.

Yet from meager beginnings in the 1960s there is increasing evidence of the emergence of islands of renewal. In certain neighborhoods, private-market initiatives are leading to revitalization. The crude statistics of population decline mask other data that carry within them countervailing indicators. In many "declining" cities the number of households has actually increased. Metropolitan Chicago's population increased only 1.8 percent between 1970 and 1980, yet the number of households increased by 13.9 percent and housing units (occupied plus vacant) by 15.1 percent. In metropolitan Pittsburgh population declined by 5.7 percent; households increased by 9.1 percent; and housing units increased by 10.8 percent. In their respective central cities, Chicago's population declined by 10.8 percent and housing units by 2.9 percent; and Pittsburgh's population declined by 18.5 percent and housing units by 5.6 percent. But in both of these central cities the numbers and the percentages of young adults increased, particularly those engaged in the white-collar and professional occupations that have grown in downtown Chicago and have been central to Pittsburgh's two-phased "Renaissance," the transformation of a blue-collar steel city into a far-reaching headquarters city and administrative hub.

Conventional wisdom has it that these young professionals are the driving forces of "gentrification," the private-market revitalization that has produced the islands of renewal within the seas of decay. In what follows, this conventional wisdom will be assessed and additional causal elements suggested. I first review the currently available literature on the topic and then examine two derivative hypotheses about timing and location: first, the demand-shift idea associated with young professionals of the baby boom generation; and second, supply-side notions involving the pace of filtering and the magnitude of the price differentials for suburban and central-city housing. The essay concludes by linking the changes to the knowledge- and information-based postindustrial revolution that is now transforming the American economy and society.

Studies of Revitalization

Since the early 1970s the news media have chronicled the renewal of certain neighborhoods in U.S. central cities. The appearance of young professionals (a sort of newly arrived gentry) and of refurbished homes in deteriorated neighborhoods has provided sharp contrast to the overwhelming decline of central-city housing. Renewed interest in what was considered obsolete housing has captured the journalistic imagination and has become the hope for the eventual turnaround of central-city living environments and their residential tax bases.

Preservation of vintage housing near the traditional central business areas of American cities is, of course, a longer-term phenomenon than popularly reported. Early models predicted deterioration of central neighborhoods as upwardly mobile families moved to new housing at the developing periphery, but resistance to this tendency was soon noted. Neighborhoods in Central Boston's Back Bay and historic neighborhoods near the Common, Beacon Hill, and the Charles River were able to resist change and retain their historic values.[3] Georgetown, in Washington, D.C., exhibited early resistance to decapitalization as strong efforts were made by residents for preservation both through traditional zoning and by means of new federal legislation.[4] Such early resistance was restricted to areas occupied by the elite. Current private-market rehabilitation by young artisans or professionals is a new and significantly different force, however.

Anecdotal reporting by the media and follow-up study raise a variety of questions, including the extent of revival, the factors influencing it, neighborhood conditions during the process, and the effects on neighborhoods. Recurring themes are these: Is the phenomenon a back-to-the-city movement? Does it offer a prospect for reversing central-city decline and shoring up sagging tax bases? Is the interest in central-city housing a reflection of changing preferences in housing and life-styles, or is it due simply to a shift in relative housing prices between the suburbs and the central cities?

Extent of Revival

The earliest studies of neighborhood revitalization examined the extent of revival in older New York and Philadelphia neighborhoods.[5] There were important relationships between the location of the neighborhoods and the presence of social and employment opportunities in the central core: a later study confirmed that a weak urban core precluded revival.[6]

The first cross-city studies were undertaken in the 1970s. A landmark

3. Walter Firey, "Sentiment and Symbolism as Ecological Variables," *American Sociological Review*, vol. 10 (1945), p. 142.

4. Eileen Zeitz, *Private Urban Renewal* (Lexington, Mass.: Lexington Books, 1979), pp. 64–65.

5. Edgar M. Hoover and Raymond Vernon, *Anatomy of a Metropolis* (Harvard University Press, 1959); and William G. Grigsby, *Housing Markets and Public Policy* (University of Pennsylvania, Institute for Urban Studies, 1963).

6. Bernard J. Frieden, *The Future of Old Neighborhoods* (MIT Press, 1964), p. 128.

Urban Land Institute study examined private market housing renovation in 260 central cities having populations over 50,000.[7] Forty-eight percent of the respondents said that there was some renovation taking place within their city; the total number of units being renovated was barely 50,000, however, averaging 441 units per city. A National Urban Coalition study of the 30 largest central cities showed similarly modest levels of revitalization, restricted to only 100 neighborhoods overall.[8] The percentage of cities reported to be experiencing renovation increased with size and was higher in the North and South than elsewhere. Units being rehabilitated were predominantly single-family, located within areas of local or national historical importance (possibly having received historic designation), and were close to the city's central business district.[9]

An examination of the twenty largest standard metropolitan statistical areas for 1960–70 produced similar findings.[10] Certain cities with strong cores (New York, Washington, and Boston) showed extensive areas of housing improvement; in others, improvement was restricted to one or two neighborhoods near the core if the core was healthy. When the core was stagnant or deteriorating, there was little rehabilitation. Cities with the highest rates of central white-collar employment and the greatest commuting distances to new housing developments had the strongest, highest-status cores and the greatest volumes of renovation activity.

The extent of revitalization reported is not large. Renovation so far appears to have affected less than 0.5 percent of the central-city housing stock.[11] Continuing outmigration from central cities and disinvestment in housing appear to serve as brakes on private investors because the renovation that has been taking place is risk sensitive and, in most cases, limited in intensity.[12] As Sternlieb has noted; "While much has been made of the relatively few cases of middle class stabilization and/or return to the city

7. Thomas J. Black, "Private-Market Housing Renovation in Central Cities: A ULI Survey," *Urban Land*, vol. 34 (November 1975), p. 7.

8. National Urban Coalition, *Displacement: City Neighborhoods in Transition* (Washington, D.C.: National Urban Coalition, 1978).

9. Black, "Private-Market Housing Renovation," pp. 6–7.

10. Gregory S. Lipton, "Evidence of Central City Revival," *Journal of the American Planning Association*, vol. 43 (April 1977), pp. 136–47.

11. Phillip L. Clay, *Neighborhood Renewal* (Lexington, Mass.: Lexington Books, 1979), p. 17.

12. Howard J. Sumka, "Neighborhood Revitalization and Displacement: A Review of the Evidence," *Journal of the American Planning Association*, vol. 45 (October 1979), pp. 480–87.

. . . as yet these are relatively trivial. The decade of the 1970s . . . has given little promise of mass revival in the major central cities."[13]

Speculations about Causes

What precipitates the decision to renovate a central-city home? Locational, aesthetic, social, and economic factors have been cited. Convenience to place of employment (usually white-collar or professional) in order to reduce commuting distance is the most often quoted reason for moving into a central-city neighborhood.[14] Families in revitalizing neighborhoods rank nearness to employment among the first three reasons for moving into the area.[15] Other factors include nearness to commercial or institutional centers and presence of other than residential rehabilitation. In New Orleans, renovation was viewed more positively than new construction. Nonresidential upgrading occurred near 81 percent of the improved neighborhoods.[16]

Aesthetics (that is, the character of the neighborhood and style of the house) also appears to be critical in selection of a neighborhood for renovation. In virtually all areas being improved, the house is of a significant architectural style. Victorian designs are especially favored in neighborhoods that were built originally to house upper-middle-class families and have filtered yet remain basically sound. The reversal of the filtering process is in many ways due to the recognition of their earlier value and the expectation that house and neighborhood could be returned to their former state. Claims to particular historical significance have tended to reinforce the value of distinctive architecture, most dramatically in Washington, D.C.[17]

13. George Sternlieb, *The Maintenance of America's Housing Stock* (Rutgers University, Center for Urban Policy Research, 1980).

14. Lipton, "Evidence of Central City Revival"; Clay, *Neighborhood Renewal*; Dennis E. Gale, "Middle Class Resettlement in Older Urban Neighborhoods: The Evidence and the Implications," *Journal of the American Planning Association*, vol. 45 (July 1979), p. 297; and Deborah Auger, "The Politics of Revitalization in Gentrifying Neighborhoods: A Case of Boston's South End," *Journal of the American Planning Association*, vol. 45 (July 1979), pp. 515–22.

15. Clay, *Neighborhood Renewal*, p. 15.

16. Ibid., p. 47.

17. Gale, "Middle Class Resettlement in Older Urban Neighborhoods"; and Dennis E. Gale, "Neighborhood Resettlement in Washington, D.C.," in Shirley B. Laska and Daphne Spain, eds., *Back to the City: Issues in Neighborhood Renovation* (Pergamon, 1980), pp. 95–115.

Closely related are social factors—attitudinal and life-style changes among a portion of an emerging group in demand of housing.[18] Many researchers have hypothesized that young, professional, childless couples with college educations and two incomes hold an entirely different set of preferences than was common a generation ago.[19] These persons favor life-styles associated with aesthetics, the excitement of central-city living, and proximity to their places of professional or white-collar employment.

The shift in housing preference by this group is part of an expressed quest for a new set of social values. The appeal of an integrated neighborhood has drawn some young couples, although the level of integration appears to decline as gentrification runs its course.[20] Another attraction is nearness to adult-oriented activities and the city's cultural life.[21] The development of pro-urban values and the desire to reside in mixed ethnic and cultural environments are particularly strong stimuli.

Economic factors are vocalized least by survey respondents. However, one study of Washington, D.C., found them ranked prominently, with respondents naming the investment potential and the affordable price as the reason for selecting neighborhoods undergoing gentrification.[22] According to other studies, the baby boom population entered the housing market when new construction was low and suburban housing was relatively expensive, making the central city a sensible choice, and this opportunity for good, stylish housing at bargain prices is considered a key explanatory variable.[23] Outward shifts in housing and jobs cause a net drop in housing demand in the central city, and a comparison of housing value and potential capital growth makes central-city housing a wise investment.[24]

The potential renovator senses the increased viability of central-city housing and observes higher costs elsewhere as well as the high cost of commuting. In five major cities (Boston, Dallas, San Francisco, Atlanta, and St. Paul), due to the high cost of both new construction and existing

18. Sumka, "Neighborhood Revitalization."

19. Clay, *Neighborhood Renewal*, p. 16.

20. Gale, "Middle Class Resettlement in Older Urban Neighborhoods"; and Gale, "Neighborhood Resettlement in Washington, D.C."

21. Lipton, "Evidence of Central City Revival," p. 138.

22. Gale, "Middle Class Resettlement in Older Urban Neighborhoods"; and Gale, "Neighborhood Resettlement in Washington, D.C."

23. Sumka, "Neighborhood Revitalization," p. 482; and Clay, *Neighborhood Renewal*, p. 4.

24. Anthony Downs, "Key Relationships between Urban Development and Neighborhood Change," *Journal of the American Planning Association*, vol. 45 (October 1979), pp. 462–71; and Anthony Downs, *Neighborhoods and Urban Development* (Brookings, 1981).

suburban housing, the inner cities offered the home buyer more. A wide variety of convenient, reasonably priced houses in neighborhoods with high vacancy rates (for example, homes that were almost fully depreciated and outwardly uninhabitable in Boston's South End) were available for several thousand dollars.[25] Viewed in such a light, private market rehabilitation is not a chance phenomenon, but an investment decision. Movement of capital to the suburbs results in depreciation of central values and a "rent gap." When the gap is large, rehabilitation investments challenge the rates of return available elsewhere and capital returns to the city.[26]

Another factor widely hypothesized to be influential is rapidly rising commuting costs brought on by energy price increases. During the energy crisis, respondents did not want to live far from their jobs.[27] Energy costs have not been ranked significantly in many studies, however. But an alternative transportation cost rationale explaining the original movement of the affluent to the periphery and their subsequent return to the central city has been postulated.[28] It is rooted in the differential effects of price changes on income groups, not in preferences. The reversal in the location of the well-to-do is explained by a continuation, not a reversal, of the price changes that caused the flight to the periphery. Expensive transportation innovations always gave initial competitive advantages in location to the wealthy, but eventually the lower cost of that transportation allowed the poor to follow. Historically, a succession of innovations allowed the rich to maintain their superior locational advantage. But no innovation has replaced the automobile, and rich and poor now approach equal access to housing opportunity. As a result, a reversal in housing patterns is now occurring, because the rich are substituting locational for technological advantage.

Is There a Back-to-the-City Movement?

Much has been made of inner-city revitalization as a back-to-the-city movement. Early reporting by national and regional media developed the theme that private rehabilitation was being undertaken by families who had at one time turned their backs on the city and were now returning,

25. Black, "Private-Market Housing Renovation."

26. Neil Smith, "Toward a Theory of Gentrification," *Journal of the American Planning Association*, vol. 45 (October 1979), p. 545.

27. Black, "Private-Market Housing Renovation," p. 8.

28. Stephen LeRoy and Jon Soustelie, "Paradise Lost and Regained: American Cities in the 1970s" (University of California–Los Angeles, 1979).

disillusioned by suburban life-styles, housing costs, and increasing costs of commuting.

This hypothesis has been tested. People moving to rehabilitated neighborhoods were questioned around the country. Their responses seem to support an alternative hypothesis, because for the most part they came from other parts of the central city. It appears to be a stay-in-the-city rather than a back-to-the-city movement.

One comparative study of Atlanta, New Orleans, New York, St. Paul, Boston, Cambridge, and Washington, D.C., showed only a minority (20 percent) of the new households coming from the suburbs. From 50 to 90 percent of new households questioned had come from somewhere else in the central city. Most were first-home buyers. A large majority of the families (60 to 90 percent) had spent their childhood in rural, small town, or suburban areas, though. They came to the city for college or employment and when ready to make an investment in housing chose the city as an environment preferable to the suburbs.[29]

In Washington, D.C., there was not so much a back-to-the-city movement as there was an investment in permanent homes by former renters.[30] Only 10 percent of new white households in the central city were returning from the suburbs, a similar percentage to that for Philadelphia, where only 14 percent of rehabilitators came from the suburbs, 72 percent came from elsewhere in the city, and 11 percent were upgrading their long-term residence.[31]

A stay-in-the-city phenomenon is thus more likely than a return from the suburbs. Newly established city families have strong reasons to stay in the city and to find investment opportunities there compatible with their needs. Established suburban dwellers, securely settled in their own housing market, employment, and social routines, have little incentive to return to the city.[32] The life-cycle change when young adults leave their parents' homes does place large numbers of youths in the city as they begin their careers or higher education, however.[33] The expansion of central-city office space and managerial and professional occupations is very at-

29. Gale, "Middle Class Resettlement in Older Urban Neighborhoods"; and Gale, "Neighborhood Resettlement in Washington, D.C."

30. George Grier and Eunice Grier, *Movers to the City: New Data on the Housing Market for Washington, D.C.* (Washington Center for Metropolitan Studies, 1977).

31. Smith, "Toward a Theory of Gentrification," p. 539.

32. Herbert Gans, "Why Exurbanites Won't Reurbanize Themselves," *New York Times*, February 12, 1977.

33. Larry H. Long, "Back to the Countryside and Back to the City in the Same Decade," in Laska and Spain, eds., *Back to the City*, pp. 61–76.

tractive to young college-trained couples.[34] Centers of employment, two-wage-earner households, and the rising prices of suburban housing keep these families in the city. Surveys of central-city neighborhood attitudes report a strong satisfaction with neighborhood life among these residents. Even though residents feel the city is declining, they expect to remain.[35] Their confidence is in the neighborhood and not the city.

Stages of Revitalization

According to many observers, the revitalization process changes dramatically as it progresses, producing an environment quite different from the one envisioned by the first renovating families.[36] The stages of the process are distinguished primarily by the actors involved and the extent of renovation accomplished.

STAGE ONE. A few households (either oblivious to or acceptant of the risks involved), usually singles or childless couples, purchase homes in a deteriorated neighborhood and begin renovating for their own use. These are often design professionals or artists, each one employed, who share a desire to live in a mixed ethnic neighborhood in a part of the city exhibiting popularized urban cultural values and who express their design aptitudes by restoring classic homes. Since neighborhood vacancy rates are high and the houses are often gutted shells, the cost is very low and there is little displacement of existing neighborhood residents. As a result, there is little resentment or hostility on the part of the indigenous population. Little public attention is aroused by the initial activity. The newcomers rely on private capital sources, "sweat equity" investment, and informal neighborhood organizations for support. Efforts are generally confined to a two-to-three block area.

STAGE TWO. After six months to a couple of years, knowledge of neighborhood rehabilitation spreads. Many of the same types of families are attracted, plus a new group of "risk takers"—upper-middle-income management or professional types. The price, investment potential, and neighborhood cultural, architectural, and locational characteristics are appealing,

34. Laska and Spain, eds., *Back to the City*.

35. Ibid.

36. A four-stage process was proposed by Pattison, elaborated by Clay, and refined to three stages by Gale. See Timothy Pattison, "The Process of Neighborhood Upgrading and Gentrification" (M.A. thesis, Massachusetts Institute of Technology, 1977); Clay, *Neighborhood Renewal*; Gale, "Middle Class Resettlement in Older Urban Neighborhoods"; and Gale, "Neighborhood Resettlement in Washington, D.C."

but capital still is not freely available due to continuing uncertainty. Realtors become involved in subtle promotional activities, and small-scale developers begin renovating for speculation, but in limited amounts because of a lack of institutional investment capital. The media begin to take note of the scale of rehabilitation, and the boundaries of the area expand. Vacant housing quickly disappears, and displacement begins to occur among rentals where low-income, elderly, and transient populations reside. Those who move in at stage two are not as accepting of class and cultural differences, and the indigenous population begins to express resentment as invasion threatens their stability.

STAGE THREE. There is major media and government interest in the neighborhood. Physical improvements are visible. Active governmental intervention begins. Prices escalate, developers begin larger-scale renovations, conversion of rental units to condominiums begins in force, and commercial redevelopment spreads. The area is "greenlined" by financial institutions, and investment and home improvement capital becomes more readily available. Newer groups of residents appear, including older and more affluent executives and administrators who are risk averse. They pay top prices and effectively displace most of the remaining indigenous residents. The newcomers establish their own neighborhood organizations or effectively dominate or change the character of pioneer organizations. They make demands for public resources, protection, and land use restrictions. Social service institutions and public housing or low-income housing assistance programs are resisted.

The Revitalizing Neighborhood

What is evident from the foregoing is that there is a private-market process that is successfully running counter to the dominant forces of deconcentration and downward filtering of older housing. Residential deterioration is arrested, upgrading takes place, and the rich displace the poor.

What characteristics do revitalizing neighborhoods share in common? In the nation's thirty largest central cities, 46 percent of the structures in revitalizing areas were at least one hundred years old and another 27 percent were at least seventy-five years old.[37] The area represented the cities' most distinctive architecture, generally Victorian. Most neighbor-

37. Clay, *Neighborhood Renewal*, p. 18.

hoods were dominated by one- or two-family structures, a characteristic that was maintained through the process. Seventy-eight percent of the housing was judged to be deteriorating before investment. In about half the neighborhoods, the cost of acquisition was less than $15,000.

Changes due to rehabilitation include improvements in both buildings and public facilities. Structural improvements range from less expensive cosmetic improvements to authentic restoration or gut rehabilitation, including major structural and utilities replacement. As revitalization reaches advanced stages increasing pressure is exerted by neighborhood organizations or local government for public improvements. Demands are made and met for street and sidewalk resurfacing or replacement with paving stones, fashionable lighting, landscaping, and improved public services such as police patrols and sanitary disposal. Rehabilitators generally do not seek improvements in public education, however, since they either have few children or use private schools.[38]

The value of improved units increases rapidly. Demand for the units is brisk, and early investment and sweat equity pay off handsomely. Values in one Washington, D.C., area increased at twice the city rate.[39] There are preconditions for this success, however. The neighborhood must have definable boundaries so that there is reasonable anticipation of consolidation and stability. The housing stock must have residual strengths—a high percentage with special characteristics or potential for rehabilitation. The area must be of special historical importance or qualify for historical district designation. It must be favorably located near the central business district. There should be expectations that significant rehabilitation will take place and that government services can be improved. Influential neighborhood groups are essential. These are conditions necessary for later stages of revitalization and are seldom considered important to investment by "risk-oblivious" pioneers.[40]

What about the human characteristics of upgraded neighborhoods? The general nature of social change was outlined earlier. A detailed insight into a classic case of social interaction, confrontation, and use of organizational influence was provided in a study of the transition of Boston's South End.[41]

38. Ibid., p. 63.

39. Zeitz, *Private Urban Renewal*, p. 49.

40. Black, "Private-Market Housing Renovation," p. 7; and Paul Porter, "Neighborhood Interest in a City's Recovery," *Journal of the American Planning Association*, vol. 45 (October 1979), pp. 473–79.

41. Auger, "The Politics of Revitalization in Gentrifying Neighborhoods."

Before rehabilitation, residents were a racially mixed combination of settled families, singles, elderly people, and transients. Employed persons were generally blue-collar workers, clerks, and low-skilled laborers. Population densities were higher at this time than at any period later in the process.[42] In contrast, those moving in were predominantly childless, white adult households, together with many single parents in their late twenties or early thirties, professionals or managers, well educated (up to 80 percent with college degrees), affluent enough to handle self-financing, and highly motivated politically and socially.[43]

After rehabilitation was complete, about half of the neighborhood was composed of younger couples and half was of mixed age but significantly younger than the previous residents. Professional and white-collar employees assumed control of neighborhood politics and pressure group activities for public improvements.[44] The activism was short-lived, however. Once the improvements were secured, involvement by the latecomers declined. Typically, latecomers are not as neighborhood-based as the pioneers were. Their associations are based on work, and they look outside the neighborhood for recreation and consumer goods and services. Their higher-status tastes exceed what the neighborhood can provide. They prefer political issues to personalities and interest group lobbying to clubs or populist vehicles, and thus stay independent of neighborhood organizations.[45]

Positive and Negative Impacts

Though the extent of gentrification is not great, the available literature suggests that it has substantial impacts, both positive and negative, on the central city. Positive effects are decreases in vacancy rates, increases in property values, stability in once-declining neighborhoods, encouragement of other forms of development in or near the neighborhoods, and rekindled interest in the central city as a place to live—a real locational and economic alternative to housing in the suburbs. The positive aspects are welcomed by the city, development and business interests, and established and

42. Zeitz, *Private Urban Renewal*, pp. 39–40.

43. Grier and Grier, *Movers to the City*; Sternlieb, *The Maintenance of America's Housing Stock*; and Black, "Private-Market Housing Renovation," p. 7.

44. Zeitz, *Private Urban Renewal*, pp. 71–72.

45. Clay, *Neighborhood Renewal*, p. 65.

prospective residents, and they are lauded by the media and students of urban research.

Negative aspects, with the possible exception of displacement, are often overlooked by those interested in the benefits of rehabilitation. The costs of increased demands for service, infrastructure, and amenities and the impact on existing public services have not been studied, nor have the opportunity costs of investment capital or the problem of speculative increases in blighted property values that might be unsupportable in the long run.[46]

Of all of the problems accompanying private-market renewal, the most serious is displacement. The first to be displaced are renters. A National Urban Coalition Study found that these predominantly minority, elderly, and transient groups are always forced out, casualties of owner capitalization of depreciated structures, escalating demand in a market of fixed supply, and increasing code enforcement.[47]

Accurate study of the extent of this neighborhood displacement is difficult. The cost and effort of tracing the displaced families has discouraged systematic analysis. Small samples and intuitive judgment are the basis of most conclusions. The results are as ambiguous as data on the real extent of revitalization.

Data from the Census Bureau's *Annual Housing Survey* indicate that 1 million households were displaced between 1974 and 1976, yet one study indicated the problem to be relatively small in scale, affecting 100 to 200 households per year in any city.[48] Studies of Washington, D.C., suggest that the problem grew significantly there during the 1970s, compounded by low vacancy rates due in part to suburban development moratoria that reduced housing starts. On the other hand, another study suggests that where rehabilitation occurs at a moderate pace and vacancy rates approximate the national average, the impact of displacement is modest, although the effects on affected individuals may be profound.[49]

46. Black, "Private-Market Housing Renovation," p. 9.

47. Cushing N. Dolbeare, "Involuntary Displacement: A Major Issue for People and Neighborhoods," report prepared for the National Commission on Neighborhoods (Government Printing Office, 1978); and National Urban Coalition, *Displacement: City Neighborhoods in Transition.*

48. Grier and Grier, *Movers to the City.*

49. Gale, "Middle Class Resettlement in Older Urban Neighborhoods"; and Gale, "Neighborhood Resettlement in Washington, D.C."

Demand-Side Dynamics: The Gentrification Hypothesis

A picture begins to emerge: amidst pervasive depopulation of central cities some neighborhoods in some of these cities are beginning to attract private capital and along with it the mainly white middle class. Alliterative labels abound—rehabilitation, reinvestment, revitalization, even renaissance—but the most evocative term is the one imported from London: *gentrification.*

By conjuring the image of an aristocratic landed gentry, the gentrification label suggests that the new urban gentry are somehow different from and more exotic than normal people. An unexamined folklore has sprung up. According to the oral tradition, the urban gentry are overwhelmingly young, affluent, and nomadic. Many are artists, architects, or self-employed professionals. They include homosexuals or "swinging singles" drawn to the nightlife and the sexual marketplace of the city. Those that are married are likely to be childless two-earner couples. But this given wisdom about the new urban gentry has not been subjected to much empirical scrutiny. What literature exists on the topic tends to rely upon impressionistic and anecdotal observations, rather than on a systematic comparison of the social worlds of comparably affluent urban and suburban dwellers.

To the extent that more systematic inquiry is now being undertaken, it centers on the gentrification hypothesis: that the key role in the rehabilitation of decaying homes and the restoration of blighted neighborhoods is being played by relatively affluent childless two-worker families—"yuppies."[50]

Attributes of the New Gentry

For example, one effort to model the sources of the city's upper-income renaissance concludes that upper-income residence in the city usually requires the following observable attributes:

1. Childless households. The decision to raise children implies a substantial commitment to activities focused on home and family. Individuals and couples who have not made this commitment can be expected to seek

50. Martin T. Katzman, "Gentrification of Cities and the Changing Composition of American Families" (University of Texas, School of Social Sciences, 1979).

both more diversions and more social relationships outside the home than those who have. The social, cultural, and entertainment facilities of the city center can provide both things to do and opportunities for making and maintaining friendships. For individuals and couples in childless households, these facilities' marginal utility should be high and remain high even with frequent use. On the other hand, reductions in residential density are apt to provide relatively modest and rapidly declining increments to satisfaction for childless households. Exterior space where children can play safely without supervision is of obvious value where children are present, but irrelevant when children are absent from the household.

2. Unmarried adults. An interest in social relationships outside the home and in opportunities for meeting and entertaining one another should be particularly strong among unmarried adults, even when they are heads of families with children.

3. Higher educational levels. Besides the skills it develops, higher education seeks to enhance understanding and appreciation of a wide variety of cultural experiences and historical properties and neighborhoods that are most frequently found in the central city. It should therefore increase the pleasure such experiences provide and sustain it during repeated attendance or exposure that would quickly bore the uninitiated.[51]

Childlessness is a particularly important factor because childless families are relatively impervious to the turmoil in big-city school systems associated with the desegregation that has led to white flight.[52] Childlessness, in turn, flows directly from shifts in the composition and life-styles of the American population. The continued development of American society has resulted in increased economic parity for women; this enables them to have the option of roles other than those of housewife and mother. In consequence, men and women lead more independent lives and are able to exercise more options. Increasing number of couples live together without the formal ties of marriage. The direct and opportunity costs of child rearing are rising; birth control technology has improved; and abortion laws have been liberalized. Hence the birthrate is dropping. There are increasing numbers of families with two or more workers and more working wives than ever before.

The literature on residential mobility states that changes in family status—such as marriage, birth of children, or dissolution of marriage—

51. Clifford R. Kern, "Upper Income Renaissance in the City: Its Sources and Implications for the City's Future," *Journal of Urban Economics*, vol. 9 (January 1981), pp. 106–24.

52. Katzman, "Gentrification of Cities."

raise the probability that a given family will change its residence; that families in different stages of the life cycle differ in their sensitivity to particular neighborhood characteristics (such as crime rates or school quality); and that families are residentially segregated on the basis of their stage in the life cycle.

In residential choice theory, a family is presumed to observe an array of neighborhoods that differ in quality of the housing structures (space, comfort); physical aspects (location, site amenities); social character (class, ethnic, and racial composition); municipal services (quality of schools, police protection, tax rates); and housing prices. Families presumably attribute different importance to these characteristics, depending upon their stage in the life cycle, socioeconomic status, race, or ethnicity. High-income families with school-age children may place greater weight on safe streets than do low-income families without children. Or, because their wages are higher and time is more valuable, high-income families may be more willing to avoid commuting costs than low-income families.

Within the spectrum of neighborhood choices available, the reduction in fertility and the rise in female labor force participation produce a situation in which affluent, childless, two-worker families appear to be attracted to neighborhoods offering: (1) geographic clusters of housing structures capable of yielding high-quality services; (2) a variety of public amenities within safe walking distance of these areas, such as a scenic waterfront, parks, museums or art galleries, universities, distinguished architecture, and historic landmarks or neighborhoods; and (3) a range of high-quality retail facilities and services, including restaurants, theaters, and entertainment.

These neighborhoods are more often than not close to downtown and tend to have older housing, higher crime rates, worse air pollution, and schools that are perceived as worse than those in the suburbs. These factors are almost fully reflected in housing prices. For example, houses in school zones attended by low-income minorities generally command lower prices than houses located in zones attended by upper-middle-income whites. This price differential presumably reflects the competition by families with school-age children for housing in the "better" school district. Families without children have no special reason to pay a premium for living in the neighborhood with better schools and find the neighborhood with poor schools less expensive, other factors being equal. A flight of middle-class families with children from downtown neighborhoods to the suburbs thereby creates potential housing bargains for affluent families without children.

This potential is realized if other relevant urban-suburban differences in neighborhood quality, such as safety and cleanliness of the streets, are reduced.[53]

Affluent, two-worker families may, of course, inherently be attracted to near-downtown residences because of the proximity to their jobs in government, communications, finance, or law. These activities are still heavily concentrated in the central business districts of many older cities despite the long-term suburbanization of employment. Indeed, analyses of centrifugal patterns of metropolitan growth through the 1960s have identified the professional-managerial group as the biggest losers: because of the high degree of centralization of their jobs in some cities, this group may face the longest commute. The situation is even more acute for two-worker professional families. Living in the peripheral suburbs, such families often spend twice as much time and money in commuting downtown as a one-worker family. Even if the secondary worker does not work downtown, a more central location provides greater access to the metropolitan labor market. Finally, peripheral residence restricts access to cultural amenities and recreational opportunities that loom large in the budgets of the more affluent.

Such observations serve to affirm one scholar's conclusion that the cities with strong upper-income neighborhoods close to downtown were, in 1960–70, dominantly those with administrative central business districts, minimal heavy industry, and long commuting distances to the suburbs.[54] Conversely, industrial cities with weak central business districts and dispersed industrial locations were unable to retain or attract the professional middle class.

Cohort Effect or Long-Term Change?

According to one line of argument, the continued decline in fertility, the prolongation of childlessness, the growth of female labor force participation, and the emergence of high-service downtown economies all bode well for the cities. Indeed, it is argued that the changes in family composition of the 1970s and 1980s may have far more impact on returning the middle class to the central city than all the urban redevelopment programs of the

53. Ibid.
54. Lipton, "Evidence of Central City Revival."

1950s and 1960s.[55] A question that then arises is whether these changes will remain in the long term or simply are an effect associated with the baby boom cohort that will pass as members of that generation age.

Demographers note that even in the 1960s young people (aged 20 to 25) expressed some preference for city living.[56] Cities have long served as "staging areas"—places where young middle-class adults, while renting, could meet and marry before settling down to raise families in the suburbs. If the age-specific preferences of past decades remained the same, the maturation of the baby boom cohort would, in itself, swell the ranks of young city dwellers (though not necessarily of young central-city home buyers), but the effect would pass.

Thus one view is that reduction in urban household size represents a postponement of marriage and childbearing in the baby boom cohort, rather than a permanent shift in family patterns. The argument continues that the 1980s may see an acceleration of urban out-migration rates as the children of the baby boom years move through their own childbearing period.

In the same vein, another scholar argues that the most important influence on residential location is accessibility to the workplace, and so long as downtowns continue to lose professional and managerial jobs to the suburbs, the accessibility factor will work to the disadvantage of gentrification. He also observes that while safer neighborhoods are more important to families with children than to childless families, the difference is slight, as are the differences in preferences for neighborhood racial composition between families varying by number of children and number of workers.[57]

But others demur, arguing that the baby boom cohort is behaving differently from preceding cohorts and will continue to do so.[58] The sheer size of the cohort is said to condemn its members to perpetual relative economic disadvantage—a disadvantage that has prompted falling fertility rates, declining household size, increased female labor force participation, and a reluctance to make long-term commitments to marriage and family. This demographic determinism suggests that the tastes and preferences of

55. Richard A. Easterlin, *Birth and Fortune: The Impact of Number on Personal Welfare* (Basic Books, 1980); and William Alonso, "The Population Factor and Urban Structure," in A. P. Solomon, ed., *The Prospective City: Economic Population, Energy, and Environmental Developments* (MIT Press, 1980), pp. 32–51.

56. Long, "Back to the Countryside and Back to the City."

57. Katzman, "Gentrification of Cities."

58. Easterlin, *Birth and Fortune*.

the maturing baby boom generation will not change drastically, and that its members will likely remain in the city longer than those favoring the temporary nature of the cohort effect might imagine.

Supply-Side Forces: A New Interpretation

The gentrification hypothesis suggests a variety of reasons why childless two-worker professional households are likely to be drawn to certain kinds of inner-city neighborhoods, while the combination of the large baby boom cohort and the rapid growth of professional employment in the last two decades indicates why this particular set of demands has grown. But why has gentrification occurred only in certain central cities? A new supply-side interpretation helps to answer this question.

The classical supply-side argument has two components. The first rests on the observation that although more households are added to the ranks of homeowners during high construction years than during low construction years,[59] rehabilitation expenditures have classically been countercyclical.[60] This observation has led to the conclusion that the forces guiding home seekers to the central city have been greatest in periods of economic downturn and in the metropolitan housing markets where the new housing industry is weakest.

The second component is the effects of rapid increases in both building costs and housing prices in the face of increasing demand. The baby boom children graduated from high school between 1965 and 1982, so the housing market is now experiencing the full impact of that cohort. The logical resolution of the conflict between higher suburban building costs and increasing numbers of home seekers should be to increase the demand for lower-cost central-city housing or to stimulate provision of alternatives, such as factory-built (mobile) homes and condominium or cooperative ownership. This force should be greatest, according to this argument, in the housing markets with the greatest cost and demand pressures. Together, the two supply-side components lead to a prediction that gentrification is

59. Dowell Myers, "Back-to-the-City: New Measurements in Three Cities," paper prepared for the 1980 conference of the American Planning Association.

60. Franklin J. James, "Private Reinvestment in Older Housing and Older Neighborhoods," statement before the Senate Committee on Banking, Housing and Urban Affairs, July 10, 1977; and Franklin J. James, "The Revitalization of Older Urban Housing and Neighborhoods," in Solomon, ed., *The Prospective City*, pp. 130–60.

most likely in housing markets with weak new housing industries faced by both rapidly rising construction costs and housing demand and should occur countercyclically, at low points in the economic cycle.

In what follows I argue to the contrary. It is the housing markets in which the new housing industry has created the largest surpluses and in which the forces of inner-city abandonment are greatest that one finds the most extensive and sustained processes of gentrification, subject to the condition that there also be significant office growth in the central business district.

The Magnitude of Excess Supply

The U.S. home-building industry has responded to strong housing demand in the last thirty years by constructing new homes at rates substantially greater than the rate of household growth. The amount by which new construction exceeds household growth in any housing market can be called the excess supply. Excess supplies will result either in increased vacancies or in withdrawals of older units from the housing stock as households move into the better units and the market attempts to bring demand and supply back into balance. Vacant units may also be removed from the housing stock so that in certain housing markets withdrawals from the stock may exceed excess supply by the amount by which vacancies are reduced.[61]

Nationally, some 20 million new housing units were built in the 1970s (nearly double the increase of the 1960s), so that by 1980 one in every five American households was able to reside in a home that was less than ten years old. Close to 7 million older housing units were removed from use as places of residence, although rates of displacement from housing that was condemned, demolished, or for some other reason removed from the inventory were lower than during the 1960s, when urban renewal and

---

61. In equation form, the accounting equality is that units built (U) minus household growth (H) equals excess supply (E), and excess supply in turn equals withdrawals from the stock (W) plus vacancy increase ($+V$) in the case that some of the excess remains vacant, and minus vacancy change ($-V$) in the case that there are net withdrawals from the vacancy pool:

$$U - H = E$$
$$E = W \pm V$$
$$U = H + W \pm V.$$

Tabulations of excess supplies and withdrawals from stock for the nation's "million plus" metropolitan areas for the decades 1960–70 and 1970–80 are available from the author.

slum clearance programs were at a peak.[62] As a result, the availability of housing increased from 284 units per 1,000 people in 1940 to 338 in 1970 and 389 in 1980. Average household size fell from over 3.5 to 2.5 between 1940 and 1980.[63] Another result was the removal of large numbers of housing units that were no longer useful because of their absolute age and obsolescence or their configuration. If all central-city housing is taken as a group, in the brief period from 1970 to 1974, filtering made possible by excess supply produced substantial upgrading on most indices of housing quality: there was a reduction of over 25 percent in the number of units lacking some or all plumbing and in units with more than one person per room, while the number of units having no bathrooms or shared bathrooms was reduced by more than one-third.[64]

For many of the excess housing units filtered out at the unwanted end of the nation's housing chains, abandonment preceded withdrawal from the stock.[65] Technically, abandonment describes structures that are largely unoccupied and whose original use is no longer economically viable. The owners have walked away and the services that normally keep them intact are no longer being provided, property taxes are frequently unpaid, and the city may be in the process of taking title to the properties via tax foreclosure. Ultimately, most such abandoned buildings are demolished. But abandonment may also be viewed in terms of the scrappage rate familiar

62. In 1950–60, programs for the renewal of deteriorated commercial and residential areas, highway construction, and other land use clearance projects contributed to the removal of an estimated 10 million housing units from the nation's housing inventory. See the Advisory Commission on Intergovernmental Relations, *Relocation: Unequal Treatment of People and Businesses Displaced by Governments* (GPO, 1965); Martin Anderson, *The Federal Bulldozer: A Critical Analysis of Urban Renewal, 1949–1962* (MIT Press, 1964); and Cincinnati Department of Urban Development, *Family Relocation Patterns in Cincinnati* (City of Cincinnati, 1973).

63. Donald C. Dahmann, *Housing Opportunities for Black and White Households: Three Decades of Change in the Supply of Housing*, Special Demographic Analyses of the Bureau of the Census (U.S. Department of Commerce, 1981); and George E. Peterson, "Federal Tax Policy and the Shaping of the Urban Environment" (Cambridge, Mass.: National Bureau of Economic Research, 1977).

64. Dahmann, *Housing Opportunities for Black and White Households.*

65. George Sternlieb and Robert W. Burchell, *Residential Abandonment: The Tenement Landlord Revisited* (Rutgers University, Center for Urban Policy Research, 1973); Bruce Bender, "The Determinants of Housing Abandonment" (Ph.D. dissertation, University of Chicago, 1976); Michael J. Dear, "Abandoned Housing," in John S. Adams, ed., *Urban Policymaking and Metropolitan Dynamics* (Ballinger, 1976), pp. 59–99; U.S. Department of Housing and Urban Development, *Residential Abandonment in Central Cities* (GPO, 1977); and U.S. General Accounting Office, *Housing Abandonment: A National Problem Needing New Approaches* (GPO, 1978).

to businessmen: the proportion of an inventory that is removed on an annual basis. The housing scrappage rate that manifests itself in end-of-the-line abandonment approximates 1 percent of the housing stock per year, an annual loss of 600,000–800,000 units.[66]

Withdrawals from Stock and Contagious Abandonment

When new construction is suburban and the least desirable stock is older and more central, it is easy to see how the phenomenon of inner-city abandonment—the seas of decay—can arise. As more desirable housing units are occupied and less desirable ones left behind, excess supplies of housing will show up in withdrawals from the inner-city housing stock and depopulation of the central city. This can happen in an atmosphere of general "looseness" of the housing market, when many units need to be withdrawn from the stock to bring demand and supply into balance but vacancies still increase, or when there is a "tightening" of the market because both excess supplies and some of the existing vacancies are removed as the market readjusts toward equilibrium. In the first case, the inner city will have increasing numbers of vacant and boarded-up buildings; in the second, there will be vacant lots and empty spaces.

In the extreme case, abandonment develops a dynamic of its own, becoming a contagious process—a spreading blight that leads to the removal of far more units from the housing stock than would be warranted by smooth filtering of excess supplies to the oldest units and neighborhoods, those most in need of scrappage and replacement.[67] Contagious abandonment can lead to the removal of the good along with the bad and can rapidly transform a situation of substantial excess supply into one of significant tightness.

The Conditions for Gentrification

The classical supply-side argument, stated above, was that gentrification should be characteristic of housing markets where the new housing industry is weakest or faced by the greatest demand pressures. Yet if one considers the cases where significant gentrification has been recorded (for example, New York, Philadelphia, San Francisco, Boston, Washington, St. Louis,

66. Sternlieb, *The Maintenance of America's Housing Stock.*
67. Dear, "Abandoned Housing."

and Atlanta),[68] my research reveals that a different dynamic is taking place. Gentrification has its onset in some of the housing markets in which the housing industry is producing substantial excess supply by building far more units than the growth in the number of households requires—markets that one would expect to be among the nation's loosest. Which are being gentrified? The process appears to be limited to those housing markets in which even larger volumes of the older housing stock are being scrapped (typically as an outcome of contagious abandonment), and there is a resultant tightening of the market as the pool of vacancies is reduced.

However, the list of gentrification-eligible housing markets tightened by contagious abandonment also includes such examples as Detroit, Cleveland, and Newark, where significant gentrification has not yet occurred. This leads me to the conclusion that supply-side factors set a necessary but not a sufficient condition for gentrification to take place. There must be an additional triggering mechanism that separates the markets with the necessary combinations of excess supplies, scrappage rates, and vacancy changes into those with and those without gentrification.

The missing link has been alluded to earlier: significant central business district growth, focusing professional and white-collar jobs downtown. What separates the Cleveland, Detroit, and Newark cases from those such as Boston, Philadelphia, and Atlanta is the growth of central business district office space, averaging barely 20 percent in the cases without gentrification, but 33 percent in those with it in 1970–78 (figure 1). Excessive scrappage of inner-city housing is indeed a necessary but not sufficient supply-side condition for gentrification to occur; the process has to be activated by demand-side shifts rooted in professional job growth anchored in downtown offices and by baby boom life-style shifts.

These shifts, in turn, have their own roots in the emergence of a modern service economy after World War II and the concentration of corporate activities and key producer services in selected cities. Some of those cities—those with the necessary housing market conditions—also had gentrification. The services revolution has been charted by Thomas M. Stanback, Jr., and his associates.[69] The main points of their arguments are as follows.

1. Between 1948 and 1978 the share of services in U.S. employment increased from 54 percent to 67 percent. The most significant change was

68. Laska and Spain, eds., *Back to the City.*
69. Thomas M. Stanback and others, *Services: The New Economy* (Totowa, N.J.: Allanheld, Osmun, 1981); and Thomas M. Stanback, Jr., and Thierry J. Noyelle, *Cities in Transition* (Totowa, N.J.: Allanheld, Osmun, 1982).

Figure 1. *Growth in Central Business District Office Space in Thirty-one U.S. Cities, 1970–78*

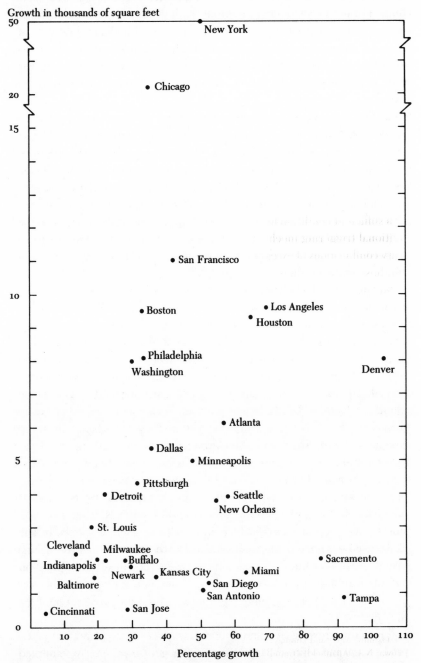

Growth in thousands of square feet

Percentage growth

Sources: Survey data provided by the Urban Land Institute, Washington, D.C., for all cities except New York, Detroit, San Francisco, St. Louis, and Milwaukee, which were based on survey data provided by the Regional Plan Association of New York.

the rapid emergence of producer services designed to assist private-sector firms and public-sector and nonprofit institutions in carrying out administrative, developmental, and financial functions. This change brought with it a shift from blue-collar to white-collar jobs, a major expansion in the employment of women, and new characteristics relating to working conditions, terms of employment, and the distribution of earnings among workers.

2. The new jobs in corporate and producer services concentrated disproportionately in selected urban centers—what Stanback terms the nation's *nodal centers*, metropolitan areas strongly specialized and diversified in the distributive services and in corporate activities. These include four national centers—New York, Los Angeles, Chicago, and San Francisco—and nineteen regional centers, such as Boston, Philadelphia, and Atlanta. Other places affected have been a few key specialized centers characterized by the articulation of administration, research, and production in selected industrial complexes, such as Pittsburgh in steel and Rochester in scientific and office equipment.

3. The concentration of many of the growing services in the downtown areas of the nation's principal organizational and control centers, which has thus focused jobs and residential choices of young white-collar and professional workers, has arisen from very traditional pulls: those of agglomeration economies that accrue to firms when they congregate. In this respect, the role of corporate headquarters, divisional offices, and other specialized service installations is of particular importance. As developmental and administrative functions have become more important, major corporate offices have increasingly been located near large banks, insurance companies, legal firms, and other producer services. In turn, they have fostered the growth of these services. These agglomeration tendencies do not simply benefit the relationship between producer services and corporate headquarters or divisional offices, however. They also attract a host of private-sector, public-sector, and nonprofit services. Specialty retail stores, fancy restaurants, theaters, universities, major hospitals, or specialized governmental services tend to locate more frequently in large places because of the larger markets to be served. In turn, corporations and their attendant producer services are drawn to these places because of the larger support system of consumer and not-for-profit services that they find there.

It is in this growing complex of modern service-sector activities that the professional and white-collar jobs supporting gentrification have emerged.

To turn the supply-side argument around, the nation's key "command and control" centers provide a sufficient demand-side trigger for gentrification, provided that the necessary supply-side housing market characteristics also are present.

Conclusions

Certain neighborhoods in certain central cities are experiencing a new form of private-market revitalization—gentrification. The process is limited to urban centers of strategic national and regional importance in which the expansion of modern headquarters complexes and related producer services has led to significant new central business district growth, producing the demand-side trigger of young professional and white-collar workers. It also is limited to housing markets in which new construction substantially exceeds household growth, but in which scrappage (perhaps in the form of contagious abandonment) exceeds the excess housing supply. The result is that the markets are tightened and older central-city housing becomes an attractive option.

It is the intersection of the two sets of forces that is of interest. Central business district growth in Sun Belt urban centers lacking the necessary housing market conditions is not accompanied by gentrification. Neither is there gentrification in older urban regions where abandonment proceeds apace, but the central business district remains moribund. Both the necessary and the sufficient conditions must be satisfied for a process of gentrification to begin.

Once the process takes hold, it serves to heighten the contrast between renewal and decay. The cities that have shifted most sharply to a service employment base have at the same time experienced the most dramatic losses of their middle-income manufacturing jobs. As a result, their labor markets have become increasingly polarized between well-paying white-collar and professional employment and low-paying service jobs. The overall trend among the service industries has been toward the development of more polarized earning structures and truncated occupational systems. Most service firms tend to be structured in such a way that the two poles of their occupational system are dependent upon one another to ensure the existence and functioning of the firm, yet are rarely linked internally by ladders of upward mobility. As a result, what appears to be emerging is a situation in which two labor markets and, by extension, two societies coexist, increasingly divorced from each other.

The contrast between, yet interdependency of, the islands of renewal and seas of decay is therefore one of the manifestations of this polarization, for the most fundamental axiom of both urban geography and urban sociology is that the urban landscape is a mirror reflecting the society that maintains it.[70] To reiterate, on the demand side the services revolution contributed to the shifts in preferences and behavior of the baby boom generation that are central to the gentrification hypothesis. Yet the effect of the services revolution has been concentrated in and around the downtowns of relatively few metropolitan areas, those in which withdrawals from stock have been greater than relatively high rates of excess supply. This has led to the apparent contradictions but logical links between suburban overbuilding, contagious inner-city abandonment, decreasing vacancies and tightening markets, and gentrification.

Whether or not gentrification will become more widespread depends in turn on whether or not service-related changes in job markets continue to reinforce polarization; whether the aging baby boom generation changes preferences; whether housing markets tighten or loosen; whether polarization creates such strains that it pushes top-echelon employees and jobs to decentralize; and whether technological change in communications facilitates interaction without the need for concentration, which could lead to the dissolution of central business district agglomerations. Each of these issues must be the subject of continuing research and monitoring if society hopes to anticipate change, measure the course of its direction, and attempt to reshape it for alternative ends.

70. D. T. Herbert and R. J. Johnson, "Spatial Processes and Forms," in D. T. Herbert and R. J. Johnson, eds., *Social Areas in Cities*, vol. 1 (Wiley, 1976), p. 5.

PART TWO

The Impact
of Racial Change

ELIJAH ANDERSON

Race and Neighborhood Transition

AROUND the nation, urban residents feel intimidated by their streets, parks, and other public places, particularly after dark or when too many strangers are present. The national public problem of safe streets has become especially acute in urban areas adjacent to large ghetto communities undergoing racial, class, and cultural transition. Occasionally, the margins of these areas are becoming "gentrified," being slowly absorbed by the wider community, which is made up primarily of middle- and upper-income people who are for the most part white (see the essay by Brian Berry).[1]

The housing units in these areas are relatively inexpensive, but promise a high return on the initial investment. The housing is generally old, even of antique vintage, which for many is part of the attraction; the area's novelty and social diversity are also often valued. The newcomers and the wider society increasingly place high value on such old dwellings, particularly when they are beautifully restored to something approaching their original splendor and are inhabited by well-to-do people. Significantly, such people, because of their professional status and, usually but not always, their skin color, are able to alter the general perception and thus the value of such areas by buying homes and moving into them. As they occupy and make visible use of the neighborhood, they imbue it with a certain social

Work for this paper was supported in part by a grant (80-NI-AX-0003) from the National Institute of Justice.

1. Howard J. Sumka, "Neighborhood Revitalization and Displacement: A Review of the Evidence," *Journal of the American Planning Association*, vol. 45 (October 1979), pp. 480–87; and Dennis E. Gale, "Middle Class Resettlement in Older Urban Neighborhoods: The Evidence and the Implications," *Journal of the American Planning Association*, vol. 45 (July 1979), pp. 293–304.

distinction and reputation. They join others of their class and form through their individual purchases and collective residence a subcultural community of financially well-off people, who in time threaten to displace the original residents.

In such transitional areas, the financially well-off sometimes move in right next door to relatively poor people. And with the establishment of their presence they make social, cultural, economic, and territorial claims on the area, which sometimes confuse and upset their neighbors. In time, property values rise and taxes follow. Formerly nonexistent home improvement loans become available, houses get refurbished, long-vacant apartment buildings are renovated, and the neighborhood is physically improved. The city services begin to be revitalized, and local schools become more attentive to their charges, although the newcomers only cautiously approach these institutions. What was an urban area on the verge of becoming a slum slowly turns around, in time to be redefined as quaint, historic—and desirable. And the poorer people, unable to keep up with the rising taxes and property values, often find themselves moving, at times into an adjacent ghetto area.

Meanwhile, residents of the general community are concerned about crime and safe streets. In their conversations with neighbors, residents presuppose the offenders to be young, black, and male; some refer to them as "kids." Yet they tend to think of the street criminal as someone who recognizes no bounds. It is money, and sometimes thrills, that he is after. Many know him as a figure lurking in the shadows of dark streets, hiding in a doorway or behind a clump of bushes, ready to pounce on a victim. Or they know "them" as a small group of young black males out to hit (mug) anyone who seems vulnerable; thus it is important not to seem vulnerable. And residents, black and white, male and female, young and old, become suspicious of strange black males they encounter in public. Such black males evoke fearsome images, which are often in the minds and on the tongues of residents as they venture into the streets at night, wondering if they or their loved ones will return home safely. Many residents at times wonder if they will be next. In trying to be careful, some residents agonizingly work to keep strange black males at a comfortably "safe" physical and social distance, succumbing to a kind of racial prejudice peculiarly adapted to public places in the area. Others appear comfortable with such distancing behavior, viewing it simply as an urban survival tool. While many middle-income white and black people simply give up and flee the area, apologizing to the neighbors and friends they leave behind and bewailing inadequate police protection and the frequency of crime, others tough it out, learning and adopting a peculiar etiquette for surviving in the streets and other public spaces.

A Community in Transition

A prototype of the urban areas facing the problems that accompany racial and class transition is the "Village-Northton," a community of "Eastern City."[2] Northton is predominantly black and low income. The Village is at present racially integrated, while becoming increasingly white and middle to upper income. The history of both areas is interrelated with the growth and expansion of Eastern City.

Early History

The Village was first settled in the 1800s by well-to-do people who could afford to commute across the Tyler River to the center of Eastern City or to maintain summer homes along the river's western bank. The first landowners built large houses on their estates, but in time these holdings were cut up and additional homes were built on the properties. Neighborhoods developed, with general stores, churches, and schools. During the 1850s, 1860s, and 1870s, many fancy Victorian houses were built. Some inhabitants branched out farther west into an area that is to this day wealthy and suburban.

During the late 1800s and early 1900s the area to the north and west of the Village was overtaken by industrial development. Small factories emerged and nearby homes were built at a rapid pace. Accompanying the new industries were working-class neighborhoods, and one of the most prominent was Northton, just north of what was to become known as the Village.

2. "Village-Northton" and "Eastern City" are fictionalized names deemed convenient for description, since the real community in question has qualities of smallness, quaintness, and a certain intimacy so often associated with villages, and the area is located in a large eastern city. These names are used to maintain the privacy and anonymity of the community residents. The information presented here as history is based on accounts collected through extensive interviews with longtime residents of both the Village and Northton. Though the facts of the various accounts sometimes differ, it is coherent with regard to ideals and impressions that the fieldworker here is after. In a sense the history presented here is a kind of lore that is remembered to be true, what has come down through the years as a guiding ethos and neighborhood identity.

Village. They called themselves the Village Friends, and they passionately supported pacifism, racial integration, and economic egalitarianism. The Village Friends invited blacks and others to live in their communal dwellings. They condoned interracial and interethnic marriages among their members. The group even began buying dilapidated buildings in the Village, refurbishing them and renting them out to the "right kind of people," including university students of color and others who had difficulty finding decent housing in the Village or in the immediate area. It was the time of the "beat generation," and the Village Friends developed their own version of such Bohemian values, watered down to fit with their own commitments to liberalism on racial equality and other issues. In this regard they actively supported the civil rights movement, including open housing, school integration, and other issues. Because they were especially concerned with brotherhood and equality between the races, their most immediate mission was in the Village.

Their neighbors, the conservative middle-class Irish and German Villagers, looked on the Friends with suspicion, if not outrage, calling them "communists" and "nigger lovers." But despite such criticism, the Friends adhered to their stated goals: "to keep the Village from becoming a land speculator's paradise" and "to make the Village the kind of place where all different kinds of people can live."[4]

Meanwhile, the Bell Weather Street boundary was showing increasing signs of weakness. Numbers of poor blacks were concentrating on the periphery of the Village. The slumlords continued to buy run-down buildings, making the minimum of cosmetic repairs and renting them to the poorest class of blacks from Northton and other areas of the city. The middle-class Irish and Germans as well as the Village Friends could rally together against this trend, for neither wanted the "wrong kind of blacks" for neighbors. As the Friends negotiated with the other whites for control over Village resources, the hidden restrictions in their own notions of who and what kind of blacks were to be tolerated became evident. They were most hospitable to "educated" or "decent" blacks who would contribute to neighborhood stability and an ambience of racial integration and harmony.

An association of concerned Villagers, the Village Development Association, sprang up. Individuals and families contributed to the association's fund for buying up properties, renovating them, and selling or renting to

4. As told to me by a longtime Village resident and informant who participated in the general movement.

one walks the streets and learns, "This was the 3820 Co-op," or "That's the old headquarters for the MCCO." Many praise the Village as the most liberal-radical part of the city and would never consider living in any other area. As some of the former squatters have been transformed into renters, they have moved numerous times to different buildings or houses within the Village. As one informant said, "There's something about the Village and the Village person. This is the greatest place to live. I wouldn't live anywhere else. You couldn't pay me to live out there among the squares and 'burbs."

Under the influence of the Quakers and a tradition of liberal political and social values, the Village has developed a reputation in the wider society of being a laid-back area, where a variety of people leading diverse life-styles are tolerated, if not accepted and encouraged, including gays, hippies, students, interreligious and interracial couples, and political liberals and radicals. Among the long-time residents are college professors, architects, lawyers, garbage men, cleaning ladies, automobile mechanics, carpenters, dishwashers, taxi drivers, and factory workers. The Village has the well-deserved reputation for being one of the most ethnically and culturally diverse areas of the city. In line with this reputation, the Village has developed a seemingly endlessly mutable credo of "live and let live." Over the years, however, the Village's black residents have only slowly come to take part in this collective definition of the situation, and they are thus the ones who probably know best that the openness has its restrictions, the tolerance its limitations, and the espoused egalitarianism its shortcomings.

The New Invasion

Today, the Village is again being invaded, this time by young to middle-aged, primarily white, professionals often in search of elegant homes and promising real estate investments. Many choose the Village because it is relatively close to the cosmopolitan center of the city, but also because of its unique offerings of large yards and homes and the promise of an urban setting in which to raise children, grow gardens, and have pets, all important aspects of suburban life. Many of the newcomers to the Village come from suburbs that as a general rule are ethnically and racially less complex than the Village-Northton area.

The newcomers' presence in the area, both current and anticipated, has contributed to a rise in real estate values and rents, thus affecting the present and future makeup of the Village. As housing values increase, institutions on the periphery of the area expand, and investors and speculators seek to take advantage of these developments, the area promises to become increasingly middle to upper income and predominantly white—but within a local area bounded on two sides by long-standing high-crime and economically depressed black ghetto communities of Northton.

Sharing the Public Space

Today, with the general perception of increasing black youth unemployment and rising crime on Village streets, feeling safe on the streets and in one's home has become a central concern for even the most devoted supporters of openness and tolerance. Residents must daily confront the fact that public space in the community must somehow be shared, sometimes closely, by all kinds of people, rich and poor, black and white, including the sometimes desperate. Such concerns become complicated by issues of race and class in the community. To many residents, race becomes confused with class. Interaction on the streets is often significantly influenced by a person's skin color and gender. The communal acknowledgment of these differences expresses itself not only in behavior in public places, but also in sociability patterns peculiar to this racially and culturally diverse area.

What users of the Village streets usually want is safe passage—to and from work, school, and recreational areas where others of their own kind gather—but to effect this they must learn whom to trust, whom to avoid, and what preventive measures are appropriate for helping them to avoid trouble. In short, they must resolve the social problem of navigating the public streets safely. With this general goal in mind, as well as an often vague notion of "community," they closely observe public situations of everyday life, exchange social information about the streets and local neighborhoods, read the daily papers, and listen attentively to television and radio reports. From all of this, they often generalize and attempt to fit the information to their immediate experiences as they try to plan their itineraries to maintain safety for themselves and their loved ones.

Making Mental Notes

In attempts to learn and know the area, the streets and public places are used and carefully observed, and various types of people are mentally noted. Social information on various kinds of people and the areas they occupy and frequent, including the times they are likely to be there, may be stored. Through observation over time, people may be determined to have a place. Certain individuals may then be viewed as people to avoid, while others may be held in a kind of social reserve as potential future allies or friends on the streets or in the neighborhood more generally. This amounts to a process of social typing as a means of making sense of the public areas, which then provides a basis for trusting the immediate public environment.

The local urban environment of a highly heterogeneous population of unknown people inspires this process of mental notation, which prepares the foundation for trust between strangers, dictated by the situation and proceeding by means of repeated face-to-face encounters. This social process works to form what may be viewed as the basis of public community within the immediate neighborhood. In effect, residents and users of public spaces come to know and trust the territory, particularly the various kinds of people who come with the territory.

The process begins something like this: One person spots another walking down a certain street alone, with another person, or perhaps even with a few others. The person or persons spied might be engaged in some noteworthy activity, such as getting out of an unusual car, riding a bicycle, walking a particular kind of dog, taking the run of the grounds of a particular dwelling in the neighborhood, simply crossing a street at the light, or leaving a store with bags of groceries. People repeatedly engaging in such everyday activities help to convey what may be interpreted as a usual picture of public life, or what is to be taken as normal happenstance in the immediate area. In such circumstances, skin color, gender, age, dress, and styles of comportment can become important as markers, which then help to characterize and define the area.

At times, depending on an individual observer's biases, such specific markers can become the most important characteristics determining the status of those being observed, often superseding other meaningful attributes of the person in question.[5] The most important aspect of the situation is simply that the observer makes note of the other person: some significant social contact, not necessarily reciprocal, is made. It is in this way that the person spotted or the category he is believed to represent comes to be seen as an ordinary part of the common picture of this public environment.

5. See Everett Cherrington Hughes, "Dilemmas and Contradictions of Status," *American Journal of Sociology*, vol. 50 (March 1945), pp. 353–59.

Although such initial contact is important, it is not the most crucial element in publicly "knowing" others and ultimately feeling comfortable in the area. Rather, the initial contact situation helps set the social context for any meaningful subsequent interaction, unilateral or bilateral; this gives observers a sense of who may be expected here, and when. The primary significance of the initial encounter is contingent upon the kind and quality of subsequent meetings and interactions. If the person spotted is never seen or heard from again, then the initial spotting may gradually lose its power. On the other hand, if the observer spots the person again or is reminded by others of the kind of person seen, the impression has the chance of developing and becoming stronger. The strength of such impressions, nurtured through repeated encounters, observations, and talk with other residents, builds.

All of this serves to form a kind of social bond that slowly works to knit the highly heterogeneous neighborhood into a series of often overlapping public communities wherein people keep familiar others in mind as potential threats, friends, or even allies on the streets in times of need. Though initially superficial, this form of knowing, and the mental maps it helps to foster, allows strangers of diverse life-styles and backgrounds to navigate the Village streets with a certain reserve of social knowledge that in time grows into trust.

For instance, a stranger may be first seen in one context, then in another, then a third. In time, the observer might say to himself, "Do I know that person?" and answer, "Yes." For on a certain level he does know that person—if only by sight. He has mentally noted him many times in various contexts in the neighborhood, although perhaps unwittingly. But with each successive encounter he has become increasingly familiar with him and the class of others he may represent. Based primarily upon unilateral observations and perhaps visual exchanges, this familiarity has yet to reach the verbal level; the persons are not on speaking terms. They may have exchanged knowing looks or initial looks important enough to establish at least the minimal basis for trust. If asked directly, the observer might say, "Yeah, I've seen him around." But a particular stimulus or provocation is often required, say an emergency or a major coincidence, to bring such knowledge to the surface to help make a meaningful connection. And there is indeed a distinct possibility that the people involved will never reach speaking terms. Yet on a visual level, strangers may know one another and obtain a degree of territorial communion without ever having spoken a word.

But there are those circumstances in which the social gap between visual and verbal interaction in public is pressed and the relationship between incomplete strangers is required to go further. People sometimes feel silly continually passing without speaking to others whom they know well by sight. They may experience a certain discomfort that may be resolved either by greeting the other person or by avoidance. Many choose simply to speak and perhaps to unwittingly commit themselves to what may amount to a series of often obligatory public greetings.

Or when visual interaction becomes rich enough, when it has occurred repeatedly over time and a context has been established, then the stranger may be placed in a kind of social reserve until opportunity or need arises. Background information and knowledge, gradually built up and refined through communication, may become useful for social connection and possible subsequent interaction. Though the connection is made quite often by chance, it is of importance for an emerging sense of community within the area. For instance, during emergencies such as house fires, crimes on the street in which someone is clearly in need of help, or some other focus of attention in which incomplete strangers have an opportunity to gather and compare notes with their neighbors, they may stumble a bit and seem embarrassed, saying, "Hello. My name is ——."

A similar kind of introduction sometimes occurs when two people have been taking note of each other in the neighborhood for some time and then happen to meet inadvertently in a different part of town and, somewhat embarrassed, become constrained to greet each other like long-lost friends. Perhaps in the Village they had not yet reached the point of speaking but had only warily acknowledged one another with knowing looks, perhaps stolen looks, or even the customary offensive-defensive scowl usually reserved for keeping strangers distant. After a meeting and verbal exchange, say downtown, two such previously socially distant Villagers may begin to exchange verbal greetings on the streets of the neighborhood on a regular basis. It is in just this way that a basis for interpersonal trust can be established between strangers who may then come to know one another, sometimes intimately.

The social knowledge gained through this process of mental notation seems to be situation-specific, and until times of emergency or coincidence it usually takes on no great significance for the observer. It remains in a kind of mental reserve, to be recalled in situations that demand it. A Villager may call up such knowledge and experience when he shares with others certain tales of strangers noticed on the streets. Such group talk and shared stories often serve as a means of confirming and consolidating observations, contributing to a mental picture of the public culture of the community.

The primary consequence of so much mental notation is the building of familiarity with and trust of the local environment. A shared sense of public community and positive feeling about the area develops. Such feelings allow many to relax and to become cautiously open with others they encounter on the streets and in public places. But when a mugging, killing, or rape occurs in the neighborhood, residents often tense up and begin taking defensive action on the streets again. For the moment, many distrust the area and feel uncomfortable on the streets, particularly after dark. They become especially suspicious of strangers they encounter, particularly black males. However, the environment is slowly reused, retested, and made note of again. Neighbors talk and socialize. After a period of time, when diverse kinds of people have repeatedly used the public space uneventfully, memory of the initial incident fades. Feelings of suspicion and distrust subside. Familiarity rebuilds and a shared sense of trust is gradually restored.

In this way, social knowledge of the immediate area is refined. Context is gained as stories are shared and retold, and in this process a group perspective on the area gradually emerges. It is from this perspective and the necessity of dealing with actual encounters that a set of informal rules emerges among residents and users of the streets and public areas. These rules, discussed among friends and refined through practice, allow diverse kinds of people orderly passage with the promise of security or at least the minimum of trouble or conflict. The general result amounts to perhaps a deceptive appearance of an effortlessly ordered and racially tolerant public space. In fact, however, color, gender, and other considerations and prejudices are much at work in the public ordering of the community area.

Stereotypic Perceptions

By living in the neighborhood and partaking of its lore, residents develop very localized stereotypic attitudes and expectations about what certain kinds of people are likely to do on the streets. For instance, an unknown black teenager wearing sneakers and bouncing a basketball might dictate one course of action to a watchful resident; the same person without the basketball, loitering in front of a vacant house, might dictate quite another. In some areas of the Village the police might be called, basketball or no, just to check things out. The time of day, the season of the year, the neighborhood's social history—of the past thirty years or even a few days—and involvement with the adjacent neighborhoods affect the meaning this black teenager has for the residents who watch and informally guard the local streets and other public spaces.

Throughout the Village, young black male street groups often predominate, some lounging on street corners, others casually moving about. The black youths are stereotypically thought to be unemployed, and often are. Some young black males often wear sneakers, "gangster caps," and sunglasses and carry large portable radios. In this uniform, suggestive of an urban underclass, these young men are generally presumed to be involved in criminal activity or to be up to no good until they demonstrate otherwise. These working conceptions and behaviors of the streets are a source of sometimes subtle but enduring racial and class distinctions, if not overt hostility, within the community.

The law-abiding members of the community tend to hold such youths responsible for street crimes in the vicinity. Particularly on dark streets, these young men and others who resemble them are held suspect in chance encounters by most others who use the streets, whites as well as blacks. Many of the youths are indeed unemployed and are left to gain money any way they can. Some of the most desperate are involved in the underground economy and are known to man certain street corners and to set themselves up as community protectors and gatekeepers, at times tacitly offering to ensure safe passage for money.[6] Many residents thus become intimidated and are inclined to limit their use of the streets to daylight hours, to remain indoors after dark, to travel in small groups, to walk with a dog, or even to arm themselves in order to navigate the streets in security.

Drawing Color Lines

Though the Village is generally viewed as perhaps the most racially tolerant area of the city, its public spaces and streets are places where distinctions are very often made along the lines of color. There is prejudice, to be sure, but it must be distinguished from a traditional kind of racial prejudice that was perhaps more deep-seated and profound in its total

6. See Elijah Anderson, "Some Observations on Black Youth Employment," in Bernard E. Anderson and Isabel V. Sawhill, eds., Youth Employment and Public Policy (Prentice-Hall, 1980), pp. 64–87.

emotional content and effects on the general relations between the races.[7]
The prejudice here seems to emerge not so much out of deep-seated racial
hatred and hostility, but rather seems to become prominent as it is felt
useful for safe passage and security on the public streets. But this situation
can and often does degenerate into racial hostility when blacks feel they
are being overly scrutinized by whites or when whites blame blacks for
feelings of humiliation and harassment as they are required to expend an
enormous amount of psychic energy in figuring out and abiding by the
informal rules of the streets—or suffer certain consequences.

Hence, in an unexpectedly practical manner, the residents' cognitive
maps of the area tend to be color-coded, contributing a situational and
selective aspect to their dealings with co-users of the public spaces.[8] To
be sure, this color-coding has as a basis an inordinate fear of blacks and a
very strong association of black males, especially youths, with street crime.
And along with this fear, residents feel a need to place distance between
themselves and others who might mean them harm. Black middle-income
people often appear as eager as whites to prejudge, avoid, and even defer
to strange black males in the interest of safe passage on the streets.

As a general rule of the public order, blacks tend to be more suspect
than whites. The unknown or strange black male, particularly the youth,
is to be heavily scrutinized. Not to be trusted, his commitment to civility
is easily questioned. When he approaches, people sometimes cross the
street. Women sometimes tense up and clutch their purses or move them
around to their other side. The following fieldnote is relevant:

At 7:30 on a sunny Thursday morning, I was jogging through the Village
neighborhood. I am black, male, 5'11", and weigh about 180 pounds. Dressed in
a blue jogging suit and running shoes, I was running on the sidewalk as I occasionally
do to avoid cars. I spied a young white man and a young white woman walking
ahead of me, their backs to me, approximately thirty-five yards away. The man
was walking on the inside with the woman on his left and near the street. They
looked over their shoulder and spotted me. Our eyes met. As I approached towards
the outside, still a good twenty-five yards away, the man immediately, and perhaps
instinctively, traded places with the woman, pushing her to the inside, in a grand
protective gesture. She clutched her pocketbook. As I passed, both people looked
at me. I looked back over my shoulder. They were still watching me.

7. See Thomas F. Pettigrew, "Prejudice," in Stephan Thernstrom, ed., *Harvard En-
cyclopedia of American Ethnic Groups* (Harvard University Press, 1980), pp. 820–29; and
Herbert Blumer, "Race Prejudice as a Sense of Group Position," *Pacific Sociological Review*,
vol. 1 (Spring 1958), pp. 3–7.

8. For an elaboration of the concept of cognitive maps, see Gerald D. Suttles, *The Social
Construction of Communities* (University of Chicago Press, 1972), pp. 32–33.

Still others, including some black females, often cut short their looks at black males, averting their glance, and gazing at something apparently far away. As one young white female informant reported: "I must admit, I look at [male] blacks on the streets just for a few seconds. Just long enough to let him know I know of his presence, and then I look away."

While members of all groups are inclined to engage in defensive behavior toward the stereotypic black male, many blacks and street-wise whites attempt to be selective, deliberately and carefully choosing those blacks and others whom they will approach with caution. On the public streets, most are on the lookout for those displaying threatening symbols, including black skin color, youth, unconventional dress, and incivility. Many such symbols possess a certain ambiguity—and felt risk; people often say they don't know what to expect from strange black youth on the streets. Consequently, many whites, and an increasing number of blacks, tend to cast a broad net of defensive prejudice around themselves, thus holding suspect numerous black male strangers they encounter.

To be sure, black males are not equally distrusted. While younger males seem to warrant keen scrutiny in this area, those who are known stand to be trusted. Moreover, those who display the emblems and uniforms of the overclass (particularly suits, ties, briefcases, and books) and who conform to a certain level of propriety may be granted a measure of trust on the streets. Older black men tend to earn a greater degree of trust through their appearance and demeanor, suggesting maturity and even a caretaking role toward others on the streets. Strikingly, they often become guardians of the public peace, showing concern for the safe passage of others. They inform strangers about certain corners, at times warning them of where not to go. But most often, the advice they offer is only to whites who they presume are ignorant of the ways of the streets, yet it is offered out of sincerity and genuine concern.

It is clear that black males' presentation of self is crucial for gaining trust from their counterparts on the streets. Many black youth exude an offensive-defensive posture because they themselves regard the city streets as a jungle. And their pose is generally not intended for people who are not aggressive toward them; it is usually intended for other youth who may threaten them. And yet this pose encourages fear, circumspection, and anxiety by law-abiding residents, black and white, whose primary concern is safe passage on the streets. An overwhelming number of younger black males are indeed committed to civility on the public streets, but they tend to have a difficult time convincing others of this because of the social meanings often attributed to their youth and their color. Many youths simply give in to the negative stereotypes, becoming angered by the scrutiny and the presumptions they know others have about them; at times, they may attempt to get even by scaring or ridiculing those who clearly operate with such prejudgments. This is illustrated in the following narrative by a young white female.

> I went out for something at the store at about 9 P.M., after it was already dark. And when I came back, there was no place to park in front of my house anymore. So I had to park around the corner, which I generally don't do because there's a greater chance of getting your car broken into or stolen over there, since a lot of foot traffic goes by there at night. So I parked the car, turned out all of the lights and got out of the car. And I began walking across the street, but I got into a situation I don't like to get into—and I've been into it a couple times before—of having there be some ominous-looking stranger between me and my house. So I have to go around him or something. And he was a black fellow between twenty and thirty, on the youngish side. He certainly wasn't anybody I knew. So I decided not really to run, just sort of double time it, so I wouldn't meet him at close distance at the corner. I kinda ran diagonally, keeping the maximum distance between him and me. And it must have been obvious to him that I was running out of fear, being alone at night out in the street. He started chuckling, not trying to hide. He just laughed at what I was doing. He could tell what he meant to me, the two of us being the only people out there.

In response to such attitudes and behavior, many law-abiding and civil black males find themselves needing to publicly disavow criminality and incivility in their interactions with complete strangers. Middle-class blacks often feel a great need to distance themselves publicly from members of the black underclass. And consequently many males find themselves working hard to put other strangers at ease about their own presence on the streets as they attempt to manage their black skin color in the public places of the Village.[9] Such disavowals are in stark recognition of what seems to be a general rule of the public order: that trust for whites is an ascribed characteristic, while trust for blacks must be achieved, which is not easy to do.

Class Differences

Class seems to be significant in determining how residents approach strangers and how they adjust to the problematic Village streets. Middle-

9. See Erving Goffman, *Stigma: Notes on the Management of Spoiled Identity* (Prentice-Hall, 1963).

class people, regardless of color, seem much more cautious on the streets than those of the working class or those of the urban counterculture. Middle-class people, for instance, tend to be very careful with their children, even in broad daylight; they walk their children on a remarkably short invisible tether. Middle-class children are also usually very well supervised at play. Working-class blacks, on the other hand, appear comfortable and at ease on the streets and allow their children to roam more freely. It may be that these differences are strongly associated with relative differences about the sense of respective life chances in society. To be middle-class in the Village, regardless of race, is to have some particular sense of program or outlook toward the wider society. It is perhaps this sense, and the future it promises, that brings the middle-class person alive to the physical and social precariousness of the public environment of the Village, even highlighting his sense of self-worth. With a strong sense of something of value to protect and to defend, he becomes acutely aware of those people and public situations that might threaten his opportunities for the good life.

As the working-class black person navigates the streets in a seemingly relaxed and carefree manner, it is not that he cares less for himself and his children than does his middle-class counterpart. Rather, in the general scheme of things he may simply not possess the same heightened sense of self-importance, hopes, expectations, and returns on his investment in living. And to him, feeling he is among his own in the general area, the streets are somehow relatively less suspect and more tolerable, though never completely trustworthy. This difference in class and racial outlook makes for important differences in views of the precariousness of the Village environment.

The Hegemony of Blacks in Public Spaces

Another important reason for this relative difference in orientation to the street culture is the general feeling of public hegemony of blacks. White residents often defer to blacks in the public places of the Village. This is indicated in the following fieldnotes:

It was a warm evening in May. A middle-aged white Villager was gardening in his front yard, which opens on relatively quiet Linden Avenue. The street was calm, for the real traffic had not yet begun. He went to his work, busily digging with his hand trowel. Suddenly, out of nowhere, three black youths appeared. One carried a large radio, turned off, one carried a basketball, and a third youth simply walked. They were dressed in jeans, light jackets, and sneakers. One wore a dark blue cap. They talked among themselves and appeared to be enjoying one another's company. As the youths approached, the white man acted very much involved in his work, though he could see them from the corner of his eye. They noticed him but continued on their way. As soon as their backs were to the man, however, he stopped his gardening and took a long scrutinizing look, watching them until they were out of sight. Then he returned to his work.

And on another occasion:

Near the local high school, not far from the trolley tracks, stood five black teenage girls. The girls were lighting up and passing around a pack of cigarettes. Each took one and passed the pack on. On the other side of the street walked two white girls on their way to the Village. One of the white girls looked intently at the group of black girls. Then came this from one of the black girls: "What you lookin' at?" "Yeah," chimed in another. Laughter mixed with mean looks and scowls came from the group of black girls. Something had been started. The white girl immediately looked away, perhaps wishing she had never looked at the group. Visibly shaken, she and her friend hurriedly walked toward the Village.

And again:

On a warm summer day, my two-and-one-half-year-old daughter and I approached the local community minipark in the center of the Village. The park, which is understood to be open to all residents of the community, has a swing, old tires for climbing, and other play equipment for children. Sitting on the swing was a three-year-old white boy with his father close behind him. Near them was a white woman of about twenty-five with her four-year-old daughter, and a black woman of about thirty with her four-year-old son. My daughter and I acknowledged the others, and she began to play. Soon she was involved with the equipment and the little girl. This went on for about half an hour. Then two black boys of seven or eight arrived. In a while a twenty-five-year-old black man and his four- and six-year-old daughters appeared. The group lasted for about five minutes after his arrival, which apparently tipped the acceptable balance between the races. At this point the whites began trickling away, and soon the park was totally occupied by blacks. My daughter and I stayed about thirty minutes longer and witnessed the arrival of two other black children, but no whites. As I spoke with residents about the park and observed it over time, the racial use of the park that my daughter and I had witnessed seemed to be a patterned occurrence.

While use of the park is not supposed to be restricted to any one race, there are differences in usage that seem racially determined. Often the people using the park are either all black or all white. It seems that when blacks are present whites somehow know they are to stay away. But when whites are occupying the park and using the equipment, it is not a signal for the blacks to stay away. Usually the blacks approach the park regardless of who is there, do what they want for as long as they want, and leave when *they* are ready. Consequently, blacks are put in the role of invaders and successors. The relative usage of the public space and the resulting social distancing behavior of whites toward blacks may be viewed in the context of some vague but generalized notion of accepted territorial prerogatives. The dominant community impression may be that blacks have a free hand with the public space, using it whenever they please, while whites are more limited in their use. Thus whites readily defer to blacks, forfeiting rights to public spaces at the slightest hint of contest. Interestingly, whites appear emboldened when they are in numbers (particularly young white males), when they walk their dogs, or when the police are generally present.

Race and Street Crime

It is important to remember that there exists a general assumption among residents, black and white, that young blacks are primarily responsible for street crime in the area, and that blacks are somehow not as likely to assault other blacks on the streets when whites are available. In reality, though, middle-income blacks in the Village, who often share a victim mentality with middle-income whites, appear just as distrustful of black strangers as their white neighbors, if not more so. They find themselves at parties and other gatherings discussing a recently experienced close call and then instructing inexperienced whites in the ways of the streets, at times taking on a certain strong sense of outrage mixed with moral guilt for the street crimes of young blacks. On the streets, the blacks express this attitude as they work at maintaining a certain distance toward certain black strangers whom they know only too well.

A felt deterrent to black-on-black crime in this area is the possibility that the victim will recognize his assailant later. It may be that the possibility of recognition causes the potential black mugger, if only for a crucial moment, to think twice before robbing a black person. Not only may the victim bump into his assailant again, but there may be a chance the victim will recognize and, equally important, "take care of him" personally. Many a mugger would not like to carry such a burden, especially when there are so many whites around who are often assumed, if erroneously, to be easier to rob, unlikely to bump into and recognize him, and certainly not as likely to be after him. Further, there is a sense in which membership in the black community is presumed to transcend other considerations in potential stickup situations, a presumption made by many black potential victims. It may be that such a sense of racial group belonging allows blacks who walk the streets the pretense that they are less likely to become actual victims than their white counterparts.

But such a racial interpretation of cultural responses to crime is much too simple. It is a convenient confusion of blacks and street criminals, reifying a "we-they" dichotomy between whites and blacks. One may argue that the average mugger is much more concerned with the prospective trouble or ease of taking his victim's property and perhaps secondarily with the possible personal consequences of his actions. Given the important differences in the economic and social circumstances of blacks and whites in the Village, and the mugger's interpretation of them, whites may be viewed as easier and better targets, race in itself notwithstanding.

The changing racial and class composition of the Village may also be a factor in the choice of victims of street crime: not only do the perpetrators of crime often view new people as invaders of the community, they also tend to see them as "people who got something" and yet as inexperienced in the ways of the street. And the new residents, because of their actual and supposed inexperience, their relative wealth, and to some degree their skin color, are viewed as easy marks and often easily become victims.

Yet many residents, black and white, succumb to the simple and convenient view of street crime as primarily a racial problem, though many whites who feel this way are inclined to keep such riskily "racist" views to themselves unless convinced they are in sympathetic company. In this racially tolerant area, speaking in a racially mixed group in a way that associates young blacks with street crime seems to be a liberty reserved to blacks only, for the black person who voices such opinions is supposedly not capable of the prejudice so often attributed to whites. Such widely held opinions are thought to contribute to the general public conception of strange black youth as the primary perpetrator of street crime, especially against whites. But with a belief in their immunity from the charge of racism, Village blacks make some of the same, if not more incisive, public observations concerning blacks and crime in the streets.

That whites and blacks have common concerns about such issues suggests a certain social commonality and co-presence in the same moral community. Such a view allows them the sense, albeit limited, that as residents of the same community area they have the same problems of street navigation. But this ultimately breaks down, affecting neighborhood trust and the social integrity of the community. For in fact the actual experiences and problems of a person with dark skin on the streets are often, though not always, very different from those of a person with white skin. The idea of a moral community gives individuals an interest in interpreting such experiences similarly. And black and white residents sometimes at community meetings entertain the fiction that "we're all in this together." But this fiction is strained, if not exposed, when people are required to figure out and adopt the appropriate etiquette in order to be safe on the streets. This effort at times requires enormous energy mixed with a certain humiliation and sense of harassment, which serves to generate prejudice and exacerbate racial tensions.

Street Etiquette

While the Village's neighborhoods are affected by citywide and even nationally held stereotypes, the area imbues its residents with a peculiar and very local code of street etiquette—its own system of behavioral prescriptions and proscriptions for handling others on the streets with a minimum of trouble. Such a code might well be viewed as a collective response to the common problems local people face each time they venture into the streets. How much eye contact to give or allow from what sort of person on what streets at what time of day, whom to talk with and what to say, where not to walk the dog, how to stand at the corner, the safest though sometimes quite indirect route to one's destination, how to carry one's pocketbook, how much money to carry (in case of a mugging), or the appropriate way to behave in a stickup situation all have their place in the street code of the Village.

By closely observing everyday life in public places and exchanging social information and opinions about the way things happen and why they do, residents gain and elaborate a perspective on the public areas and the streets they must use.[10] It is primarily through neighborly talk and information exchange that inhabitants of the Village provide new arrivals as well as established residents with informal rules concerning the best approaches to the area and the streets at different times of the day. But

10. For a discussion of the concept of group perspectives, see Howard S. Becker and others, *Boys in White: Student Culture in Medical School* (University of Chicago Press, 1961), pp. 36–37. Notably, "Group perspectives are modes of thought and action developed by a group which faces the same problematic situation. They are customary ways members of the group think about such situations and act in them. . . . Perspectives contain definitions of the situation." Also note the discussion of the differences of attitudes and values from perspectives: perspectives are defined as situationally specific, including modes of action, as well as collectively arrived at out of a group's felt need. Also see Tomatsu Shibutani, "Reference Groups as Perspective," *American Journal of Sociology*, vol. 60 (May 1955), pp. 562–70.

residents chiefly learn from the mental notes of their own experiences. It is with the give and take of conversations relating to such personal experiences, including close calls and horror stories, and their explanations that neighborly communion may be initiated and affirmed. It is in this way that a neighborhood perspective may be offered and gained.

A young couple moving in from the suburbs learns from an upstairs neighbor that the reason Mrs. Legget, an elderly white woman, walks with a cane is not just that she is eighty-five years old. Until several years ago, Mrs. Legget took her regular afternoon walk unaided by the thick wooden stick she now relies on to get up and down the stairs to her second-floor apartment. Then one afternoon she was knocked to the pavement by "a couple of kids" outside Mel's, the neighborhood market where black high school students from the Village and Northton stop for candy and soda and usually congregate on their way home from school. In the scuffle, Mrs. Legget's purse was snatched. The police took her to the hospital, where it was discovered she had a broken hip.

Since her injury, Mrs. Legget's gait is less steady. She still takes her walks, but she now goes out earlier and avoids Mel's at the time school lets out. When the new couple ask about the circumstances of her mugging, she is unwilling to describe the "kids" who knocked her down. She only smiles and gestures toward the small, low-slung cloth bag in which she now carries her valuables. "This one is mug-proof, they tell me," she says, a glimmer in her eye. It is a poignant lesson for the young couple: purse straps should be worn around the neck and across the chest, bandolier style, not carelessly hooked over the arm. And perhaps Mel's is worth avoiding at three in the afternoon.

As time goes by the young couple will come to understand the special meaning of the term "kids," which Villagers, particularly whites, often use to avoid direct reference to a young assailant's blackness. The special social history of the Village helps make certain euphemisms or code words preferable to more openly racial descriptions. So "kids" used in a story about street mugging generally means "black kids," and Villagers know it.

Such words and phrases are generated and refined during neighborly social intercourse behind closed doors of middle-class Village homes. At various social gatherings, including block meetings, cocktail parties, dinner parties, and small get-togethers, Villagers gather and exchange stories about urban living in general and life in the Village in particular. The streets and crime are often prime topics of both pointed narratives and casual conversations. People are often found comparing their actual experiences and passing on hearsay. They commiserate with victims of the streets, casting themselves and others with whom they identify in the role of the oppressed. Recent stickups, rapes, burglaries, and harassments are subjects that make them sit up and listen, taking special note of where certain kinds of trouble occurred and in what particular circumstances.

By engaging in such talk and sociability, not only do they learn about the streets, but they also often affirm personal conceptions that city people are somehow special, deserving commendation for putting up with the many problems of being middle class in an environment that must be shared with the working class and the poor. As one middle-class, middle-aged white woman said while fertilizing the geraniums on her front porch: "I'm convinced that city people are just so much more ingenious. We *have* to be."

In contrast, city living, and the urban streets in particular, appear not to be the same problem for many blacks and former hippies in the Village. At their gatherings, the streets are seldom a central topic, but are discussed more casually. Working-class Village blacks see their neighborhood as "nice" and "decent" compared with the streets of Northton, where many were raised. The former hippies, on the other hand, who often view themselves as the vessels of the unique hip Village neighborhood identity, pride themselves on knowing the streets. They generally consider theft and harassment facts of life in the city to which one must adapt in order to survive. Hence they display little interest in stories of "who did what to whom." Said one thirtyish former draft counselor of a block meeting entitled "Violence in the Village" scheduled by concerned Villagers: "It's always a lot of 'who got mugged where and when.' " She did not plan to attend the meeting.

At times the young blacks and the young white former hippies even come together in apartments or spontaneous intrabuilding get-togethers and lament the recent influx of middle-class suburbanites, whom they see as responsible for rent increases and stricter standards of porch and yard maintenance. They talk about the newcomers as "squares" or "uptight," believing their fears about theft and violence are not to be taken too seriously. Many of these self-proclaimed veterans, and even the young blacks to a certain extent, act as public models and agents of socialization for the newcomers who so desperately need to get a handle on the streets.

But even if the dangers of the streets are played down by the hippies and the blacks, they, along with the newcomers, follow certain rules in order to navigate the streets in safety. Women, especially as they remain longer in the Village, tend to adopt a style of dress designed to negate stereotypical female frailty and to symbolize aggressiveness. Many attempt to desexualize their appearance. For many of the veterans, up to age forty, plain blue jeans are the mainstay of Village casual street garb. Denim jackets and unisex nylon parkas, heavy boots, sneakers, and unshaven legs are all part of the urban female costume.

Along with their appearance goes a certain demeanor or strategy intended to allow them safe passage on the streets. When walking alone at night, some street-wise women will keep up with strangers who seem to be "all right." Especially at night, they sometimes will walk toward the center of particularly dark streets and try to walk only on those that are well-lighted, though such streets may be indirect routes to their destinations. They avoid high bushes, large trees, and dark doorways. Some carry whistles and Mace. When a large, dark figure is spotted approaching, many women will cross the street, walk up to someone's lighted porch, or even run. The following story by a twenty-eight-year-old black male is relevant:

A white lady walkin' down the street with a pocketbook. She start walkin' fast. She got so paranoid she broke into a little stride. Me and my friends comin' from a party about 12:00. She stops and goes up on the porch of a house, but you could tell she didn't live there. I stop and say, "Miss, you didn't have to do that. I thought you might think we're some wolf pack [small groups of black youths who have been known to assault and rob people in public places]. I'm twenty-eight, he's twenty-six, he's twenty-nine. You ain't gotta run from us." She said, "Well, I'm sorry." I said, "You can come down. I know you don't live there. We just comin' from a party." We just walked down the street and she came back down, walked across the street where she really wanted to go. So she tried to act as though she lived there. And she didn't. After we said, "You ain't gotta run from us," she said, "No, I was really in a hurry." My boy said, "No you wasn't. You thought we was goin' snatch yo' pocketbook." We pulled money out. "See this, we work." I said, "We grown men now. You gotta worry about them fifteen-, sixteen-, seventeen-year-old boys. That's what you worry about. But we're grown men." I told her all this. "They the ones ain't got no jobs; they're too young to really work. They're the ones you worry about, not us." She understood that. You could tell she was relieved and she gave a sigh. She came back down the steps, even went across the street. We stopped in the middle of the street. "You all right, now?" And she smiled. We just laughed and went on to a neighborhood bar.

The long-time Village men, many of whom are between thirty and forty, also tend to wear jeans on the public streets and to employ survival strategies similar to those of females. Many will attempt to display, in trying circumstances, a tough or masculine appearance. Some take to the streets with a determined set to their jaws, displaying a dead serious look that can be interpreted as something between a frown and a scowl; among black youths, this behavior is referred to as "gritting." In planting such looks on their faces to ward off undesired advances by strangers, they may ward off potential friends; this has implications for the emergence in public of spontaneous relationships.

In time, the newcomers accept and adopt the rules for avoiding crime in the area. As they adapt to what is thought of as a "high-crime area," the newcomers learn to park their cars on certain east-west streets (ones with relatively little traffic from Northton) to avoid having them broken into at night. They find themselves purchasing crime locks and hood locks for their cars, precautions people of the suburbs tend not to take. They buy chains for their bicycles, bars for their first-floor windows, and dead bolts for their back doors. Yet they continue to feel not quite secure. They constantly talk and worry about getting ripped off. They sometimes build high fences to supplement the quaint waist-high wrought iron fences from the early 1900s, when the well-to-do still claimed hegemony within the area. Furthermore, they learn the schedule of the nearby black high school, enabling them to avoid the well-traveled north-south streets when the high school students are there in force.

In addition, the newcomers work hard to know the general area, which eventually pays off in a slowly building measure of trust, allowing them to feel somewhat more at ease. They come to recognize other Villagers and frequent visitors from Northton, even though they may not always be fully aware that they know them. The more general neighborhood color-coding, which people in racially homogeneous areas can more easily apply in making decisions about strangers, goes through a refinement process in the Village, due to the strong tradition of tolerance of diversity in life-styles, class, and race.

Conclusion

Gentrifying community areas may be of importance for the American urban landscape for years to come. Though the ultimate consequences remain to be seen, the more immediate implications seem clear. With the invasion of young, predominantly white, middle- to upper-income professionals, the phrase *inner city* increasingly takes on a new meaning.

Before the onset of gentrification, the setting described in this essay was probably the most socially diverse and tolerant area of the city. As the newcomers move in, their presence threatens to alter the heterogeneous character of the neighborhood many of them may want to preserve: in time the area is likely to become increasingly homogeneous. They also value the area's proximity to the cosmopolitan center of the city. But this means they must tolerate an urban environment whose security is uncertain at best and for which many of them are unprepared. Many sell out and move, often to the suburbs, when they are no longer able to stand the crime (which many blame on the diversity of the area), or they tire of living in such close proximity to "so many suffering people," or their children reach school age.

Those who remain adopt a peculiar public etiquette in order to navigate the streets and public spaces of the general area. This etiquette is color-coded and relies upon prejudicial thinking in encounters with young black males and other strangers. Such prejudice is often troubling to those who entertain it and is a source of tension with blacks of the area, though many blacks take similar precautions and make similar adaptations to the problems of street navigation.

The longer such people remain in the area the greater chance they have of coming to trust the public spaces they use repeatedly. As their numbers gradually increase, and as they make use of the streets and public areas, they pay close attention to others who make up the community, mentally noting fellow users of the public spaces in a variety of situations. In effect, they mentally document such experiences, store their impressions, and recall them to help make sense of an otherwise dubious public environment. With this method, they slowly grow to trust the area, feeling increasingly secure, though they find themselves required to explain this sense of security to friends, family, and other outsiders who lack familiarity with the area they have come to trust.

But when a serious crime, such as a rape, mugging, or killing, has been committed, they tend to tense up and may even question their decision to live in this area. They then take some extra precautions, and as time passes they become reaccustomed to the area, being mindful of the spot where the latest crime occurred. In time, many find themselves learning the area and getting to know their neighbors; they form a subculture of sorts and sometimes develop a sense of affiliation with the area and respect for its unique diversity.

The new invasion profoundly affects the social definition of the area, not only in the eyes of its residents, but also in those of local business and government officials. For instance, mortgages and home improvement loans that would have been denied a few years earlier now become readily available. Further, the new residents press government officials for increased municipal services, including police protection, for the area. These demands are often met, and the area benefits. The once-segregated schools gain some white students, whose parents involve themselves in the schools and require them to be responsive to their needs. Thus the schools improve. But with all of these improvements, housing costs increase and so do taxes. The poorer people trickle out, unable to afford to live in the area they have helped to create. Additional middle- and upper-income people are attracted to the area, and the neighborhood is gradually but surely transformed.

For centuries blacks and whites have resided in separate communities, a separation that has been institutionalized and even supported in law until only recently. Generally, the development of each group has been both separate and unequal. Today, those blacks and whites who come together and reside in inner-city areas do so almost by historical accident. Their communities may be referred to as "integrated," but this is often deceptive. Such areas are usually in transition, from black to white and from lower income to upper income. And the very few black professionals who reside in such communities and are presumed likely to remain with others of their class, color notwithstanding, must often resist the strong attraction of the suburbs and other residential situations. In time, this dynamic leaves the community area predominantly white, but as a consequence of class factors rather than primarily racial considerations.[11] As W. E. B. DuBois so presciently said, "the problem of the color line" still exists in 1985, but it is a problem increasingly compounded by considerations of social class.

11. For an elaboration of this point with respect to recent historical changes in American institutions, see William Julius Wilson, *The Declining Significance of Race: Blacks and Changing American Institutions*, 2d ed. (University of Chicago Press, 1980).

WILLIAM JULIUS WILSON

The Urban Underclass
in Advanced Industrial Society

THE social problems of urban life in the United States are, in large measure, associated with race. The rates of crime, drug addiction, teenage pregnancies, female-headed families, and welfare dependency have risen dramatically in the last several years, and they reflect a noticeably uneven distribution by race. Liberal social scientists, journalists, policymakers, and civil rights leaders have nonetheless been reluctant to face this fact. Often analysts make no reference to race at all when discussing issues such as crime and teenage pregnancy, except to emphasize the deleterious effects of racial discrimination or of the institutionalized inequality of American society.

Indeed, in an effort to avoid the charge of racism or of "blaming the victim," some scholars have refrained from describing any behavior that might be construed as stigmatizing or unflattering to particular racial minorities. Accordingly, the increase among blacks in crime, female-headed families, teenage pregnancies, and welfare dependency has not received careful and systematic attention.

Such neglect is relatively recent. During the mid-1960s scholars such as Kenneth B. Clark, Lee Rainwater, and Daniel Patrick Moynihan forthrightly examined the cumulative effects of racial isolation and class subordination on life and behavior in the inner city.[1] As Clark described it:

This chapter is based on a larger study, *The Hidden Agenda: Race, Social Dislocations, and Public Policy in America* (University of Chicago Press, forthcoming).

1. Kenneth B. Clark, *Dark Ghetto: Dilemmas of Social Power* (Harper and Row, 1965); Lee Rainwater, "Crucible of Identity: The Negro Lower Class Family," *Daedalus*, vol. 95 (1966), pp. 176–216; Daniel P. Moynihan, *The Negro Family: The Case for National Action* (Washington, D.C.: Office of Policy Planning and Research, U.S. Department of Labor, 1965); and Moynihan, "Employment, Income and the Ordeal of the Negro Family," in Talcott Parsons and Kenneth B. Clark, eds., *The Negro American* (Beacon Press, 1965), pp. 134–59.

"The symptoms of lower class society afflict the dark ghettos of America—
low aspiration, poor education, family instability, illegitimacy, unemployment, crime, drug addiction and alcoholism, frequent illness and early
death. But because Negroes begin with the primary affliction of inferior
racial status, the burdens of despair and hatred are more pervasive."[2] In
Clark's analysis of psychological dimensions of the ghetto and Rainwater's
and Moynihan's examinations of ghetto family patterns, the conditions of
ghetto life "that are usually forgotten or ignored in polite discussions"[3]
were vividly described and systematically analyzed.

All of these studies linked discussions of the experiences of inequality
to discussions of the structure of inequality. In other words, they attempted
to show the connection between the economic and social environment into
which many blacks are born and the creation of patterns and norms of
behavior that, in the words of Clark, took the form of a "self-perpetuating
pathology."[4] The studies by Clark and Rainwater in particular not only
sensitively portrayed the destructive features of ghetto life but also com-
prehensively analyzed those structural conditions, including changing economic relations, that combined with race-specific experiences to bring
about these features.

One of the reasons social scientists have lately shied away from this line
of research may perhaps be the virulent attacks on the "Moynihan report"
concerning the Negro family in the latter half of the 1960s.[5] There is no
need here for detailed discussion of the controversy surrounding the report,
which like so many controversies over social issues raged in great measure
because of distortions and misinterpretations. However, it should be pointed
out that various parts of Moynihan's arguments had been raised previously
by people such as Clark, E. Franklin Frazier, and Bayard Rustin.[6] Like
Rustin, Moynihan argued that as antidiscrimination legislation breaks down

2. Clark, *Dark Ghetto*, p. 27.
3. Rainwater, "Crucible of Identity," p. 10.
4. Clark, *Dark Ghetto*, p. 81.
5. For an excellent discussion of the Moynihan report and the controversy surrounding
it, see Lee Rainwater and William L. Yancey, *The Moynihan Report and the Politics of
Controversy* (MIT Press, 1967).
6. E. Franklin Frazier, *The Negro Family in the United States* (University of Chicago
Press, 1939); Kenneth B. Clark, *Youth in the Ghetto: A Study of the Consequences of
Powerlessness and a Blueprint for Change* (Harlem Youth Opportunities [HARYOU] Report,
1964); and Bayard Rustin, "From Protest to Politics: The Future of the Civil Rights Movement,"
Commentary, vol. 39 (February 1965), pp. 25–31.

barriers to black liberty, issues of equality will draw attention away from issues of liberty; in other words, concerns for equal resources enabling blacks to live in material ways comparable to whites will exceed concerns of freedom. The simple removal of legal barriers will not achieve the goal of equality, he maintained, because the cumulative effects of discrimination make it very nearly impossible for a majority of black Americans to take advantage of opportunities provided by civil rights laws. He observed, in this connection, that "the Negro community is dividing between a stable middle-class group that is steadily growing stronger and more successful, and an increasingly disorganized and disadvantaged lower-class group."[7]

Like Clark, Moynihan emphasized that family deterioration—as revealed in urban blacks' rising rates of broken marriages, female-headed homes, out-of-wedlock births, and welfare dependency—was one of the central problems of the black lower class. And as had Frazier, Moynihan argued that the problems of the black family, which present major obstacles to black equality, derive from previous patterns of inequality that originated in the slavery experience and have been maintained and reinforced by years of racial discrimination. He concluded his report by recommending a shift in the direction of federal civil rights activities to "bring the Negro American to full and equal sharing in the responsibilities and rewards of citizenship" and thereby to increase "the stability and resources of the Negro American family."[8]

The vitriolic criticism of the Moynihan report, which paid far more attention to Moynihan's unflattering depiction of the black family in the urban ghetto than to his historical analysis of the black family's special plight or to his proposed remedies, helped to create an atmosphere that discouraged many social scientists from researching certain aspects of lower-class black life.[9] This atmosphere was enhanced by the emergence of a "black solidarity" movement in the second half of the 1960s that, among other things, proffered a new definition of the black experience in the United States as the "black perspective." This new definition was popularized by militant black spokesmen during the mid-1960s and was in-

7. Moynihan, *The Negro Family*, pp. 5–6.
8. Ibid., p. 48.
9. It is interesting to point out that President Lyndon B. Johnson's widely heralded Howard University commencement speech on human rights, which was partly drafted by Moynihan, drew heavily from the Moynihan report when it was still an in-house document. The speech was uniformly praised by black civil rights leaders.

corporated as a dominant theme in the writings of young black intellectuals by the early 1970s.[10] Although the black perspective represented a variety of views on racial matters, the trumpeting of black pride and black self-affirmation was a characteristic feature of the speeches and writings that embodied the intellectual component of the black solidarity movement. Accordingly, the emphasis on the positive aspects of the black experience led to the uniform rejection of earlier arguments, which asserted that some aspects of ghetto life were pathological, in favor of those that accented strengths in the black community. And arguments extolling the "strengths" and "virtues" of black families replaced those that described the deterioration of black families. In fact, features of ghetto behavior characterized as pathological in the studies of the mid-1960s were reinterpreted or redefined as functional because, argued some black perspective proponents, blacks were displaying the ability to survive and even flourish in an economically depressed environment. Ghetto families were described as resilient and capable of adapting creatively to an oppressive, racist society. In short, these revisionist studies purporting to "liberate" the social sciences from the influence of "racism" effectively shifted the focus of social science analysis away from discussions of the consequences of racial isolation and economic class subordination to discussions of black achievement.

Also consistent with the dominant theme of racial solidarity in the writings of the black perspective proponents was an emphasis on "black" versus "white" and "we" versus "they." Since the focus was overwhelmingly on race, neither the social and economic differences within the black community nor the economy's problems received major attention. Thus the promising move to outline programs of economic reform by describing the effects of American economic organization on the minority community in the early and mid-1960s was cut short by calls for "reparations," or "black control of institutions serving the black community" in the late 1960s. This is why Orlando Patterson lamented, in a later analysis, that black ethnicity had become "a form of mystification, diverting attention from the correct kinds of solutions to the terrible economic condition of the group," thereby

10. See, for example, Joyce Ladner, ed., *The Death of White Sociology* (Random House, 1973); Robert B. Hill, *The Strength of Black Families* (New York: Emerson Hall, 1972); Nathan Hare, "The Challenge of a Black Scholar," *Black Scholar*, vol. 1 (1969), pp. 58–63; Abdul Hakim Ibn Alkalimat (Gerald McWorter), "The Ideology of Black Social Science," *Black Scholar*, vol. 1 (1969), pp. 28–35; and Robert Staples, "The Myth of the Black Matriarchy," *Black Scholar*, vol. 2 (1970), pp. 9–16.

making it difficult for blacks to see "how their fate is inextricably tied up with the structure of the American economy."[11]

Meanwhile, during this period of black glorification, significant developments were unfolding in ghetto communities across the United States that profoundly affected the lives of millions of blacks and dramatically revealed that the problems earlier described by Clark, Moynihan, and others had reached catastrophic proportions. To be more specific, one-quarter of all black births were outside of marriage in 1965, the year Moynihan wrote his report on the Negro family, and by 1980 over half were; in 1965 nearly 25 percent of all black families were headed by women, and by 1980 41 percent were; and, partly as a result, welfare dependency among poor blacks has mushroomed. And perhaps the most dramatic indicator of the extent to which social dislocations have afflicted urban blacks is crime, especially violent crime, which has increased sharply in recent years. Finally, these growing social problems have accompanied increasing black rates of joblessness.

Although these problems are heavily concentrated in urban areas, it would be a serious mistake to assume that they afflict all segments of the urban minority community. Rather, these problems disproportionately plague the urban underclass—that heterogeneous grouping of inner-city families and individuals who are outside the mainstream of the American occupational system. Included in this population are persons who lack training and skills and either experience long-term unemployment or have dropped out of the labor force altogether; who are long-term public assistance recipients; and who are engaged in street criminal activity and other forms of aberrant behavior.

The Tangle of Pathology in the Inner City

When figures on black crime, teen-age pregnancy, female-headed families, and welfare dependency are released to the public without sufficient explanation, racial stereotypes are reinforced. And the tendency of liberal social scientists either to ignore these issues or to address them in circumspect ways does more to reinforce than to undermine racist perceptions.

11. Orlando Patterson, *Ethnic Chauvinism: The Reactionary Impulse* (Stein and Day, 1977), p. 155.

These problems cannot be accounted for simply in terms of racial discrimination or in terms of a culture of poverty. Rather, they must be seen as having complex sociological antecedents that range from demographic changes to problems of economic organization. But before turning to these explanatory factors, I should like to sketch the growing problems of social dislocation in the inner city, beginning first with violent crime.

Race and Violent Crime

Only one of nine persons in the United States is black; yet in 1980 nearly one of every two persons arrested for murder and nonnegligent manslaughter was black, and 44 percent of all victims of murder were black. As Norval Morris and Michael Tonry indicate, "Homicide is the leading cause of death of black men and women aged 25 to 34." Furthermore, nearly 60 percent of all persons arrested for robbery and 36 percent of those arrested for aggravated assault in 1980 were black. Moreover, the rate of black imprisonment in 1979 was 8½ times greater than the rate of white imprisonment.[12]

The disproportionate involvement of blacks in violent crime is clearly revealed in the data on city arrests collected by the Federal Bureau of Investigation (FBI). Blacks constitute 13 percent of the population in cities, but, as reported in table 1, they account for nearly half of all city arrests for violent crimes. More than half of those arrested in cities for murders and nonnegligent manslaughter, more than half of those arrested for forcible rape, and 61 percent of those arrested for robbery are black. The rate of black crime is even greater in large urban areas where blacks constitute a larger percentage of the population. Although the FBI does not provide data on arrest by size of city and race, the magnitude and social significance of the problems of violent black crimes in large metropolises can perhaps be revealed by examining data on murder rates provided by the Chicago Police Department.[13]

The 1970s was a violent decade in the history of Chicago. The number

12. U.S. Department of Justice, *Uniform Crime Reports for the United States, 1980* (Washington, D.C.: Government Printing Office, 1981); and Norval Morris and Michael Tonry, "Blacks, Crime Rates and Prisons—A Profound Challenge," *Chicago Tribune*, August 18, 1980, p. 2.

13. My discussion of violent crime in Chicago is indebted to Rick Greenberg, "Murder Victims: Most Blacks, Latinos Now Surpassing Whites," *Chicago Reporter: A Monthly Information Service on Racial Issues in Metropolitan Chicago*, vol. 1 (January 1981), pp. 1, 4–7.

Table 1. *Arrests in Cities, by Type of Offense and Race, 1980*
Percent

			Racial distribution	
Offense	White	Black	American Indian or Alaskan native	Asian or Pacific Islander
Violent crime	49.9	48.7	0.8	0.6
Murder and nonnegligent manslaughter	43.8	54.8	0.7	0.8
Forcible rape	45.0	53.5	0.8	0.7
Robbery	38.0	60.8	0.5	0.7
Aggravated assault	58.3	40.1	1.0	0.5
Property crime	65.7	32.5	0.9	0.9
Burglary	65.6	33.2	0.7	0.6
Larceny-theft	65.7	32.3	1.0	1.0
Motor vehicle theft	64.7	33.3	0.9	1.0
Arson	75.3	23.9	0.4	0.4
Crime total index[a]	62.6	35.7	0.9	0.8

Source: Federal Bureau of Investigation, *Uniform Crime Reports for the United States, 1980* (Government Printing Office, 1981), p. 216. Figures are rounded.
   a. Percentage of all crimes committed by each ethnic group.

of violent crimes in the city began to rise in the mid-1960s and reached record levels in the 1970s. The number of homicides jumped from 195 in 1965 to 810 in 1970. During the severe recession year of 1974, the city experienced a record 970 murders (30.8 per 100,000 population) and 4,071 shooting assaults. Despite the record number of homicides in Chicago in 1974, Chicago's murder rate was actually lower than those in Detroit, Cleveland, Washington, and Baltimore (see table 2). In 1979, another recession year, 856 murders were committed in Chicago, the second highest number ever; yet its rate placed Chicago only sixth among the ten largest urban areas in the country.

In Chicago, like other major urban centers, blacks are not only more likely to commit murder, they are also more likely to be victims of murder. During the 1970s, eight of every ten murderers in Chicago were black, as were seven of every ten murder victims.[14] In 1979, 547 blacks, 180 His-

14. As pointed out in ibid., p. 7, "In its yearly murder analysis, the Chicago Police Department defines the killer of an individual as someone who has been arrested for the crime or is a prime suspect. Because there are a number of unsolved murders each year, calculations of 'who killed whom' are based only on the number of murders in which the police knew or suspected whom the offender was, not on the total number of homicide victims in any racial or ethnic group."

Table 2. *Murder Rates per 100,000 Population of Ten Largest U.S.*
Cities, 1974–79[a]

City	1974 Rate	1974 Rank	1975 Rate	1975 Rank	1976 Rate	1976 Rank	1977 Rate	1977 Rank	1978 Rate	1978 Rank	1979 Rate	1979 Rank	Six-year average Rate	Six-year average Rank
Detroit	51.8	1	45.5	1	50.8	1	38.0	2	40.3	1	38.3	3	44.2	1
Cleveland	46.3	2	45.1	2	33.9	2	40.2	1	34.1	2	50.0	1	41.6	2
Washington	38.3	3	32.9	3	27.1	3	28.0	3	28.4	4	24.6	9	29.9	3
Houston	26.2	6	22.3	7	22.3	7	24.4	6	30.9	3	41.4	2	28.4	4
Baltimore	34.1	4	30.6	4	23.8	6	22.4	7	24.8	7	31.1	5	27.8	5
Chicago	30.8	5	26.4	6	26.5	5	26.9	4	26.0	6[b]	28.6	6	27.5	6
Dallas	22.5	8	27.4	5	26.7	4	25.5	5	26.0	5[b]	34.4	4	27.1	7
New York	21.4	9	22.6	8	20.9	8	21.7	8	21.8	9	25.8	7	22.4	8
Los Angeles	17.1	10	18.8	10	17.8	9	19.0	9	22.9	8	25.7	8	20.2	9
Philadelphia	22.8	7	19.4	9	17.5	10	18.1	10	20.1	10	22.9	10	20.1	10

Source: *The Chicago Reporter: A Monthly Information Service on Racial Issues in Metropolitan Chicago*, vol. 10 (January 1981).
  a. As of 1970 census.
  b. Chicago's rate was 25.98, Dallas's rate was 26.01.

panics, and 120 whites (other than Hispanic) were victims of murder; and 573 of the murders were committed by blacks, 169 by Hispanics, and 64 by whites. In 1970 only 56 of the murder victims were Hispanic, compared with 135 white and 607 black victims. Age changes in the Hispanic population accounted in large measure for their increased involvement in violent crimes—a matter that will be discussed later in greater detail. Homicides in Chicago were overwhelmingly intraracial or intraethnic. During the 1970s, 98 percent of black homicides were committed by other blacks, 75 percent of Hispanic homicides were committed by other Hispanics, and 51.5 percent of white homicides were committed by other whites.

In examining the figures on homicide in Chicago it is important to recognize that the rates vary significantly according to the economic status of the community, with the highest rates of violent crime associated with the communities of the underclass. More than half the murders and shooting assaults in Chicago in the first ten months of 1980 were concentrated in seven of the city's twenty-four police districts, the areas with a heavy concentration of low-income black or Latino residents.

The most violent area is the overwhelmingly black Wentworth Avenue police district on the South Side of Chicago. "Within this four-square-mile area an average of more than 90 murders and 400 shooting assaults occur each year; and one of every 10 murders and shooting assaults in Chicago occurred there during the 1970s. Through mid-November of 1980, Wentworth saw 82 murders (almost 12 percent of the city-wide total) and 309 shooting assaults (11.3 percent of the city total)."[15]

The Wentworth figures on violent crime are high partly because the Robert Taylor Homes, the largest public housing project in the city of Chicago, is located there. Robert Taylor Homes is a complex of twenty-eight sixteen-story buildings covering ninety-two acres. The official population in 1980 was almost 20,000, but, according to a recent report, "there are an additional 5,000 to 7,000 adult residents who are not registered with the housing authority."[16] In 1980 all of the more than 4,200 registered households were black and 72 percent of the official population were minors. The median family income was $4,925. Women headed 90 percent of the families with children, and 81 percent of the households received aid to families with dependent children (AFDC).[17] Unemployment was estimated to be 47 percent in 1980. Although only a little more than 0.5 percent of Chicago's more than 3 million people live in Robert Taylor Homes, "11 percent of the city's murders, 9 percent of its rapes, and 10 percent of its aggravated assaults were committed in the project."[18]

Robert Taylor Homes is by no means the only violent large housing project in Chicago. For example, Cabrini-Green, the second largest, experienced a rash of violent crimes in early 1981 that prompted Chicago's former mayor, Jane Byrne, to take up residence there for several weeks to help stem the tide. Cabrini-Green includes eighty-one high- and low-rise buildings covering seventy acres on Chicago's near North Side. In 1980 almost 14,000 people, almost all black, were officially registered there; but like Robert Taylor Homes, there are many more who reside there but do not appear in the records of the Chicago Housing Authority (CHA). Minors were 67 percent of the registered population; 90 percent of the families with children were headed by women; 70 percent of the households were on welfare in 1980; and 70 percent received AFDC.[19] In a nine-week period beginning in early January 1981, ten Cabrini-Green residents were murdered; thirty-five were wounded by gunshots, including random snip-

15. Ibid., p. 6.
16. Nathaniel Sheppard, Jr., "Chicago Project Dwellers Live Under Siege," *New York Times*, August 6, 1980.
17. Chicago Housing Authority, *Statistical Report, 1980* (Chicago Housing Authority Executive Office, 1981).
18. Sheppard, "Chicago Project Dwellers."
19. CHA, *Statistical Report, 1980*.

ing; and the Chicago police confiscated more than fifty firearms, "the tip of an immense illegal arsenal," according to the police.[20]

Family Dissolution and Welfare Dependency

What is true of the structure of families and welfare dependency in Robert Taylor Homes and Cabrini-Green is typical of all the CHA housing projects. In 1980, of the 27,000 families with children living in CHA projects, only 11 percent were married-couple families, and 67 percent of the family households received AFDC.[21] But female-headed families and welfare dependency are not confined to public housing projects. The projects simply magnify these problems, which permeate ghetto neighborhoods and to a lesser extent metropolitan areas generally.

The increase in the number of female-headed families in the United States was dramatic during the 1970s. Whereas the total number of families grew by 12 percent from 1970 to 1979, the number of female-headed families increased by 51 percent. Moreover, the number of families headed by women with one or more of their children present in the home increased by 81 percent. If the change in family structure was notable for all families in the 1970s, it was close to phenomenal for blacks and Hispanics. Families headed by white women increased by 42 percent; families headed by black and Hispanic women grew by 73 and 77 percent, respectively.[22]

In 1965 Moynihan expressed great concern that 25 percent of all black families were headed by women. That figure rose to 28 percent in 1969, 37 percent in 1976, and a startling 42 percent in 1980. By contrast, only 12 percent of white families and 22 percent of Hispanic families were headed by women in 1980, even though each group recorded a significant increase in female-headed families during the 1970s.[23]

In 1979, 73 percent of all female householders resided in metropolitan areas (41 percent in central cities and 32 percent in the adjacent suburbs); of those who were black and Hispanic, 80 and 90 percent respectively lived

20. Paul Galloway, "Nine Weeks, Ten Murders," *Chicago Sun-Times*, March 22, 1981.

21. CHA, *Statistical Report, 1980*.

22. U.S. Bureau of the Census, *Current Population Reports*, series P-23, no. 107, "Families Maintained by Female Householders, 1970–79" (GPO, 1980).

23. Based on calculations from ibid.; U.S. Bureau of the Census, *Current Population Reports*, series P-60, nos. 116, 120, 127, "Money Income and Poverty Status of Families and Persons in the United States, 1977, 1978, 1980" (GPO, 1978, 1979, 1981); and U.S. Bureau of the Census, *Current Population Reports*, series P-23, no. 38, "The Social and Economic Status of the Black Population in the United States, 1970" (GPO, 1971).

in metropolitan areas, with 64 percent of each group in the central city. The women householders were younger than in previous years. For example, from 1970 to 1979 the number of female heads of families 45 years or older increased by only 525,000 (17 percent), while those under 45 years of age increased by 2.3 million (96 percent), resulting in a decline in the median age from 48.2 years in 1979 to 42.0 years in 1979.[24]

Even if a female householder is employed full time, her earnings are usually substantially less than that of a male worker and are not likely to be supplemented with income from a second full-time employed member of the household. For women who head families and are not employed (including those who have never been employed, have dropped out of the labor force to become full-time mothers, or are employed only part-time), the economic situation is often desperate. In 1980 the median income of female-headed families ($10, 408) was only 45 percent of the median income of husband-wife families ($23,141); and the median income of families headed by black women ($7,425) was only 40 percent of the median income of husband-wife black families ($18,592).[25] In 1978, of the roughly 3.2 million families who recorded incomes of less than $4,000, more than half were headed by women.[26]

The relationship between level of family income and family structure is even more pronounced among black families. As shown in table 3, whereas 80 percent of all black families who had incomes under $4,000 were headed by women in 1978, only 8 percent who had incomes of $25,000 or more were headed by women; in metropolitan areas, the difference was even greater.

Economic hardship has become almost synonymous with black female-headed families: only 30 percent of all poor black families were headed by women in 1959, but by 1978 the proportion reached 74 percent (though it dipped to 70 percent in 1981). By contrast, 38 percent of all poor white families were headed by women in 1978.[27] Reflecting the growth of black female-headed families, the proportion of black children in married-couple families dropped significantly, from 64 percent in 1970 to 56 percent in

24. U.S. Bureau of the Census, "Families Maintained by Female Householders, 1970–79."
25. U.S. Bureau of the Census, "Money Income and Poverty Status of Families, 1980."
26. U.S. Bureau of the Census, "Families Maintained by Female Householders, 1970–79."
27. Based on calculations from U.S. Bureau of the Census, *Current Population Reports*, series P-60, no. 138, "Characteristics of the Population below the Poverty Level: 1981" (GPO, 1983).

Table 3. *Proportion of Families at Selected Income Levels, by Race,
Head of Household, and Metropolitan Residence, 1978*
Percent unless otherwise indicated

Race and income level (dollars)	All families at level	Families at level with female heads	All families at level in metropolitan areas	Metropolitan families at level with female heads
Black				
Under 4,000	15.9	80.3	70.7	85.1
4,000–6,999	16.2	63.8	70.1	71.2
7,000–10,999	18.3	46.2	74.8	50.7
11,000–15,999	16.7	28.9	76.3	31.8
16,000–24,999	19.2	15.3	82.7	15.4
25,000 and over	13.4	7.7	88.5	7.6
White				
Under 4,000	4.3	42.2	52.4	51.0
4,000–6,999	4.7	27.6	56.2	33.7
7,000–10,999	12.7	19.5	57.7	21.8
11,000–15,999	16.9	13.4	59.9	16.7
16,000–24,999	28.8	7.2	66.0	8.5
25,000 and over	29.5	2.9	75.4	3.1

Source: U.S. Bureau of the Census, *Current Population Reports*, series P-60, no. 123, "Money Income of Families and Persons in the United States: 1978" (GPO, 1980), p. 70.

1974 and 49 percent in 1978. Moreover, 41 percent of black children under 18 years of age resided in families whose incomes were below the poverty level in 1978, and three-fourths of those were in families headed by females.[28]

The rise of female-headed families among blacks corresponds closely with the increase in the ratio of out-of-wedlock births. Only 15 percent of all black births in 1959 were out of wedlock. This figure jumped to roughly 24 percent in 1965 and 53 percent in 1978, six times greater than the white ratio. Indeed, despite the far greater white population, the number of black babies born out of wedlock actually exceeded the number of illegitimate white babies in 1978. Although the proportion of black births that are outside of marriage is, in part, a function of the general decline in fertility among married blacks (a point discussed below), it is also a reflection of the growing prevalence of out-of-wedlock births among black teenagers.

28. Based on calculations from U.S Bureau of the Census, *Current Population Reports*, series P-60, no. 124, "Characteristics of the Population below the Poverty Level: 1978" (GPO, 1980); and U.S. Bureau of the Census, "Families Maintained by Female Householders, 1970–79."

In 1978, 83 percent of the births to black teenagers (and 29 percent of the births to white teenagers) were outside of marriage.[29]

These developments have significant implications for the problems of welfare dependency. In 1977 the proportion of black families receiving AFDC slightly exceeded the proportion of white families, despite the great difference in total population.[30] It is estimated that about 60 percent of the children who are born out of wedlock and are alive and not adopted receive welfare. A study by the Urban Institute pointed out that "more than half of all AFDC assistance in 1975 was paid to women who were or had been teenage mothers."[31]

I focus on female-headed families, out-of-wedlock births, and teenage pregnancy because they have become inextricably connected with poverty and dependency. The sharp increase in these and other forms of social dislocations in the inner city (including joblessness and violent crime) offers a difficult challenge to policymakers. Because there has been so little recent systematic research on these problems and a paucity of thoughtful explanations for them, racial stereotypes of life and behavior in the urban ghetto have not been adequately challenged. The physical and social isolation of residents in the urban ghetto is thereby reinforced. The fundamental question is: why have the social conditions of the urban underclass deteriorated so rapidly since the mid-1960s?

Toward a Comprehensive Explanation

There is no single explanation for the racial or ethnic variations in the rates of social dislocations I have described. But I would like to suggest several interrelated explanations that range from the fairly obvious to ones that most observers of urban processes overlook altogether. In the process, I hope to be able to show that these problems are not intractable, as some people have suggested, and that their amelioration calls for imaginative and comprehensive programs of economic and social reform that are in

29. U.S. Department of Health and Human Services, National Center for Health Statistics, "Final Natality Statistics, 1979," *Monthly Vital Statistics Report* (GPO, 1981).

30. U.S. Department of Health and Human Services, Social Security Administration, Office of Policy, "Aid to Families with Dependent Children, 1977," *Recipient Characteristics Study* (GPO, 1980).

31. Kristin Moore and Steven B. Cardwell, *Out-of-Wedlock Pregnancy and Childbearing* (Washington, D.C.: Urban Institute, 1976).

sharp contrast to the current approaches to social policy in America, which are based on short-term political considerations.

The Effects of Historic and Contemporary Discrimination

Discrimination is the most frequently invoked explanation of social dislocations in the urban ghetto. However, proponents of the discrimination thesis often fail to make a distinction between the effects of historic discrimination, that is, discrimination before the middle of the twentieth century, and the effects of discrimination following that time. They therefore find it difficult to explain why the economic position of poor urban blacks actually deteriorated during the very period in which the most sweeping antidiscrimination legislation and programs were enacted and implemented.[32] And their emphasis on discrimination becomes even more problematic in view of the economic progress of the black middle class during the same period.

There is no doubt that contemporary discrimination has contributed to or aggravated the social and economic problems of the urban underclass. But is discrimination greater today than in 1948, when, as shown in table 4, black unemployment was less than half the 1980 rate, and the black-white unemployment ratio was almost one-fourth less than the 1980 ratio? Although labor economists have noted the shortcomings of the official unemployment rates as an indicator of the economic conditions of groups, these rates have generally been accepted as one significant measure of relative disadvantage.[33] It is therefore important to point out that it was not until 1954 that the 2:1 unemployment ratio between blacks and whites was reached, and that since 1954, despite shifts from good to bad economic years, the black-white unemployment ratio has shown very little change. There are obviously many reasons for the higher levels of black unemployment since the mid-1950s (including the migration of blacks from a rural subsistence economy to an urban economy with protected labor markets), but to suggest contemporary discrimination as the main factor is to obscure the impact of economic and demographic changes and to leave unanswered the question of why black unemployment was lower not after but before 1950.

32. William Julius Wilson, *The Declining Significance of Race: Blacks and Changing American Institutions,* 2d ed. (University of Chicago Press, 1980); and Wilson, "The Black Community in the 1980s: Questions of Race, Class and Public Policy," *Annals of the American Academy of Political and Social Science,* vol. 454 (1981), pp. 26–41.

33. Charles C. Killingsworth, Jr., *Jobs and Income for Negroes* (University of Michigan Press, 1963).

Table 4. *Unemployment Rates, by Race, Selected Years, 1948–80*

| Year | Unemployment rate[a] | | Black-white unemployment ratio[c] |
	Black and other races[b]	White	
1948	5.9	3.5	1.7
1951	5.3	3.1	1.7
1954	9.9	5.0	2.0
1957	7.9	3.8	2.1
1960	10.2	4.9	2.1
1963	10.8	5.0	2.2
1966	7.3	3.3	2.2
1969	6.4	3.1	2.1
1972	10.0	5.0	2.0
1975	13.9	7.8	1.8
1978	11.9	5.2	2.3
1980	12.3	5.9	2.1

Source: U.S. Bureau of the Census, *Current Population Reports*, series P-23, no. 48, "The Social and Economic Status of the Black Population in the United States, 1974" (GPO, 1975); and U.S. Bureau of the Census, *Statistical Abstract of the United States, 1980* (GPO, 1980).
a. The percentage of the civilian labor force aged 16 and over that is unemployed.
b. "Black and other races" is a U.S. Census Bureau designation and is used in those cases where data are not available solely for blacks. However, because about 90 percent of the population so designated is black, statistics reported for this category generally reflect the condition of the black population.
c. The percentage of blacks who are unemployed divided by the percentage of whites who are unemployed.

The question has also been raised about the association between contemporary discrimination within the criminal justice systems and the disproportionate rates of black crime. An answer was provided by Alfred Blumstein in an important study of the racial disproportionality in America's state prison populations. Blumstein found that 80 percent of the disproportionate black incarceration rates during the 1970s could be attributed to the disproportionate number of blacks arrested; and that the more serious the offense, the stronger the association between arrest rates and incarceration rates; for example, all but a small fraction of the disproportionate black incarceration rates for homicide, aggravated assault, and robbery could be accounted for by the differential black arrest rates. He points out, therefore, that discrimination probably plays a more important role in the black incarceration rates for less serious crimes. He also states that "even if the relatively large racial differences in handling these offenses were totally eliminated, however, that would not result in a major shift in the racial mix of prison populations."[34]

Thus, if a higher rate of black incarceration is accounted for by a higher

34. Alfred Blumstein, "On the Racial Disproportionality of United States' Prison Population," *Journal of Criminal Law and Criminology*, vol. 73 (1983), pp. 1259–81, quote on p. 1281.

rate of arrests, the question moves back a step: is the racial disproportionality in U.S. prisons largely the result of black bias in arrest? Recent research in criminology demonstrates consistent relationships between the distribution of crimes by race as reported in the arrest statistics of the *Uniform Crime Reports* and the distribution based on reports by victims of assault, robbery, and rape (where contact with the offender was direct).[35] "While these results are certainly short of definitive evidence that there is not bias in arrests," observes Blumstein, "they do strongly suggest that the arrest process, whose demographics we can observe, is reasonably representative of the crime process for at least these serious crime types."[36]

It should also be emphasized that, contrary to prevailing opinion, the black family showed signs of significant deterioration not before, but after, the middle of the twentieth century. Until the publication of Herbert Gutman's impressive historical study on the black family, scholars had assumed that the current problems of the black family could be traced back to slavery. "Stimulated by the bitter public and academic controversy" surrounding the Moynihan report, Gutman presented data that convincingly demonstrated that the black family was not particularly disorganized during slavery or during the early years of blacks' first migration to the urban North, beginning after the turn of the century. The problems of the modern black family, he suggests, are a product of more recent social forces.[37]

But are these problems mainly a consequence of present-day discrimination, or are they related to other factors that may have little or nothing to do with race? If contemporary discrimination is the main culprit, why did it produce the most severe problems of urban social dislocation during the 1970s, a decade that followed an unprecedented period of civil rights legislation and ushered in the affirmative action programs? The problem, as I see it, is unraveling the effects of present-day discrimination, on the one hand, and historic discrimination, on the other.

My own view is that historic discrimination is far more important than contemporary discrimination in explaining the plight of the urban underclass, but that a full appreciation of the effects of historic discrimination is

35. Michael J. Hindelang, "Race and Involvement in Common Law Personal Crimes," *American Sociological Review*, vol. 43 (February 1978), pp. 93–109; and Hindelang, *Criminal Victimization in Eight American Cities: A Descriptive Analysis of Common Theft and Assault* (Ballinger, 1976).

36. Blumstein, "Racial Disproportionality," p. 1278.

37. Herbert Gutman, *The Black Family in Slavery and Freedom, 1750–1925* (Pantheon, 1976), quote on p. xvii.

impossible without taking into account other historical and contemporary forces that have also shaped the experiences and behavior of impoverished urban minorities.

The Importance of the Flow of Migrants

One of the legacies of historic discrimination is the presence of a large black underclass in central cities. Blacks constituted 23 percent of the population of central cities in 1977, but they were 46 percent of the poor in these cities.[38] In accounting for the historical developments that contributed to this concentration of urban black poverty, I would like to draw briefly upon Stanley Lieberson's work.[39] On the basis of a systematic analysis of early U.S. censuses and other sources of data, Lieberson concluded that in many spheres of life, including the labor market, blacks were discriminated against far more severely in the early twentieth century than were the new white immigrants from southern, central, and eastern Europe. The disadvantage of skin color, in the sense that the dominant white population preferred whites over nonwhites, is one that blacks shared with the Japanese, Chinese, and other nonwhite groups. However, skin color per se "was not an insurmountable obstacle." Because changes in immigration policy cut off Asian migration to America in the late nineteenth century, the Chinese and Japanese populations did not reach large numbers and, therefore, did not pose as great a threat as did blacks. Lieberson was aware that the "response of whites to Chinese and Japanese was of the same violent and savage character in areas where they were concentrated," but he emphasized that "the threat was quickly stopped through changes in immigration policy." Furthermore, the discontinuation of large-scale immigration from China and Japan enabled those already here to solidify networks of ethnic contacts and to occupy particular occupational niches in small, relatively stable communities.

If different population sizes accounted for much of the difference in the economic success of blacks and Asians, they also helped to determine the dissimilar rates of progress of urban blacks and the new European arrivals. The dynamic factor behind these differences, and perhaps the most im-

38. U.S. Bureau of the Census, *Current Population Reports*, series P-23, no. 75, "Social and Economic Characteristics of the Metropolitan and Nonmetropolitan Population, 1977 and 1970" (GPO, 1978).

39. Stanley Lieberson, *A Piece of the Pie: Blacks and White Immigrants Since 1880* (University of California Press, 1980), quotes on pp. 368, 369.

portant single contributor to the varying rates of urban racial and ethnic progress in the twentieth century United States, is the flow of migrants. After the changes in immigration policy that halted Asian immigration to America came drastic restrictions on new European immigration. However, black migration to the urban North continued in substantial numbers for several decades. The sizable and continuous migration of blacks from the South to the North, coupled with the curtailment of immigration from eastern, central, and southern Europe, created a situation in which other whites muffled their negative disposition toward the new Europeans and directed their antagonisms against blacks. According to Lieberson, "the presence of blacks made it harder to discriminate against the new Europeans because the alternative was viewed less favorably."[40]

The flow of migrants also made it much more difficult for blacks to follow the path of both the new Europeans and the Asian-Americans in overcoming the negative effects of discrimination by finding special occupational niches. Only a small part of a group's total work force can be absorbed in such specialities when the group's population increases rapidly or is a sizable proportion of the total population.[41] Furthermore, the continuing flow of migrants had a harmful effect on the urban blacks who had arrived earlier. Lieberson points out:

> Sizable numbers of newcomers raise the level of ethnic and/or racial conscious-ness on the part of others in the city; moreover, if these newcomers are less able to compete for more desirable positions than are the longer-standing residents, they will tend to undercut the position of other members of the group. This is because the older residents and those of higher socioeconomic status cannot totally avoid the newcomers, although they work at it through subgroup residential isolation. Hence, there is some deterioration in the quality of residential areas, schools, and the like for those earlier residents who might otherwise enjoy more fully the rewards of their mobility. Beyond this, from the point of view of the dominant outsiders, the newcomers may reinforce stereotypes and negative dis-positions that affect all members of the group.[42]

The pattern of rural black migration that began with the rise of urban industrial centers in the North has been strong in recent years in the South.

---

40. Ibid, p. 377.

41. Some social scientists have attempted to explain the deterioration of the position of urban blacks as their numbers increased with the argument that there was a shift in the "quality" of the migrants. But, as Lieberson points out, "there is evidence to indicate that southern black migrants to the North in recent years have done relatively well when compared with northern-born blacks in terms of welfare, employment rates, earnings after background factors are taken into account, and so on." Ibid., p. 374.

42. Ibid., p. 380.

In Atlanta and Houston, to illustrate, the continuous influx of rural southern blacks, due in large measure to the increasing mechanization of agriculture, has resulted in the creation of large urban ghettos that closely resemble those in the North.[43] The net result in both the North and the South is that as the nation entered the last quarter of this century its large cities continued to have a disproportionate concentration of low-income blacks who were especially vulnerable to recent structural changes in the economy.

A reason for optimism is that black migration to urban areas has been minimal in recent years. Indeed, between 1970 and 1977 there was actually a net outmigration of 653,000 blacks from the central cities.[44] In most large cities the number of blacks increased only moderately or declined. Increases in the urban black population during the 1970s were mainly due to births.[45] This would indicate that for the first time in the twentieth century the ranks of central-city blacks are no longer being replenished by poor migrants. This strongly suggests that, other things being equal, the average socioeconomic status of urban blacks will in time steadily improve, including a decrease in joblessness, crime, out-of-wedlock births, teenage pregnancy, female-headed homes, and welfare dependency. Just as the Asian and newer European immigrants benefited from a cessation of migration, so too is there reason to expect that the cessation of black migration to the central city will help to improve the socioeconomic status of urban blacks. There are other factors that affect the differential rate of ethnic progress at different periods, such as discrimination, structural changes in the economy, and size of the population. But one of the major obstacles to urban black advancement—the constant flow of migrants—has been removed.

Hispanics, on the other hand, appear to be migrating to urban areas in increasing numbers. The comparative status of Hispanics as an ethnic group is not entirely clear because comparable data on their types of residence in 1970 are not available. But data collected since 1974 indicate that their numbers in central cities are increasing rapidly because of both immigration and births. Indeed, in several large cities, including New York, Los Angeles, San Diego, San Francisco, Denver, and Phoenix, "they apparently

43. As Philip M. Hauser has noted: "Data from the census indicate that blacks who migrate from nonmetropolitan areas are now going to the metropolitan centers of the South and West rather than to those of the urban North as they had in earlier decades." "The Census of 1980," *Scientific American*, vol. 245 (November 1981), p. 61.

44. U.S. Bureau of the Census, "Social and Economic Characteristics, 1977 and 1970."

45. Hauser, "The Census of 1980," p. 61.

outnumber American blacks."[46] Although the Hispanic population is diverse in nationalities and socioeconomic status—for example, in 1979 the median income of Mexicans and Cubans was significantly greater than that of Puerto Ricans—they are often identified collectively as a distinct ethnic group because of their common Spanish-speaking origins.[47] Accordingly, the rapid growth of the urban Hispanic population, accompanied by the opposite trend for the urban black population, could contribute significantly to different outcomes for these two groups in the last two decades of the twentieth century. More specifically, whereas urban blacks could very well record a decrease in their rates of joblessness, crime, teenage pregnancy, female-headed homes, and welfare dependency, Hispanics could show a steady increase in each. Moreover, blacks could experience a decrease in the ethnic hostility directed toward them, but Hispanics, with their growing visibility, could be victims of increasing ethnic antagonisms.

However, Hispanics are not the only ethnic group in urban America experiencing a rapid growth in numbers. According to the U.S. Census Bureau, Asians, who constitute less than 2 percent of the nation's population, were the fastest-growing American ethnic group in the 1970s. Following the liberalization of U.S. immigration policies, the large influx of immigrants from Southeast Asia and, to a lesser degree, from South Korea and China has been associated with reports of increasing problems, including anti-Asian sentiments, joblessness, and violent crime. According to one report, the nation's economic woes have exacerbated the situation as the newcomers have competed with black, Hispanic, and white urban workers for jobs. Moreover, the steady inpouring of immigrants from Taiwan, Hong Kong, and China has disrupted the social organization of Chinatowns. Once stable and homogeneous, Chinatowns are now suffering from problems that have traditionally plagued inner-city black neighborhoods, such as joblessness, school dropouts, overcrowding, violent street crime, and gang warfare.[48]

46. John Herbers, "Census Finds Blacks Gaining Majorities in Big Cities," *New York Times*, April 16, 1981.

47. For a good discussion of socioeconomic differences among Hispanics, see Joseph P. Fitzpatrick and Lourdes Traviesco Parker, "Hispanic-Americans in the Eastern United States," *Annals of the American Academy of Political and Social Science*, vol. 454 (1981), pp. 98–124.

48. Ralph Blumenthal, "Gunmen Firing Wildly Kill Three in Chinatown Bar," *New York Times*, December 24, 1982; Richard Bernstein, "Tension and Gangs Mar the Chinatown Image," *New York Times*, December 24, 1982; and Robert Lindsey, "Asian Americans See Growing Bias," *New York Times*, September 10, 1983.

The Relevance of Changes in the Age Structure

The flow of migrants also affects the average age of an ethnic group. For example, the black migration to urban centers—the continual replenishment of urban black populations by poor newcomers—predictably skewed the age profile of the urban black community and kept it relatively young. The higher the median age of a group, the greater its representation in higher income categories and professional positions. It is therefore not surprising that ethnic groups such as blacks and Hispanics, who on average are younger than whites, also tend to have high unemployment and crime rates.[49] As revealed in table 5, ethnic groups differ markedly in their median age and in the proportion under age 15.

In the nation's central cities in 1977, the median age for whites was 30.3, for blacks 23.9, and for Hispanics 21.8. One cannot overemphasize the importance of the sudden growth of young minorities in the central cities. The number of central-city blacks aged 14 to 24 rose by 78 percent from 1960 to 1970, compared with an increase of only 23 percent for whites of the same age.[50] From 1970 to 1977 the increase in the number of young blacks slackened off somewhat, but it was still substantial. For example, in the central cities the number of blacks aged 14 to 24 increased by 21 percent from 1970 to 1977 and the number of Hispanics by 26 percent, while whites of this age group decreased by 4 percent.[51]

On the basis of these demographic changes alone one would expect blacks and Hispanics to contribute disproportionately to the increasing rates of social dislocation in the central city, such as crime. Indeed, 55 percent of all those arrested for violent and property crimes in American cities in 1980 were under 21 years of age.[52]

Youth is not only a factor in crime; it is also associated with out-of-wedlock births, female-headed homes, and welfare dependency. Teenagers accounted for nearly half of all out-of-wedlock births in 1978, and 80 percent of all illegitimate black births in that year were to teenage and young adult women. The median age of female householders has decreased substantially in recent years; and the explosion of teenage births has contributed

49. Thomas Sowell, *Ethnic America: A History* (Basic Books, 1981).

50. U.S. Bureau of the Census, *Current Population Reports*, series P-23, no. 37, "Social and Economic Characteristics of the Population in Metropolitan and Nonmetropolitan Areas: 1970 and 1960" (GPO, 1971).

51. U.S. Bureau of the Census, "Social and Economic Characteristics, 1977 and 1970."

52. U.S. Department of Justice, *Uniform Crime Reports, 1980*.

Table 5. *Age Structure of Racial and Ethnic Groups, 1980*

Group	Under 15 years (percent)	65 years and over (percent)	Median age (years)
White	21.3	12.2	31.3
Black	28.7	7.9	23.2
Spanish origin	32.0	4.9	23.2
U.S. total	22.6	11.3	30.0

Source: Philip M. Hauser, "The Census of 1980," *Scientific American*, vol. 245 (November 1981), p. 61.

significantly to the rise in the number of children on AFDC, from 35 per 1,000 children under 18 in 1960 to 113 per 1,000 in 1979.[53]

In short, much of what has gone awry in the inner city is due in part to the sheer increase in the number of young people, especially young minorities. However, as James Q. Wilson has pointed out in his analysis of the proliferation of social problems in the 1960s (a period of general economic prosperity), "changes in the age structure of the population cannot alone account for the social dislocations" of that decade. He argues, for example, that from 1960 to 1970 the rate of unemployment in the District of Columbia increased by 100 percent and the rate of serious crime by over 400 percent, yet the number of young persons between 16 and 21 years of age rose by only 32 percent. Also, the number of murders in Detroit increased from 100 in 1960 to 500 in 1971, "yet the number of young persons did not quintuple."[54]

Wilson states that the "increase in the murder rate during the 1960s was more than ten times greater than what one would have expected from the changing age structure of the population alone" and "only 13.4 percent of the increase in arrests for robbery between 1950 and 1965 could be accounted for by the increase in the numbers of persons between the ages of ten and twenty-four."[55] Speculating on this problem, Wilson advances the hypothesis that an abrupt rise in the number of young persons has an

53. National Center for Health Statistics, "Final Natality Statistics, 1979"; U.S. Bureau of the Census, "Families Maintained by Female Householders, 1970–79"; and U.S. Bureau of the Census, *Statistical Abstract of the United States, 1980* (GPO, 1980).

54. James Q. Wilson, *Thinking About Crime* (Basic Books, 1975), pp. 16, 17.

55. Ibid., p. 17. Also see Arnold Barnett, David J. Kleitman, and Richard C. Larson, "On Urban Homicide," Working Paper WP-04-74 (Massachusetts Institute of Technology, Operations Research Center, 1974); and Theodore Ferdinand, "Reported Index Crime Increases between 1960 and 1965 Due to Urbanization and Changes in the Age Structure of the Population Alone," in Donald J. Mulvihaill and Melvin Tumin, eds., *Crimes of Violence*, Staff Report to the National Commission on the Causes and Prevention of Violence, vol. 2 (GPO, 1969).

"exponential effect on the rate of certain social problems." In other words, there may be a "critical mass" of young persons in a given community such that when that mass is reached or is increased suddenly and substantially, "a self-sustaining chain reaction is set off that creates an explosive increase in the amount of crime, addiction, and welfare dependency."[56]

This hypothesis seems to be especially relevant to densely populated inner-city neighborhoods and even more so to those with large public housing projects. Opposition from organized community groups to the construction of public housing in their neighborhoods has "led to massive, segregated housing projects, which become ghettos for minorities and the economically disadvantaged."[57] As the earlier description of Robert Taylor Homes and Cabrini-Green in Chicago suggests, when large poor families were placed in high-density housing projects in the ghetto, both family and neighborhood life suffered. High crime rates, family dissolution, and vandalism flourished in these projects. In St. Louis, the Pruit-Igoe project, which included about 10,000 adults and children, developed serious problems five years after it opened "and it became so unlivable that it was destroyed in 1976, 22 years after it was built."[58]

Wilson's critical mass theory would seem to be demonstrated convincingly in densely populated ghetto neighborhoods with large concentrations of teenagers and young adults. As Oscar Newman has shown, the population concentration in these projects, the types of housing, and the surrounding neighborhood populations have interactive effects on the occurrence and types of crimes.[59] In other words, the problems of crime, generally high in poor inner-city neighborhoods, are exacerbated by the conditions in the housing projects. In the past two decades the population explosion of young minorities in the already densely settled ghetto neighborhoods has created a situation whereby life throughout ghetto neighborhoods has come close to approximating life in the housing projects.

56. Wilson, *Thinking About Crime*, pp. 17, 18.

57. Dennis Roncek, Ralph Bell, and Jeffrey M. A. Francik, "Housing Projects and Crime: Testing a Proximity Hypothesis," *Social Problems*, vol. 29 (1981), p. 151.

58. Ibid., p. 152. See also Lee Rainwater, *Behind Ghetto Walls: Black Life in a Federal Slum* (Aldine, 1970).

59. Oscar Newman, *Defensible Space: Crime Prevention Through Urban Design* (Collier Books, 1973); and Newman, *Community of Interest* (Anchor Books, 1980). See also Roncek, Bell, and Francik, "Housing Projects and Crime"; and Dennis Roncek, "Dangerous Places: Crime and Residential Environment," *Social Forces*, vol. 60 (1981), pp. 74–96. Although crime is high in the housing projects, research by Roncek, Bell, and Francik reveals that neighborhood proximity to the housing projects has a statistically significant effect only for violent crimes in adjacent poor neighborhoods.

In both the housing projects and other densely settled inner-city neighborhoods, residents have difficulty identifying their neighbors. They are,
therefore, less likely to engage in reciprocal guardian behavior. Events in
one part of the block or neighborhood tend to be of little concern to those
residing in other parts.[60] These conditions of social disorganization are as
acute as they are because of the unprecedented increase in the number of
younger minorities in these neighborhoods, many of whom are jobless,
not enrolled in school, and a source of delinquency, crime, and unrest.

The cessation of black in-migration to the central cities and the steady
out-migration to the suburbs will partially relieve the population pressures
in the inner city.[61] Perhaps even more significant, there were 6 percent
fewer blacks aged 13 and under in metropolitan areas in 1977 than in 1970,
and 13 percent fewer in the central cities. White children in this age
category also decreased during this period by even greater percentages:
17 percent in metropolitan areas and 24 percent in the central cities. By
contrast, Hispanic children increased from 1970 to 1977 by 16 percent in
metropolitan areas and 12 percent in the central cities. Thus, just as the
change in migration flow could affect the rates of ethnic groups' involvement
in certain types of social problems, so too could changes in the age structure.
Whereas whites and blacks—all other things being equal—are likely to
show a decrease in problems such as joblessness, crime, out-of-wedlock
births, teenage pregnancy, family dissolution, and welfare dependency in
the near future, the growing Hispanic population, due to rapid increases
in births and migration, is more likely to experience increasing rates of
social dislocation.

The Impact of Basic Economic Changes

The population explosion among minority youths occurred at a time
when changes in the economy posed serious problems for unskilled individuals, both in and out of the labor force. Urban minorities have been

---

60. Roncek, "Dangerous Places"; and Newman, *Defensible Space* and *Community of
Interest.*

61. According to the U.S. Bureau of the Census, "During the 1970's Blacks have accounted
for an increasingly large proportion of the net increase in suburban population attributable
to migration. Between 1975 and 1977, for example, Black movement to suburbs accounted
for 14 percent of the net increase in suburban population attributable to migration, compared
with only 7 percent in the 1970–75 period. Blacks who moved to suburbs between 1975 and
1977 comprised 16 percent of the total Black population living in the suburbs in 1977." U.S.
Bureau of the Census, "Social and Economic Characteristics, 1977 and 1970," p. 7.

particularly vulnerable to structural economic changes, such as the shift from goods-producing to service-producing industries, the increasing polarization of the labor market into low-wage and high-wage sectors, technological innovations, and the relocation of manufacturing industries out of the central cities. These economic shifts point out the fact that nearly all of the large and densely populated metropolises experienced their most rapid development during an earlier industrial and transportation era. Today these urban centers are undergoing an irreversible structural transformation from "centers of production and distribution of material goods to centers of administration, information exchange, and higher-order service provision," as John D. Kasarda points out in his essay.[62] The central-city labor market has been profoundly altered in the process.

Roughly 60 percent of the unemployed blacks in the United States reside within central cities, mostly within the cities' low-income areas. There is much more dispersion among unemployed whites; approximately 40 percent reside in suburban areas and an additional 30 percent live in nonmetropolitan areas. Furthermore, the percentage of black men employed as laborers and service workers is twice that of white workers. The lack of economic opportunity for low-income blacks means that they are compelled to remain in economically depressed ghettos and their children are forced to attend inferior ghetto schools (see the essay by Gary Orfield). This leads into a vicious cycle, as ghetto isolation and inferior opportunities in education reinforce their disadvantaged position in the labor market and contribute to problems of crime, family dissolution, and welfare dependency.

Indeed, the problems of joblessness among blacks, especially low-income blacks, are more severe than those of any other large ethnic group in America. Heavily concentrated in inner cities, blacks have experienced a deterioration of their economic position on nearly all the major labor-market indicators. Two of these indicators are presented in tables 6 and 7, which show respectively the proportion who are in the labor force and the fraction who are employed, including those not in the labor force.

Blacks, especially young males, are dropping out of the labor force in significant numbers. The severe problems of joblessness for black teenagers and young adults are seen in the figures on changes in the male civilian

62. See also John D. Kasarda, "Urbanization, Community, and the Metropolitan Problems," in David Street, ed., Handbook of Contemporary Urban Life (Jossey-Bass, 1978), pp. 27–57; and Kasarda, "The Implications of Contemporary Redistribution Trends for National Policy," Social Science Quarterly, vol. 61 (December 1980), pp. 373–400.

Table 6. *Civilian Labor Force Participation Rates for Males Aged 16–34, by Race and Age, Selected Years, 1960–83*

Race and age	1960	1965	1968	1970	1973	1977	1983
Black and other races[a]							
16–17	45.6	39.3	37.9	34.8	33.4	30.8	26.0
18–19	71.2	66.7	63.3	61.8	61.4	57.8	55.4
20–24	90.4	89.8	85.0	83.5	81.8	78.2	77.5
25–34	96.2	95.7	95.0	93.7	91.7	90.4	88.2
White							
16–17	46.0	44.6	47.7	48.9	52.7	53.8	46.9
18–19	69.0	65.8	65.8	67.4	72.3	74.9	71.3
20–24	87.8	85.3	82.4	83.3	85.8	86.8	86.1
25–34	97.7	97.4	97.2	96.7	96.3	96.0	95.2

Sources: U.S. Department of Labor, *Employment and Training Report of the President* (GPO, 1978); and U.S. Department of Labor, Bureau of Labor Statistics, "Employment and Earnings" (GPO, 1984).
a. See footnote b, table 4.

Table 7. *Employment-Population Ratios for Civilian Males Aged 16–34, by Race and Age, Selected Years, 1955–83*[a]

Race and age	1955	1965	1973	1983
Black and other races[b]				
16–17	41.7	28.8	22.0	13.7
18–19	66.0	53.4	27.9	31.2
20–24	78.6	81.6	71.4	54.8
25–34	87.6	90.0	86.4	72.6
White				
16–17	42.0	38.0	44.8	36.3
18–19	64.2	58.3	65.1	58.0
20–24	80.4	80.2	80.2	74.3
25–34	95.2	94.8	93.4	86.7

Sources: Norman Bowers, "Young and Marginal: An Overview of Youth Employment," *Monthly Labor Review*, vol. 102 (October 1979), p. 6; and U.S. Department of Labor, Bureau of Labor Statistics, "Employment and Earnings" (GPO, 1984).
a. The employment-population ratio is the ratio of the employed civilian population to the total civilian population. This excludes those who are institutionalized or in the armed forces.
b. See footnote b, table 4.

labor force participation rates (table 6). The percentage of black males in the labor force fell sharply between 1960 and the end of 1983 for those aged 16 to 24, and somewhat less for those aged 25 to 34. Black males began dropping out of the labor force in increasing numbers as early as 1965, while white males either maintained or increased their rate of participation until 1977. Sharp declines in the three younger age categories took place from 1977 through 1983—a period plagued by a deep recession.

Figure 1. *Males Aged 16–19 with Work Experience during the Year, by Race, 1966–77*

Percent

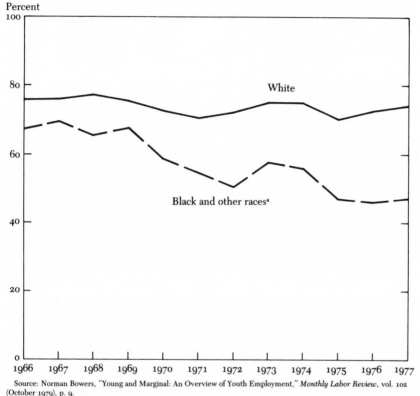

Source: Norman Bowers, "Young and Marginal: An Overview of Youth Employment," *Monthly Labor Review,* vol. 102 (October 1979), p. 9.
a. See footnote b, table 4.

But even these figures do not reveal the severity of joblessness among younger blacks. Only a minority of noninstitutionalized black youth are employed. As shown in table 7, the percentage of black male youth who are employed has sharply and steadily declined since 1955, whereas among white males it increased slightly for teenagers and virtually held steady for those aged 20 to 24 between 1955 and 1973. However, the years of recession after 1978 probably took their toll on white workers, evidenced by the noticeable increase in joblessness for all the age categories by 1983. The fact that only 55 percent of all black young adult males, 31 percent of all black males aged 18 to 19, and 14 percent of those aged 16 to 17 were employed in 1983 reveals a problem of joblessness for young black men that has reached catastrophic proportions.

Table 8. *Unemployed Blacks Aged 16–19 Living at Home,*
by School Enrollment Status and Family Income, 1977
Percent unless otherwise indicated

Family income (dollars)	Total	Enrolled in school	Not in school
Under 5,000	32.1	23.6	41.0
5,000–9,999	34.7	35.7	33.6
10,000–14,999	16.8	20.0	13.4
15,000–24,999	12.0	15.0	9.0
25,000 or more	4.4	5.7	3.0
Total	100.0	100.0	100.0

Source: Anne McDougall Young, "The Difference a Year Makes in the Nation's Youth Work Force," *Monthly Labor Review*, vol. 102 (October 1979), p. 38.

Finally, the discouraging employment situation for young blacks is further demonstrated by the data on work experience (figure 1). The percentage of young blacks obtaining any work experience at all has generally declined. The proportion of white male teenagers with work experience changed very little from 1966 to 1977, but the proportion of black male teenagers with work experience decreased from 67 to 47 percent during the same period.

The combined indicators of labor force participation, employment-population ratios, and work experience reveal a disturbing picture of black joblessness, especially among younger blacks. If the evidence presented in recent longitudinal research is correct, joblessness during youth will have a long-term harmful effect on later success in the labor market.[63] Increasing joblessness during youth is a problem primarily experienced by lower-income blacks—those already in or near the underclass. To illustrate this fact, table 8 provides data on unemployed teenagers living at home. Of the unemployed teenagers living at home in 1977, 67 percent were from families with incomes below $10,000. And among those unemployed teenagers living at home and not enrolled in school, 75 percent were from families with less than $10,000 income and 41 percent from families with less than $5,000.

The changes associated with the cessation of black migration to the central city and the sharp drop in the number of black children under age 13 may increase the likelihood that the economic situation of urban blacks will improve in the near future. However, the current problems of black joblessness are so overwhelming that it is just as likely that only a major

63. Brian Becker and Stephen Hills, "Today's Teenage Unemployed—Tomorrow's Working Poor?" *Monthly Labor Review*, vol. 102 (January 1979), pp. 67–71.

program of economic reform will be sufficient to prevent a significant proportion of the urban underclass from being permanently locked out of the mainstream of the American occupational system.

The Role of Ethnic Group Culture

In advancing different explanations of the social dislocations of the urban underclass, I have yet to say anything about the role of ethnic group culture. Even after considering discrimination, flow of migrants, changes in age structure, changes in the economy, and the problems of joblessness, some would still maintain that ethnic groups' cultural differences account in large measure for their variations in certain social problems. But any cultural explanation of group differences in behavior would have to consider, among other things, the often considerable variation within a group. For example, as pointed out earlier, although 85 percent of urban black families with incomes below $4,000 were headed by women, only 7 percent of those with incomes of $25,000 and more were headed by women. The better the economic position of black families, the higher the percentage of two-parent households. Also, the percentage of black children born out of wedlock is partly a function of the sharp decrease in fertility among married-couple black families, who have on average a higher economic status in the black community. If blacks and other ethnics are treated as monolithic groups, this overlooks the fact that high-income blacks, Hispanics, and Indians have even fewer children than their counterparts in the general population.[64]

But in the face of some puzzling facts concerning rates of public assistance and crime in the 1960s, some observers turned to the cultural explanation. More specifically, from the Great Depression to 1960, unemployment accounted in large measure for dependency: the correlation between the nonwhite male unemployment rate and the rate of new AFDC cases was close to perfect during this period. Considering this relationship, Moynihan stated: "The correlation was among the strongest known to social science. It could not be established that the men who lost their jobs were the ones who left their families, but the mathematical relationship of the two statistical series—unemployment rates and new AFDC cases—was astonishingly close."[65] Suddenly, however, the relationship began to weaken at

64. Sowell, *Ethnic America*, p. 7.
65. Daniel P. Moynihan, *The Politics of a Guaranteed Income* (Random House, 1973), p. 82.

the beginning of the 1960s, vanished by 1963, and completely reversed itself during the remainder of that decade with a steady decrease in the rate of nonwhite male unemployment and a steady increase in the number of new AFDC cases.[66]

Some observers quickly seized upon these figures to suggest that welfare dependency had become a cultural trait because, they argued, even during periods of an economic upswing minorities' public assistance rates were increasing. However, closer inspection shows that even though nonwhite male unemployment did drop during the 1960s, the percentage of nonwhite males who dropped out of the labor force increased steadily (see table 6), thereby maintaining the association between joblessness and welfare dependency. A similar argument applied to crime was presented in a recent empirical study that demonstrated that decreasing labor force participation rates, not unemployment rates, accounted for the increase in crime among youth during the last half of the 1960s.[67]

A well-founded sociological argument is that different ethnic behaviors and outcomes are largely due to different opportunities and external obstacles against advancement—which were determined by different historical and material circumstances, including different times of arrival and patterns of settlement in the United States. Furthermore, even if one were able to show that different ethnic group behavior is related to differences in values, mobility, and success, this hardly constitutes an adequate explanation. Uncovering cultural differences is only the first step in a proper sociological investigation. The analysis of their social and historical roots represents the succeeding and more fundamental step.[68]

In short, cultural values do not ultimately determine behavior or success. Rather, cultural values emerge from specific circumstances and life chances and reflect one's position in the class structure. Thus, if underclass blacks have low aspirations or do not plan for the future, it is not ultimately the result of different cultural norms but the product of restricted opportunities, a bleak future, and feelings of resignation originating from bitter personal experiences. Accordingly, behavior described as socially pathological and associated with lower-class minorities should be analyzed not as a cultural aberration but as a symptom of class inequality.[69]

66. Ibid., pp. 82–83; and Wilson, *Thinking About Crime*, p. 9.

67. Llad Phillips, Harold L. Vatey, Jr., and Darold Maxwell, "Crime, Youth, and the Labor Market," *Journal of Political Economy*, vol. 80 (1972), pp. 491–504.

68. Stephen Steinberg, *The Ethnic Myth: Race, Ethnicity and Class in America* (Atheneum, 1981).

69. Ibid.

As social and economic opportunities change, new behavioral solutions originate, develop into patterns, and are later complemented and upheld by norms. If new situations emerge, both the behavior patterns and the norms eventually undergo change. As Herbert Gans states: "Some behavioral norms are more persistent than others, but over the long run, all of the norms and aspirations by which people live are nonpersistent: they rise and fall with changes in situations."[70]

Conclusion

To hold, as I do, that changes in economic and social situations will lead to changes in behavior patterns and norms, raises the issue of what public policy can deal effectively with the social dislocations that have plagued the urban underclass for the past several years. Any significant reduction of joblessness and related problems of crime, out-of-wedlock births, teenage pregnancies, single-parent homes, and welfare dependency requires a far more comprehensive program of economic and social reform than Americans have generally deemed appropriate or desirable. In short, it would require a radicalism that neither the Democratic nor the Republican party has been bold enough to propose.

A shift away from the convenient focus on "racism" would probably result in a greater understanding and appreciation of the complex factors associated with the recent increases in the rates of social dislocation among the urban underclass. Although present-day discrimination undoubtedly has contributed to their economic and social woes in the last twenty years, I have argued that these problems have been due far more to shifts in the American economy from manufacturing to service industries, which have produced extraordinary rates of joblessness in the inner city and exacerbated conditions generated by the historic flow of migrants, and to changes in the urban minority age structure and consequent population changes in the central city.

For all these reasons, the urban underclass has not benefited significantly from "race-specific" antidiscrimination policy programs, such as affirmative action, which have helped so many trained and educated blacks. If inner-city blacks are to be helped, they will be aided not by policies addressed primarily to poor minorities, but by policies designed to benefit all of the

70. Herbert Gans, "Culture and Class in the Study of Poverty: An Approach to Anti-Poverty Research," in Daniel P. Moynihan, ed., *On Understanding Poverty: Perspectives for the Social Sciences* (Basic Books, 1968), p. 211.

nation's poor. These will need to address the broader problems of generating full employment, developing sustained and balanced urban economic growth, and achieving effective welfare reform. Unless such problems are seriously faced, there is little hope for the effectiveness of other policies, including race-specific ones, in significantly reducing social dislocations among the urban underclass.

I am reminded in this connection of Bayard Rustin's plea during the early 1960s that blacks ought to recognize the importance of *fundamental* economic reform (including a system of national economic planning along with new education, manpower, and public works programs to help reach full employment) and the need for a broad-based coalition to achieve it. And since an effective political coalition will in part depend upon how the issues are defined, it is essential that the political message underline the need for economic and social reform that benefits all groups in the United States, not just poor minorities. Politicians and civil rights organizations, as two important examples, ought to shift or expand their definition of America's racial problems and broaden the scope of suggested policy programs to address them. They should, of course, continue to fight for an end to racial discrimination. But they must also recognize that poor minorities are profoundly affected by problems in America that go beyond racial considerations. The dislocations that follow these problems have made the underclass a reality of urban life, and if left alone they will continue to do so.

GARY ORFIELD

Ghettoization
and Its Alternatives

LARGE CITIES have become increasingly black and Hispanic, while
providing homes for a small and shrinking fraction of white families. U.S.
cities have dealt with the expansion of the black population primarily by
segregation and ghettoization—the racial conversion of white areas adjoining black communities. The process of ghettoization has always been
costly and destructive, both to the old residents who have been displaced
and to the newcomers seeking to escape a cycle that they bring with them.
When this cycle comes to dominate entire cities and their institutions of
public education, the city confronts problems it cannot solve. In addition
to the problems raised by black ghettoization, many of the nation's largest
cities have been forced to manage another vast change with powerful social
effects—the long surge of Hispanic migration.

This paper argues, through a detailed examination of metropolitan
Chicago, that residential segregation is a key contemporary institution for
creating and maintaining inequality, not only for individuals and racial
groups, but also for neighborhoods and entire municipalities. Given the
nature of public beliefs and fears and the practices of major economic and
governmental institutions, this inequality is inherent and pervades many
aspects of life. The only way of controlling its destructive effects and
providing a society that offers a more genuine equal opportunity is through
a strategy of integration, as Martin Luther King, Jr., so clearly recognized
a generation ago. There are models to show that this strategy can work,
even in the heart of one of the most resistant urban areas in the United
States.

If race is a central part of the urban decline, and if identifying alternatives
to existing policies is a basic part of building a more viable urban economy,
Chicago offers important advantages as a subject of study. It is the nation's

most residentially segregated city and the center of its most segregated educational system. By many measures, inequality between whites and blacks is the highest of any large U.S. metropolitan area. Political power was long used overtly and successfully to forestall racial change. No city's racial patterns have been more intensively and continuously studied and no other city has so strongly shaped theories of urban race relations.[1] Chicago was the site of Martin Luther King's strong but futile effort to move the country to act on the problems of the urban ghetto. The area can provide not only some of the most dramatic examples of the costs of segregation, but also evidence of positive policies that surely have broader usefulness if they can survive and work in Chicago's negative social climate.

Ghettoization and Suburbanization

Since blacks first urbanized in substantial numbers, the process by which black housing needs have been accommodated has had extremely destructive social, economic, and educational effects. With the exception of servants' quarters, blacks have from the beginning been forced to reside in the least desirable neighborhoods, which in most cases are then totally removed from the white housing market. In such areas the cycle of ghettoization begins with black purchases (usually by high-status blacks), which are met by white resistance and fear. A process of racial transition follows, marked by progressive exclusion from the white housing market and inclusion in the black market. This period is often followed by a process described by sociologists as "piling up," in which the population of the area rises sharply as the aging white population is replaced by large black families eager to escape the inner ghetto. Public education in the community usually becomes almost all black during this period. As the residential market changes, so does the commercial market. Small business investment

1. Ernest W. Burgess, "The Growth of the City," in Robert E. Park, Ernest W. Burgess, and Roderick D. McKenzie, eds., *The City* (University of Chicago Press, 1925), pp. 47–62; Otis Dudley Duncan and Beverly Duncan, *The Negro Population of Chicago: A Study of Residential Succession* (University of Chicago Press, 1957); Pierre de Vise, *Chicago's Widening Color Gap* (Interuniversity Social Research Committee, 1967); Karl E. Taeuber and Alma F. Taeuber, *Negroes in Cities: Residential Segregation and Neighborhood Change* (Aldine, 1965); Thomas Lee Philpott, *The Slum and the Ghetto: Neighborhood Deterioration and Middle-Class Reform, Chicago, 1880–1930* (Oxford University Press, 1978); Richard P. Taub, D. Garth Taylor, and Jan D. Dunham, *Paths of Neighborhood Change: Race and Crime in Urban America* (University of Chicago Press, 1984); and Brian J. L. Berry, *The Open Housing Question: Race and Housing in Chicago, 1966–1976* (Ballinger, 1979).

declines, the types of businesses begin to change, churches and other institutions close or change ownership and identification, and chain supermarkets or department stores are likely, over time, to close or go into local ownership.

As time passes, the income level generally falls substantially, maintenance of housing becomes more difficult, the character of rental housing management changes, financing and insurance become more difficult or expensive to obtain, and eventually the neighborhood confronts classic ghetto conditions. Population thins out, disinvestment becomes severe and readily visible, unemployment soars, schools increasingly serve students who have little hope of success in job markets, social disorganization and crime become menacing, and the neighborhood becomes powerless. In the worst cases, the value of property in the area, even if it is near the communications center of a world-class city like Chicago, will approach zero, and abandonment and tax default will become widespread.

There is nothing new in this cycle. It has been observed and described for a half century. What is new is the scale on which it now operates, the intensity of the collapse at the center of the ghetto as black immigration to northern cities has ended, and the fact that the cycle still operates two decades after fair housing laws have been in effect in much of the nation. Also new is that at least some parts of this cycle are now affecting the rapidly growing Hispanic community in many cities.

As ghettoization undermines city neighborhoods, suburbanization separates the white middle class from the city. Suburbanization not only redistributes taxable wealth, but also redistributes jobs and educational opportunities in ways that make them virtually inaccessible to minorities confined by residential segregation to parts of the central city and declining segments of the suburban ring. It greatly increases the physical scale of racial separation, particularly for children, since middle-class white families with children become rarities in many central cities. It overlays the system of racial separation and inequality with a system of political and legal separation. Thus the best services, education, and access to new jobs are made available to affluent, virtually all-white communities that openly employ a full range of municipal powers to attract desirable jobs from the city while preventing low- and moderate-income families, or renters of any kind, from moving into the communities. As a consequence, black and Hispanic political aspirations are concentrated very largely on municipal and educational institutions that lack the tax base to maintain existing levels of services, to say nothing of mounting vast new responses to the critical problems of these expanding minority communities. Ghettoization and suburbanization have now reached a scale that threatens the economic, social, and educational viability of many central cities and emerging suburban ghettos. Outside of a few very special circumstances, there are no major countertrends that will limit the destructive impact.

Chicago's History of Racial Change

A devastating race riot in 1919 focused local and national attention on the bitter race relations that had developed in Chicago as immigration from the South surged during World War I. In subsequent generations, the scattered pockets of black settlement grew to encompass vast sections of the city and parts of the suburbs to the south and west. Chicago's black population expanded from 2.5 percent of the city total in 1910 to 23 percent in 1960 and more than 40 percent in 1980. As can be seen in figure 1, by 1980 blacks made up more than half the population in many communities on the city's South and West Sides; much of this area is virtually all-black. Since the mid-1960s the city's public schools have had a shrinking white minority. In recent years the declining white enrollment and the rising Hispanic numbers have produced a system that is more than three-fifths black, more than one-fifth Hispanic, and less than one-sixth white.[2]

Hispanic settlement in Chicago first became significant during 1916–25, with the Mexican population reaching 21,000 by 1930. Puerto Rican settlement began much later, shortly after World War II. It is difficult to discuss the settlement trends accurately because the methods of counting Hispanics in the censuses have changed continually. It is clear, however, that the major centers of Mexican settlement in the city were first established more than a half century ago. Chicago's very rapidly growing Hispanic community became the nation's fourth largest by 1980 with 581,000 Latinos in metropolitan Chicago (see figure 1) and another 47,000 across the state line in metropolitan Gary, Indiana.[3]

Population projections show that the city of Chicago is expected to

2. Diana Pearce, Joe T. Darden, and Reynolds Farley, "Housing and School Desegregation in Metropolitan Chicago," report to Chicago Board of Education, February 19, 1981; Philpott, *The Slum and the Ghetto*, p. 116; and Deborah Haines, *Black Homeowners in Transition Areas* (Chicago Urban League, 1981).

3. Gary Orfield and Ricardo M. Tostado, eds., *Latinos in Metropolitan Chicago: A Study of Housing and Employment* (Chicago: Latino Institute, 1983), pp. 11–25.

Figure 1. *Chicago Areas with 50 Percent or More Black and Hispanic Populations, 1980*

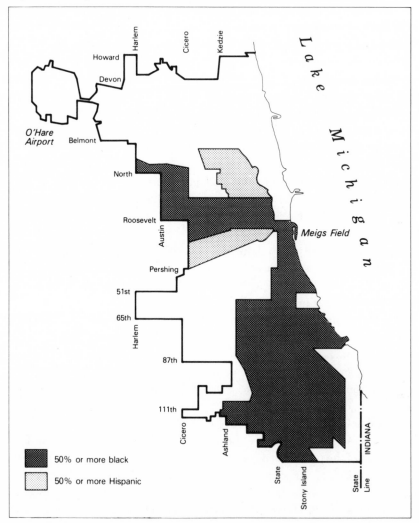

Source: Data from *Local Community Fact Book, Chicago Metropolitan Area 1980* (Chicago: Chicago Fact Book Consortium, 1984).

become more and more a minority city. Blacks will outnumber whites by the late 1980s, as the white population continues to decline. A steadily rising Hispanic population will account for at least one-third of the total city population by 2010. By 2010 the number of blacks is expected to drop somewhat from a peak in 1990, but they will be the largest population group in the city.[4]

Blacks and Hispanics made up 54 percent of Chicago's 3 million people in 1980. During the 1970s the city lost nearly one-third of its white population while gaining 9 percent more blacks and 71 percent more Hispanics (the Hispanic increase was partially due to improved counting). In spite of intense discussion of gentrification, there was no evidence of any significant countermigration of whites into the city. Considering the probable substantial undercount of illegal aliens and the evidence of continued rapid growth of Hispanic communities since the 1980 census, it is apparent that Chicago is a predominantly minority city and destined to become more so at a rapid rate. Much of the remaining white population is aging, and the city has relatively few school-age whites.

The direction of the change is underlined by the public and Catholic school statistics. Between 1971 and 1981 the Chicago public schools had a 60 percent drop in white enrollment. At the same time the city's white Catholic enrollment, in a city with a large Catholic population, dropped 47 percent. Part of this decline was a product of a dramatic drop in white birthrates and a substantial net white out-migration from the entire Chicago metropolitan area. The growth was very largely Hispanic. The city public schools gained 46 percent more Hispanic pupils, and the Catholic schools showed a 40 percent gain.[5]

In all of Cook County, an area of 5.3 million people, a clear majority of the public school students was black or Hispanic by 1981–82. More than one-third of the preschool population in the entire six-county metropolitan area was black or Hispanic by the time of the 1980 census.[6] The demographic changes were most dramatic in the city, but portions of suburbia also changed from all white to substantially integrated or even to new minority communities. In 1950, 94 percent of metropolitan Chicago blacks

4. *Chicago Tribune,* April 10, 1984; Donald Bogue and Albert Woolbright, "Population Projections: Chicago SMSA, Chicago City, and Metropolitan Ring, 1980–2000" (Chicago: Metropolitan Housing and Planning Council, 1983).

5. Marcia Turner Jones, "Chicago Area School Enrollment Trends 1970–1982" (Chicago Urban League, 1983).

6. Ibid.; and U.S. Bureau of the Census, *State and Metropolitan Area Data Book, 1982* (Government Printing Office, 1983), pp. 48, 50.

lived inside the city, as did 93 percent of a much larger black population ten years later. In 1970 the number dropped slightly to 90 percent, but the first significant decline, to 85 percent, came in 1980. Although blacks were still more concentrated in the central city than whites had been in 1950, about 200,000 blacks lived in the suburbs by 1980. Two suburban communities, Harvey and Maywood, accounted for 32 percent of the black suburban population. Smaller concentrations in eight other areas made up another 28 percent of the total. Unfortunately, much of this movement did not desegregate suburbia; it showed the rapid expansion of long-time suburban black enclaves or spillover ghettoization from the expansion of the South and West Side ghettos over the city boundary lines.[7]

Measures of Segregation

There are many ways of measuring segregation, and all show very high levels in Chicago and its suburban ring. The most commonly used measure, the dissimilarity index, shows the extent to which the actual racial distribution of populations among units of a city or metropolitan area differs from a racially random distribution of people. By this measure, the city's segregation has been extremely high for half a century and was the highest in the United States in 1980. On a scale in which 100 would be total apartheid and 0 would be a random distribution by race in all parts of the city, Chicago had a rating of 93 in 1970 and 92 in 1980. The index for the city has shown little change since 1940.[8] In 1980 this index was slightly lower for the blacks in the suburban ring, but it was still remarkably high, given the fact that blacks constituted less than 6 percent of the suburban population. For the metropolitan area as a whole, the index was 92.[9]

Another important measure is the exposure index, a measure that shows the racial composition of the block where a typical family from any racial group lives. The typical black in the city lives on a block that is 4.5 percent white, and in the metropolitan area, on a block that is 8.7 percent white.

7. Joe T. Darden, "Demographic Patterns in Housing: Changes in Chicago and the Nation Since 1950," paper prepared for conference on "Civil Rights in the Eighties," Chicago Urban League, June 15, 1984, pp. 13–18.

8. Duncan and Duncan, *The Negro Population of Chicago;* Taeuber and Taeuber, *Negroes in Cities;* and Karl Taeuber, "Appendix," in Citizens Commission on Civil Rights, *A Decent Home: A Report on the Continued Failure of the Federal Government to Provide Equal Housing Opportunity* (Washington, D.C., 1983), p. 7.

9. William C. Hogan III, "Residential Segregation in Metropolitan Chicago: 1980" (B.A. thesis, University of Chicago, 1983), pp. 35–36.

The typical block a white lives on in metropolitan Chicago is 2.6 percent black.[10] Much of the little racial contact that does exist is not due to stable integration but to temporary proximity during racial transition.

One impact of the continuing strong residential discrimination is the fact that the proportion of blacks living in virtually all-black census tracts in metropolitan Chicago actually rose from its already high level between 1970 and 1980. The number of people in all-black tracts (tracts typically contain about 4,000 people) grew 31 percent during the decade, rising from 60 percent of the area's blacks to 68 percent of a larger black population.[11]

The most common way in which people reconcile the obvious fact of continuing racial segregation with their belief that housing discrimination is a thing of the past is by asserting that the segregation is the result of income differences between blacks and whites. Obviously there is a large gap in average income between white and black households. But if an income gap were the only cause of the existing level of racial segregation in Chicago, two things would have to be true: there would have to be virtually no overlap between white and black incomes, and different areas of the city and suburbs would have to have uniformly different price structures. Neither is true.

A 1984 study examined whether the pattern of residential segregation in Chicago could be explained by economic differences. According to an econometric model developed by John Kain, the city's black population had more than 120,000 households that could not be explained by interracial income differentials or other economic factors. Each of the suburban counties, moreover, should have had three to eight times as many black families as it did have.[12]

The weakness of the economic explanation would be even more apparent if it were possible to take into account the degree to which current income inequalities are due to the cumulative effect of isolation from the best wealth-producing homeownership opportunities and from fair access to the growing areas of the suburban job market. Any reasonable estimates of those forces would increase the degree to which the present residential

10. Ibid., pp. 41–42.

11. Gary Orfield, Albert Woolbright, and Helene Kim, "Neighborhood Change and Integration in Metropolitan Chicago" (Chicago: Leadership Council for Metropolitan Open Communities, 1984).

12. John F. Kain, "The Extent and Causes of Racial Residential Segregation," paper prepared for conference on "Civil Rights in the Eighties," Chicago Urban League, June 15, 1984, tables 1 and 2.

distribution would be attributed to a history of discrimination rather than economics. Even if only current income is considered, however, economics cannot begin to explain the present extreme pattern of separation.

Perceptions and Tests of Discrimination

Blacks in the Chicago area believe that portions of the housing market are still largely closed to black home buyers and renters. This belief is both a reflection of serious problems and an important continuing cause of segregation. The validity of the black belief is supported both by the high level of agreement among whites on the existence of severe discrimination in the housing market and by direct data produced by testing of the housing market.

A 1983 survey in metropolitan Chicago found that only 9 percent of blacks and 28 percent of whites thought that blacks could "live almost anywhere" in the Chicago area. Almost nine-tenths of blacks (86 percent) and two-thirds of whites (63 percent) agreed that "there are many areas where people try to keep blacks out." A large majority of blacks (72 percent) believed that they would feel unwelcome "in most white areas if they choose to live there."[13] In the parts of the city and suburbs directly in the path of black expansion, whites perceived even more white resistance, showing both the continuing intensity of the white fear of displacement and decline because of ghettoization and the likelihood of continuation of severe conflict.

Whites who perceived more tolerance lived in areas away from the large ghettos and the path of ghetto expansion—the North Side of the city and the suburbs to the north and northwest. Upper-income whites were substantially more likely than low-income whites to believe that the housing market was open. In other words, those who lived in virtually all-white communities with little visible black presence were much more likely to be optimistic than whites near the borders of racial change. White elites, almost totally insulated from the forces of ghettoization, could express more positive attitudes with no risk of being called upon to act on them.

Upper-income and more highly educated blacks, the group for whom the question of escaping the ghetto was most urgent, had exactly the opposite beliefs from their white counterparts. As their families became more able to afford a wide array of housing their perception of discrimination

13. *Chicago Sun-Times*, October 16, 1983.

increased. There was a virtual consensus (94 percent) among blacks earning more than $40,000 a year that the housing market was not completely open to blacks.

All groups showed considerable resistance to public housing for low-income black families in their neighborhoods.[14] Subsidized housing in the city is overwhelmingly black, with 95 percent of Chicago Housing Authority family units rented to blacks.[15] Only a bare majority of blacks said that they would approve of even modest amounts of public housing units in their neighborhoods, while 63 percent of whites and 57 percent of Hispanics were opposed.[16] In a city with some of the nation's most notorious projects, public housing was widely seen as a threat to neighborhoods. The history of failure meant that few people would even consider allowing subsidized projects in their neighborhood, even the small-scale, scattered-site projects that are now being implemented.

The only way to obtain reasonably accurate measures of actual discrimination in a housing market is by tests to compare treatment given similar minority and white couples asking for similar housing. Such tests always disclose many instances of discrimination that a minority home seeker could not have detected without knowing what housing was shown on what terms to a white home seeker. Most of the testing in metropolitan Chicago in recent years has been in the southern suburbs, the suburban area experiencing the most dramatic racial change.

A 1983 analysis by University of Illinois scholars found that there was substantial discrimination in the southern suburbs and that when statistically significant differences in treatment were found "it was almost always the case that the population of black testers received poorer treatment." It found that blacks tended to be steered toward black or integrated neighborhoods and school districts in the city and suburbs, while whites were steered to all-white neighborhoods and school districts.[17]

14. The Chicago Housing Authority and the U.S. Department of Housing and Urban Development operate their programs in the Chicago area under a series of court orders growing out of the *Gautreaux* litigation, which found both guilty of the intentional segregation of the large programs of subsidized housing in the metropolitan Chicago area (*Hills* v. *Gautreaux*, 425 U.S. 284 [1976]). The remedies under these orders were resisted by city government until policy changed following the election of Chicago's first black mayor, Harold Washington, in 1983.

15. Chicago Housing Authority, *Annual Report*, 1982.

16. *Chicago Sun-Times*, October 16, 1983.

17. Dorothy Hall, William Peterman, and Judy Dwyer, "Measuring Discrimination and Steering in Chicago's Southern Suburbs," report for South Suburban Housing Center (Chicago: University of Illinois Voorhees Center for Neighborhood and Community Improvement, 1983), p. 3.

The racial composition of the school districts showed a clear pattern of racial change along a path of suburbs going from the South Side ghetto to the edge of suburban construction more than fifteen miles from the city boundaries. Just south of the city boundaries are four districts that were predominantly black by 1981. Adjoining them are four others that were 23 to 51 percent black, and there were two other such districts directly to the south. Many other districts in the south suburban region had substantial black enrollments, in contrast to the typical suburban pattern.[18]

By 1980 there were three villages in the southern suburbs that were predominantly black and five others that were 23 to 51 percent black. A number of other villages were more than one-tenth black. It was common for a village that had a large black population to be adjacent to other villages with large black populations within the north-south corridor of racial change but at the same time to have totally white suburbs to the east and west, where blacks were not shown housing.[19]

Chicago's Leadership Council for Metropolitan Open Communities, a national fair housing leader, tested the markets on the borders of black expansion in southwest and northwest Chicago and nearby suburbs in 1983.[20] The testers found extensive overt discrimination, including open refusal to show housing in white suburban areas to black home seekers. Realtors also actively discouraged whites from moving into integrated areas of the city. Particularly in the racially tense southwest neighborhoods, whites asking to look in the city were shown all-white suburbs instead. Lawsuits were filed against eight realtors who had been extensively tested in late 1983.

Racial Change: A Case Study

The dynamics of ghettoization in parts of the southern suburbs are shown in a case study of an area on the boundary of black expansion. One of the principal influences on the steering away of black home buyers from suburban neighborhoods experiencing rapid racial change was the changing enrollment pattern of one of the four high schools in the area. The Bremen Township Community High School District, about fifteen miles south of Chicago, had 5,900 students in four high schools. Although the size of the schools was similar, by the 1982–83 school year the Oak Forest School was

18. Ibid., p. 20.
19. Ibid., p. 23.
20. Leadership Council for Metropolitan Open Communities, *Action for Open Communities*, vol. 1 (1984), p. 2.

0.4 percent black while Hillcrest High was 38 percent black and rapidly changing.

The population of the Hillcrest school district was not overwhelmingly black. An analysis of the 1980 census showed that "of the 245 blocks in the Hillcrest High School attendance area, 22 were over 50 percent black and 16 were over 80 percent black."[21] In other words, about five of every six blocks in the district were predominantly white and only 7 percent were more than 80 percent black. However, white families with high school-age children were obtaining housing disproportionately in the Oak Forest district. Thus the increase in black students was almost exclusively in the Hillcrest district, which in turn was producing racially identifiable schools and sharply affecting the marketing of housing in both areas. Between the fall of 1972 and the fall of 1982 Hillcrest's white enrollment dropped 46 percent while Oak Forest's white enrollment increased 51 percent. In the meantime, Hillcrest's black enrollment was up 83 percent while Oak Forest remained virtually all white.

Systematic tests of realtors working in the area found that "realtors showing houses to white families steer them away from the Hillcrest area, often with references to the minority composition of the high school their children would have to attend."[22] Local officials were worried that real estate discrimination and the self-fulfilling prophecy of racial change in the residential market would produce a segregated school and a sizable suburban residential ghetto. Projecting the 1983 rate of change in school enrollment, it was apparent that the trend would produce a majority black school within five years.[23] That in turn would probably consolidate the steering and "self-steering" processes in the residential market, greatly reducing white demand for housing and assuring relatively rapid residential transition. It was the classic central-city racial change syndrome, played out in a different place at a later time.

Hispanic Segregation

Hispanics are seriously segregated in metropolitan Chicago, and there is evidence that their isolation is growing, particularly for the young. Among the Hispanic groups the Puerto Ricans and Mexican-Americans are the most segregated and the Cubans and Central and South Americans much

21. Jennifer Maude, report to Village of Hazel Crest, Illinois, 1983.
22. Ibid.
23. Ibid.

less so. Their level of residential and educational segregation is still far less extreme than that of the black population, but the Hispanics are highly concentrated in city and suburban areas with rapidly declining minorities of whites. Hispanics perceive very serious housing discrimination in the Chicago area, and their housing is generally older and more overcrowded than that of most blacks.

The white-Hispanic dissimilarity index in 1980 was 61 within the city and 64 in the metropolitan area—substantially below the level for blacks in the city but above the score reported for blacks in some parts of the area's housing market. The index was slightly higher for Mexican-Americans, the dominant group in the Hispanic population, and substantially higher for Puerto Ricans, reaching 81 for the metropolitan area. Hispanics in metropolitan Chicago are also extremely segregated from blacks, almost as much as whites are. This means that blacks are extremely isolated, not only from the majority group that dominates the economy and society of metropolitan Chicago, but also from a very large minority group that is growing far more rapidly than the black community.[24] The exposure indices show that although the metropolitan area population is about 8 percent Hispanic, the block the typical Hispanic lives on is 45 percent Hispanic and 56 percent total minority population. In the city it is 53 percent Hispanic and 64 percent minority.[25]

Although there were no all-Hispanic census tracts in metropolitan Chicago in 1980 and, more generally, Hispanics did not live in tracts as intensely segregated as those where most blacks lived, there was a rapid increase in the number of areas with large Hispanic majorities. The small proportion of Chicago-area census tracts that were more than 70 percent Hispanic in 1970 increased sixfold during the decade, and a solid corridor of overwhelmingly Hispanic census tracts emerged in the heart of the largest Mexican-American barrio, the Pilsen and Little Village community areas of the city. Similar concentrations, although smaller and less intensely segregated, were emerging in the Humboldt Park–Logan Square area of the Near North Side and the Back-of-the-Yards area on the South Side. Close to three-fourths of all Hispanics in the metropolitan area (71 percent) lived inside the city boundaries. A significant fraction of the remainder lived in aging satellite cities, particularly Aurora, which was 18 percent Hispanic by 1980. This meant that Hispanics, like blacks, were over-

24. Computations from 1980 Illinois census tape.
25. Hogan, "Residential Segregation in Metropolitan Chicago," p. 42.

whelmingly dependent upon the most rapidly declining sectors of the metropolitan economy and educational systems.

Consequences of Segregation

As a basic feature of urban race relations, residential segregation has a wide array of consequences. The process of racial change in a neighborhood or a municipality can transform the nature and prospects of that community. This study will look both at the consequences for blacks and Hispanics as groups and then at the consequences for areas within metropolitan Chicago. The data indicate strong effects of both kinds.

Effects on Education

Two key aspects of mobility are tied to location. Residence profoundly determines education in metropolitan Chicago, at least through the junior college level, and also helps determine accessibility to places of employment. In both respects, blacks and Hispanics are affected strongly and negatively.

The large majority of blacks and Hispanics in the Chicago area, but only a very small fraction of whites, must depend upon the Chicago public schools and community colleges for their education. Because of the concentration of blacks and the extreme segregation within the central-city system, blacks in the state of Illinois are more likely to attend intensely segregated schools (90 to 100 percent minority) than in any other state. Although a number of states have significantly higher percentages of Hispanic students, Illinois ranks fourth in the United States in segregation of Hispanics for the same reason. Black segregation has remained essentially unchanged since data first became available in the sixties. Hispanic school segregation has rapidly become worse. In the fall of 1967 the typical Hispanic child in Chicago was in a school that was slightly more than half white. During the 1983–84 school year, however, most Hispanic students were going to a school where less than one-tenth of their classmates were white. Although Hispanic families often lived in neighborhoods with a significant number of white residents, they tended to be older white ethnics. Hispanic children were growing up in severely isolated communities. In the four majority Hispanic community areas in the city, for example, an average of one-sixth of the children were white, and many of those were in private schools.[26]

The public schools were highly stratified by income as well as by race. Very large numbers of minority students (one-fourth of the black high school students, for example) in Chicago were in schools that had virtually no whites nor any students who were not classified by the schools as poor.

In metropolitan Chicago, according to a 1984 study, the racial composition of a school and its location were related to almost every significant characteristic of the school. Public schools in the Chicago school district had larger classes, teachers from the least selective colleges, fewer counselors, much higher dropout rates, fewer graduates attending four-year colleges, and much lower achievement scores. Among those schools, the all-minority, all-poor schools tended to be worst in curriculum, dropout rates, and achievement levels.[27]

Blacks and Hispanics in metropolitan Chicago do much worse than whites at every level of educational completion, and whites in the city schools fare far worse than their suburban counterparts. About half of the students in the city drop out, in comparison with one in forty in affluent DuPage County. Dropout rates are even higher for minority schools and exceed three-fourths in some low-income minority schools.[28] At the high school level the result is that the schools serving the students with the greatest need and the least help from their families often have educational programs that cannot prepare them for a college operating at a reasonably competitive level.

The high schools feed a system of public community colleges that are also defined by race and area in terms of their student enrollment, the character of their program, and the future education of their students. Enrollment data show very strong processes of channeling students from black and Hispanic areas of the city, but not from white areas, into geographically and racially defined community colleges where most of the

26. Technical Assistance Committee on the Chicago Desegregation Plan, "Integration in Chicago," report to Illinois State Board of Education, May 11, 1978; Benjamin Weinberg, calculations for Mexican American Legal Defense Fund, 1984; Gary Orfield, *Public School Desegregation in the United States, 1968–1980* (Washington, D.C.: Joint Center for Political Studies, 1983), pp. 10, 18; and Chicago Department of Planning, "1980 Census Reports, Population," pt. 1, tables 12, 13.

27. Gary Orfield, Howard Mitzel, and others, *The Chicago Study of Access and Choice in Higher Education*, report to Illinois Senate Committee on Higher Education, 1984, chap. 8.

28. Ibid.

students are from minority groups. These colleges have the least adequate curriculum, the least success in transferring students to four-year colleges, and patterns of transfer to the least selective four-year colleges in Illinois.[29] Those black city students who complete community college are most likely to enroll in the state's only black four-year institution, Chicago State University. Chicago State is the least selective public university in the state and has a high dropout rate. It becomes, in turn, the most important single source of teachers for the Chicago public schools, but for none of the eighty-five suburban high school districts.[30]

Students who grow up in segregated minority areas, particularly those within the city of Chicago, have a separate and unequal set of educational opportunities that continues throughout their schooling. One could easily argue that their educational experiences are not intended to and cannot prepare people to function in the same society and the same economy. The educational system is built on the system of residential stratification by race and tends to perpetuate both segregation and inequality.

Blacks rank below whites and Hispanics below blacks on virtually every measure of educational success in each county in metropolitan Chicago. Although there was considerable expansion of education, particularly at the college level, under the strong social and educational programs of the 1960s and early 1970s at the federal and state levels, there is considerable evidence that that process has reversed itself and that educational opportunity is diminishing, particularly for blacks. Between 1975 and 1980 the number of blacks receiving B.A., M.A., and Ph.D. degrees declined, both in Chicago and in the suburbs. Black enrollment at the leading public university in the Chicago area, the University of Illinois at Chicago, declined 38 percent between 1979 and 1983. Among the nation's seven largest urban complexes, metropolitan Chicago's Hispanics ranked lowest in educational achievement in 1980. Hispanics within the city schools now face the most severe overcrowding, the highest dropout rates, and the lowest college attendance and graduation rates of the three major racial and ethnic groups in the metropolitan area.[31]

29. Ibid., chaps. 10–13. The U.S. Department of Education ruled in 1984 that Chicago's black community colleges had less experienced and less educated faculties than their white counterparts. U.S. Department of Education, Office for Civil Rights, Region 5, "Title VI Compliance Investigation at City Colleges of Chicago, Final Letter of Findings," February 14, 1984.

30. Orfield, Mitzel, and others, chaps. 13, 15.

31. Ibid., chap. 6; Orfield and Tostado, Latinos in Metropolitan Chicago, pp. 40–46, citing statistics from census tapes; and Illinois State Board of Education data.

Effects on Employment

High school and college graduation are related to employment, occupational status, and income.[32] Unequal education is likely to become far more serious as a constraint on opportunity in the future as the low-skill, relatively highly paid jobs in Chicago's industrial economy continue to be replaced by low-wage service jobs and better jobs that have high skill requirements. In addition to the general transformation of the economy that is affecting the entire labor market, minority workers face a particularly severe disadvantage because of residential segregation (see the essay by John Kasarda). Male minority members face an additional disadvantage: entry-level, lower-paid office jobs are available to qualified minority women and account for much of the economic mobility of minority households in the past generation. There are, however, few such jobs available to men, who usually do not have the appropriate clerical training. Nor do minority men usually have the educational credentials to compete for the higher-paid, traditionally male occupations in the white-collar work force. The combination of changes in the labor market, the movement of industrial jobs to the suburbs, and the lack of adequate educational preparation contributes to the growing joblessness, downward economic mobility, and sharp decline in labor market participation for minority men. As a result, even a substantial economic recovery has little impact within the minority community. The extreme precariousness of employment for minority men further undermines family stability, the key to minority mobility.

The nature of the changing job market in major U.S. central cities is documented in Kasarda's paper. As indicated there, Chicago lost jobs in most of the major private-sector industries throughout the 1970s. Between 1972 and 1978 the city lost 83,000 manufacturing jobs while the suburbs showed a small gain. From 1979 to 1981 the city lost another tenth of its manufacturing jobs while such jobs increased in DuPage County in spite of two recessions. There were substantial losses in other fields, including wholesale and retail trade, construction, and transportation. The major growth sectors in the central-city economy were finance, insurance and real estate, and services.[33] Job growth was concentrated in the affluent

32. W. Vance Grant and Thomas D. Snyder, *Digest of Education Statistics 1983–84* (GPO, 1984), tables 150–55; and U.S. Commission on Civil Rights, *Unemployment and Underemployment among Blacks, Hispanics and Women* (GPO, 1982).

33. Illinois Bureau of Employment Security, *Where Workers Work, 1979, 1981;* and Orfield and Tostado, *Latinos in Metropolitan Chicago,* pp. 52–53.

white suburbs. During 1972–81 fourteen of these suburbs each gained 4,000–16,000 new jobs. Located primarily in DuPage County and northwest Cook County, their average black population was 0.05 percent.[34]

The 1981–83 recession showed the particular vulnerability of minority employees to economic changes. When firms were confronted with decisions on layoffs and plant closings, they typically chose to eliminate capacity in the city and later expand, if necessary, in the suburbs or elsewhere. The social consequences, particularly for minority men, were devastating.

The Illinois economy was severely damaged by the 1981–83 recession, which hit particularly hard in the city. After the low point of the 1975 recession, the city had lagged seriously in the recovery and its jobless rate had not dropped significantly for four years. For blacks, unemployment had actually increased during the first three years of the recovery. Even at the high point of expansion, in 1979, the nonwhite unemployment rate was near to its 1975 recession level: 58 percent of nonwhites in the city were employed, compared with 68 percent of all men. During 1980 the employment rate of black males fell even further, to 53 percent, and during 1982 the total nonwhite employment in the city dropped 12,000 jobs. The unemployment rate for nonwhites in the city rose 113 percent from its 1979 level, and large numbers of blacks simply dropped out of the labor market, no longer looking for work.

Things were even worse at the entry point into the job market, teenage employment. Throughout 1979–83 white teens in Chicago were about three times as likely to have a job as their nonwhite counterparts. The nonwhite teenage jobless rate rose from 40 percent in 1979 to 66 percent in 1982.[35] During the recessions the labor market for young black workers, particularly unskilled blacks, virtually disappeared in Chicago, and even at the height of expansion the unemployment rate was above depression levels. This was at a time when the Chicago public schools had a dropout rate that was 48 percent overall and considerably higher for blacks and Latinos.[36]

Part of the problem was the physical impossibility of getting to job sites from central-city neighborhoods. A 1984 analysis of the transportation dilemma showed the severity of the isolation:

The dependence of low income people on mass transit is highlighted by Chicago Metropolitan Area studies that show that twice as many blacks as whites use public

34. Author's calculation from *Chicago Sun-Times* data, October 17, 1983.
35. Wendy Wintermute, "Recession and 'Recovery': Impact on Black and White Workers in Chicago" (Chicago Urban League, 1983), pp. 1–6.
36. Illinois State Board of Education data.

transportation, and that female-headed households use such transportation more than twice as much as male heads of households. . . . Use of public transportation is inversely related to income level. . . . Transportation patterns . . . have the unfortunate effect of isolating suburban people and inner city persons from one another. Nearly 45 percent of commuters—over a million a day—both live and work in the suburbs. Another 35 percent both live and work in the city. The balance are inter-area commuters: 14 percent into the city each day, and 7 percent to the suburbs each day.[37]

The study showed that there is very little reverse commuting to jobs in spite of the vast growth of the suburbs. There is no effective way to reach most suburban jobs by mass transit. Mass transit is also considered dangerous for access to work, particularly in evening hours. A 1984 rider survey found that 59 percent of those using buses and 76 percent of those riding trains were afraid of crime on these forms of public transportation. The same survey showed that 77 percent of black riders used public transportation because they had no other option.[38] As for private transportation, the 1980 census showed that 41 percent of black households and 27 percent of Hispanic households in the Chicago area did not have cars. A 1984 computation shows that the highest unemployment areas within the city are extremely isolated from the centers of increasing job concentration. For all practical purposes, the jobs in the outer suburban areas are not accessible by public transportation from the high unemployment areas.[39]

A projection of job opportunities to 2000 shows continuation of the declining rate of job creation in Cook County (which contains more than 5 million of metropolitan Chicago's 7 million people), a continuing shift of jobs to the northwest suburbs, and a continuing replacement of manufacturing jobs with white-collar work. The county was expected to lose another 33,000 manufacturing jobs by 2000, further isolating inner-city residents from job opportunities.[40]

Effects on the Family

At the core of this changing economy were about 600,000 people in the city living in poverty, including "a full third of the black community, about

37. Quoted in *Recent Developments in Housing* (Chicago: Leadership Council for Metropolitan Open Communities, July–August 1984), p. 5.

38. *Chicago Sun-Times*, December 3, 1984. Chicago's black newspaper has reported widespread crime on the Chicago Transit Authority trains and buses and quotes some passengers as saying they are arming to defend themselves. (*Chicago Defender*, August 21, 22, 1984.)

39. Analysis of 1980 census data by James Jarusek, Northeastern Illinois Planning Commission, October 9, 1984.

40. *Chicago Sun-Times*, May 29, 1983.

a quarter of the Hispanic community, and some 10 percent of the white community," according to one study which states:

About 300,000 have been on welfare for five years or more. They are the hard core of the underclass and their ranks are growing. This new poverty of permanent unemployment and dependency has caused and is causing massive social damage. . . . This poverty of uselessness, of having no function or place in society, has eroded hope, self respect and social standards. Family structure has weakened as we see in the massive growth of female-headed families which now dominate the poverty rolls, in the growth of illegitimacy, teenage pregnancy, crime and violence, and our 50 percent dropout rate.[41]

The economic differences between city and suburbs were apparent in the responses to a *Chicago Tribune* poll shortly before the 1984 election. Suburban residents were almost twice as likely as city residents to believe that the economy had improved in the last four years, while city residents were more than three times as likely to believe that things were getting worse. City residents saw unemployment and education as the most important problems.[42]

A survey of Chicago families in the fall of 1983 by Northwestern University researchers reported: "The distribution of income appears to have become more unequal during the 1980s. The rich appear to have gained slightly while the poor have lost quite a lot." Black female-headed households reported the largest losses since 1981. More than one-third of black households spent less than the minimum necessary for an adequate food supply. About one-fifth of all renters in the city were not able to pay their rent at some point during 1982 or 1983. The growing problems were blamed on the severe recession, the simultaneous cut in federal aid, and the substantial decline in the real level of payments for aid to families with dependent children (AFDC).[43]

As jobs have left the city and minority unemployment has remained at extraordinary levels, the median family income for both blacks and Hispanics in Chicago has dropped. During the 1970s it fell 6.4 percent in real dollars for Hispanics and 12 percent for blacks.

These economic problems have in turn contributed to the collapse of the black family structure and increased problems among formerly stable

41. John A. McDermott, "The Changing Nature of Race Relations in Chicago," address to Chicago United, February 3, 1984.

42. *Chicago Tribune*, October 2 and 4, 1984.

43. Fay Lomax Cook and others, "Economic Hardship in Chicago: 1983," Research and Policy Reports (Northwestern University, Center for Urban Affairs and Policy Research, April 1984).

families in the Latino community. The result is very large numbers of very poor female-headed families who are highly concentrated in minority areas and almost wholly cut off from the private economy. The economic situation of these families then further restricts their residential choice and increases dependence on the ghetto or barrio and the poorest inner-city schools. As these problems become dominant realities in large parts of the city, the resources of the neighborhoods and eventually the entire city are further depleted, and the proportion of the population living in almost total dependence on public assistance and governmental services increases rapidly. The rise of severe social disorganization, gangs, and violent crime and the collapse of the market for private property in the neighborhood creates a powerful cycle of increasingly severe disinvestment and eventual abandonment.

Policy Responses to Racial Change

From a social and economic perspective the great questions about the impact of segregation may be questions of attitudes, social and economic mobility, and effects of ghettoization. From a policy perspective, however, the most important questions are different: What policies have been designed to address these problems and why haven't they worked? Are the processes that produced these problems still clearly dominant or are there real alternatives? Are there policy alternatives that could fundamentally alter the outcomes? Do local governments have the capacity to change the processes of racial change or must they simply accept the process as it transforms their communities more and more?

Leveling the Ghetto

The dominant answer in Chicago and most other cities from the beginning of major black immigration to the outlawing of restrictive covenants in 1948 was that organized white resistance was the only way to preserve white communities from the devastation that accompanied racial change and that it was appropriate for government to play a role in supporting white resistance, at least through court enforcement of covenants. From the late 1940s, open advocacy of officially supported segregation went out of fashion in the North, but it was replaced by overt segregation of subsidized housing and a variety of indirect measures to move blacks away from strategic parts of the cities and to create physical barriers separating black and white communities. Urban renewal, slum clearance, code enforcement, and highway construction all led to the elimination of concentrations of low-income blacks that were seen as threatening the vitality of downtown and near-downtown areas or the viability of desirable white residential communities.

The city of Chicago was a national leader in embracing urban renewal and slum clearance policies. Many square miles of the city were transformed by renewal and highway projects, and thousands of people, disproportionately black, were forced to move. These projects also created some very desirable new close-in residential locations for upper- and middle-income professionals and made it more feasible to live far out in the suburbs and commute to jobs in the city.

The tendency, in Chicago and other cities, was to focus attention only on the before and after pictures taken of the particular plot of land being cleared and redeveloped. The fact was that redevelopment forced the people from the slum being cleared to move to another neighborhood, thereby creating a new slum. Massive new vertical slums were created when Chicago's vast public housing program operated under policies that permitted white neighborhoods to veto the kind of low-density development on open land that would have made sense for families. The result was massive displacement to obtain public housing sites, extreme segregation, and the creation on the South Side of what amounted to a city within the city occupied entirely by poor black families. This city was filled with high-rise projects that were unmanageable and unsuitable for families and that soon became dangerous and frightening vertical ghettos.[44]

Punishing the Villains

If the urban renewal strategy could be called one of leveling the ghetto, the other major policy response was one of punishing the villains, who were blamed for causing destructive neighborhood change in communities that otherwise would not have been affected. The "block buster" and the "panic peddler" were the particular targets of these policies. Other villains

44. Martin Mayerson and Edward C. Banfield, *Politics, Planning and the Public Interest: The Case of Public Housing in Chicago* (Free Press, 1955); Peter H. Rossi and Robert A. Dentler, *The Politics of Urban Renewal: The Chicago Findings* (Free Press, 1961); and Devereux Bowly, Jr., *The Poorhouse: Subsidized Housing in Chicago, 1895–1976* (Southern Illinois University Press, 1978).

were added later—particularly the banks that withdrew financing from communities after racial change began and the Federal Housing Administration, which after refusing to finance black suburbanization suddenly began to finance large numbers of unqualified black buyers in integrated communities in ways that produced both rapid racial transition and precipitous economic decline.

Ghettoization was always happening in Chicago somewhere along the peripheries of minority expansion, but it tended to become a public issue only when it was particularly sudden or dramatic or when someone effectively targeted a villain. It could not be a constant story because there were no proposals to radically alter the housing market in any way that might end the necessity for continually converting white neighborhoods to black areas. Attention came when organized neighborhood groups or journalists thought that they had spotted a particular form of unethical behavior that was destroying an otherwise sound community.

The major offenses, in the minds of the critics, were letting in too many low-income blacks and stirring up white fears in a way that generated panic, produced a large glut of white housing for sale at low prices in the black housing market, and ended in tumultuous and even violent change. They perceived as villains the people who sold white housing near ghettos to blacks, not those who excluded them from other areas.

During the 1970s, in one Chicago neighborhood after another, there were publicized incidents of realtors exploiting white property owners' racial fears to persuade them to sell their homes in a panic. In turn there were numerous attempts by both property owners and public officials to put an end to such practices. The same complaints were being made and the same villains being identified, but still racial change continued, although it became less sudden and vicious in some neighborhoods. The official promises to attack the problem might change the actions of some of the participants, but the end result was not much different. Treating the symptoms of the ghettoization process does not eliminate the fear or the self-fulfilling prophecies that are deeply rooted in communities near Chicago ghettos.

Policy Failure

The problem with both the slum-leveling and villain-punishing policies, of course, was their failure to recognize that, given the nature of the housing market and white attitudes, eliminating ghettos or preventing the transition of a white neighborhood somewhere would only move the dynamic of ghettoization somewhere else. Blacks had to live somewhere, and middle-class blacks were eager to escape ghetto conditions. If there were no significant access to white or stably integrated areas, black expansion would always take the form of ghetto expansion. The policies would only affect where it happened, not whether it happened.

From the black perspective, a basic problem is that discrimination is still commonplace, many blacks are afraid to move outside the path of racial change, and there is little effective fair housing enforcement activity, even when black families confront violence. The Illinois Department of Human Rights reported an all-time peak of housing discrimination complaints in the first part of 1984. The city's leading fair housing group, the Leadership Council for Metropolitan Open Communities, reported a number of complaints of violence against black households in the second quarter of 1984, including bombings, gunshots, and burning crosses. In most cases, according to the council, police failed to provide adequate help to the families and, in two cases, police contributed to the problem.[45] At the same time that a number of white neighborhoods saw too much minority housing demand focusing on their area to allow maintenance of stable integration, blacks found themselves constrained and threatened in the housing market. Both perceptions are true. They show that unless the segregated housing market is attacked directly the groups on both sides of the racial boundary line will be continually harmed.

For such an attack to succeed there must be a real alternative. For the first time in Chicago history there is now evidence that there is a real alternative already present on a significant scale, and that it makes a dramatic difference to a community.

Successful Racial Change

Determining the patterns of racial change in Chicago and the social, educational, and economic impacts of that change across a metropolitan area of more than 7 million people poses difficult problems of analysis. I have participated in a research project that combined 1970 and 1980 census data on race and a large number of other variables, permitting comparison among seven kinds of census tracts: segregated black in both decades,

45. *Chicago Defender*, August 8, 1984.

segregated white, "panic" tracts experiencing extremely rapid racial ghettoization, black transitional tracts experiencing large but slower racial
change, Hispanic transitional tracts, and stably integrated tracts that had
a substantial white and black or Hispanic population before the 1970 census
and now show racial stability.[46]

The analysis shows that a growing fraction of both blacks and Hispanics
live in highly isolated minority communities ranked below other parts of
the metropolitan area in education, income, employment, and other key
measures. This is not surprising. It shows both the continuity and the cost
of Chicago's racial patterns.

The surprise in the data is the existence of 61 stably integrated black-
white communities and 135 stably integrated Hispanic-white communities
in the metropolitan area (see figures 2 and 3). About one-tenth of the
metropolitan Chicago white population in 1980 lived in areas where there
had been a significant black or Hispanic population for more than a decade
and no major racial change was taking place. Another considerable surprise
is that these communities tended to be predominantly white but to have
significant numbers of both blacks and Hispanics, in spite of the overall
high segregation of blacks from Hispanics.

The 1980 census showed that 528,000 whites, 102,000 Hispanics, and
87,000 blacks lived in stably integrated tracts. Blacks and Hispanics living
in the suburbs were far more likely to live in stably integrated areas,
suggesting that the city pattern need not be replicated in the suburbs,
particularly if appropriate strategies to support integration were put in
place. The large majority of Hispanics in the suburbs lived in stable rather
than transitional tracts, and there was no panic transition for blacks anywhere in the suburbs in the 1970s though suburban transition was occurring
in parts of the path of the South and West Side ghetto expansions.

The data suggest that some renewal and redevelopment plans could
have a positive racial impact. Redevelopment and gentrification have
created a cluster of stably integrated communities close to the Loop on all
sides, in Hyde Park, and in the Near North Side. There was no evidence
of a significant decline in the proportion of blacks in such communities in
the 1970s, though there were a few areas on the Near North Side that
showed a substantial loss of Hispanics. Many of the small number of stably
integrated city neighborhoods in which blacks were the largest minority

46. Orfield, Woolbright, and Kim, "Neighborhood Change and Integration in Metropolitan Chicago."

Figure 2. *Types of Racial Change for Blacks and Hispanics in Census Tracts in Chicago Suburbs, 1970–80*[a]

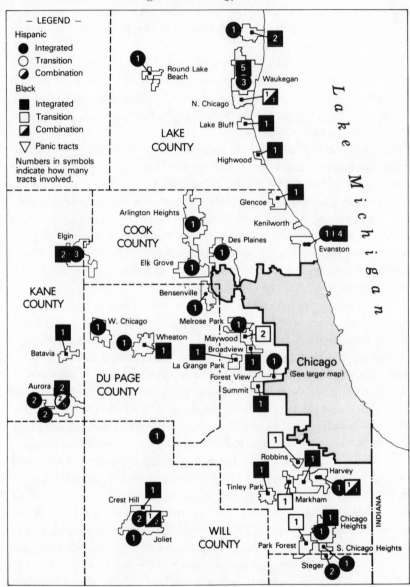

Source: Gary Orfield, Albert Woolbright, and Helene Kim, "Neighborhood Change and Integration in Metropolitan Chicago" (Chicago: Leadership Council for Metropolitan Open Communities, 1984).
a. The communities shown here are only those in which there was some racial change before 1970.

Figure 3. *Types of Racial Change for Blacks and Hispanics in Census Tracts in City of Chicago, 1970–80*[a]

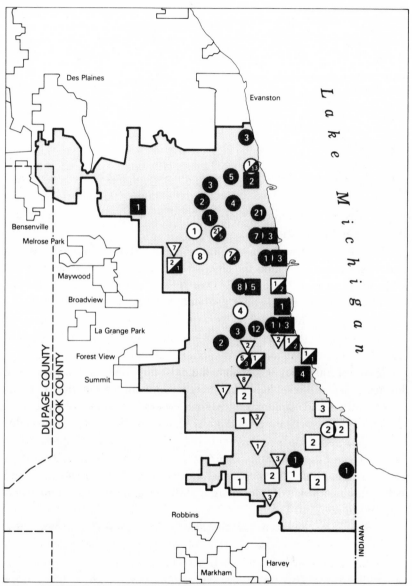

Source: Orfield, Woolbright, and Kim, "Neighborhood Change and Integration in Metropolitan Chicago."
a. The communities shown here are only those in which there was some racial change before 1970.

Table 1. *Educational and Economic Levels of Census Tracts in Chicago,*
by Level of Black-White Integration, 1980

Percent

Racial categoriza- tion of tract	High school graduates	College graduates	Profes- sional managers	Poverty	Unem- ployed
Integrated	66.6	23.5	26.9	9.5	7.1
Transitional	63.4	13.9	20.6	15.1	11.8
Panic	56.5	5.8	24.6	20.3	15.2
Black	46.1	5.1	12.1	36.3	18.2
All white	76.3	22.7	28.5	2.4	4.2
Metropolitan totals	67.5	18.5	24.3	8.8	4.5

Source: Gary Orfield, Albert Woolbright, and Helene Kim, "Neighborhood Change and Integration in Metropolitan Chicago" (Chicago: Leadership Council for Metropolitan Open Communities, 1984).

group were in communities that had been targeted for major public investment and renovation.

Hispanic racial transition was primarily limited to the old core barrios and expansion areas within the city. Stable integration for Hispanics was widespread in many areas of the North Side and in the much smaller secondary centers of Hispanic settlement in the satellite cities in the suburban ring. (The "stability" in some of these communities may, of course, be due to the relatively small size of the settlement or the stage of migration, rather than a long-term accomplishment.)

From a social policy standpoint, the most important findings were not the existence of these stable integrated communities but the contrasts between them and communities that had experienced other forms of racial change. When tracts are compared by characteristics that measure education, job status, and employment, stably integrated tracts appear to be better off along every measure than tracts that experienced racial transition (see tables 1 and 2). Tracts that had a racial panic in the 1970s rank well below those with slower transitions, and the all-minority tracts rank worst along all dimensions.

These relationships do not prove that integration causes better outcomes. No doubt some of the conditions that contribute to stable integration, such as a high educational level, also help account for the positive outcomes on other measures. Two things are clear, however. In 1970, there were considerable similarities between the communities that were to go through transition during the next ten years and those that stabilized. By some measures the transitional communities were actually stronger. Stably in-

Table 2. *Educational and Economic Levels of Hispanic Census Tracts in Chicago, by Level of Integration, 1980*

Percent

Racial categorization of tract	High school graduates	College graduates	Unemployed
Integrated			
All residents	61.1	17.3	7.4
Hispanics	36.7	6.3	10.8
Transitional			
All residents	33.2	4.9	11.9
Hispanics	23.8	2.5	13.4

Source: Orfield, Woolbright, and Kim, "Neighborhood Change and Integration in Metropolitan Chicago."

tegrated communities where blacks were the largest minority had an average gain in the proportion of blacks of 5.4 percent during the decade (from 16.4 percent in 1970 to 21.8 percent in 1980), while the average transitional community changed from 24 percent black to 80 percent black. In 1980 transitional communities were considerably less well off, not only among their overall population but also for the black households within the community. Second, a considerable fraction of the loss of white residents from Chicago during the 1970s is accounted for by racial transition. The city's twenty-nine racial panic tracts, for example, accounted for a loss of 112,000 whites during the decade and the black transition tracts for another 83,000.[47] When the loss of whites in the Hispanic transition areas is added in, it is clear that more than a third of the total decline in white population, the "white flight" from the city, is accounted for by the failure to handle the process of ghetto and barrio formation in relatively small areas on the peripheries of established segregated minority areas.

The Policy Choice

The only real alternative to ghettoization is integration. Choosing not to work for integration is not choosing the status quo, it is choosing a continuation of the ghetto-creation process. With the exception of court action to order desegregation of public housing, integration has never received serious attention as an alternative from city, state, or federal agencies in Chicago. In fact, the city and its school board have led the

47. Ibid.

battle against the efforts to desegregate the schools and subsidized housing. Neither the city nor the school board has made a serious effort to aid the neighborhoods threatened by ghettoization.

There are powerful interests that should support policies for integration, if they could only recognize the nature of the actual long-term choice the city and major portions of suburbia face. They are the major institutions that will be most hurt by continuation of the present process: the city government, the city board of education, local governments and school boards in parts of the southern and western suburbs, city businesses and property owners, and the state government, which will be expected to pick up the pieces if the city resources deteriorate further.

Some of the lessons about better policies could be learned close to home. A few integrated communities within the city and in the suburbs— such as Hyde Park–Kenwood, Oak Park, and Park Forest—are national leaders in the development of techniques for defeating the forces of re-segregation and creating stable integration. These communities have had the internal resources to attack each part of the ghettoization syndrome in order to break its momentum and create the expectation that the future would bring not a ghetto but stable integration in a middle-class community. It required sophisticated intervention in the real estate market, ability to target public investments to avoid signs of decay, intensive police work, active community organization and public relations, and, very important, maintenance of good integrated public schools. Few communities have the resources to do these things on their own or to convince other levels of government to do them. If the city and the school board would work together to focus resources toward the communities threatened by the ghettoization process and would make commitments, such as the main-tenance of substantially integrated schools, there would be a much better chance of spreading integration in the city's remaining middle-class areas and persuading white families to make permanent commitments to neigh-borhoods being revitalized.

If integration is to stabilize without putting the burden on black and Hispanic families who need more housing, there must be a far more aggressive drive to open up housing opportunities for minority families outside the traditional paths of expanding segregation. This must be done both in the city and in the suburbs, particularly the outlying suburbs that remain highly segregated and are the location of many of the desirable manufacturing jobs. Local governments and major private interests that would be hurt by unstable racial change should have a strong vested interest in encouraging integration through aggressive fair housing enforcement. Strengthening and professionalizing the existing civil rights agencies and providing community development funds for fair housing activities would be among the appropriate responses.

One housing integration experiment has been carried out successfully in metropolitan Chicago. After the 1976 Supreme Court decision on segregation of Chicago's public housing, federal and local fair housing experts began implementing a program that allows some city tenants waiting for public housing or living in housing projects to move to subsidized units of private housing, mostly in the outer suburbs. At first it was difficult to persuade low-income female-headed families to consider such a location, given an intensely segregated housing market where many blacks are fearful of white resistance. By 1984, however, the number of families placed in this program had passed 2,000. The demand for the available spaces each year has been overwhelming. When families who had moved to the suburbs were interviewed, four-fifths were satisfied with their new homes and neighborhoods and nine-tenths were satisfied with the local schools and teachers. Early participants in the program reported experiencing very little white hostility in their new neighborhoods. The families' employment had increased, and only 2 percent said they were interested in returning to the city. If funds and appropriate housing units were available, this approach could be greatly expanded.[48]

Local school boards that must carry the burden of desegregating schools attended by children who live in segregated public housing should demand that the Department of Housing and Urban Development, the local housing authorities, and the state housing development agency follow practices that aid integration. (The St. Louis School Board, for example, is now in court seeking such an order against housing agencies, and the Memphis school board is committed to this policy. In San Francisco, a plan is being developed under a consent agreement, and in Denver, planned residential and educational integration of a large new development is under way.)

There is a need in the Chicago area for a much more sophisticated understanding of the way in which schools fit into the process of integrating

---

48. U.S. Department of Housing and Urban Development, Office of Policy Development and Research, *Gautreaux Housing Demonstration* (GPO, 1979); James E. Rosenbaum, Marilynne J. Kulieke, Leonard S. Rubinowitz, and Dan A. Lewis, "The Effects of Residential Integration on Black Children," paper presented at annual meeting of American Educational Research Association, March 1982; Leadership Council for Metropolitan Open Communities, "Minority Families, Assisted Housing and the Suburbs," April 1, 1982.

or segregating neighborhoods, and thus how they affect the future of the city. Neighborhoods with virtually all-minority schools will not attract or retain white families with children in most circumstances. In the long run, as the neighborhoods become increasingly dominated by poor minority families, local schools and eventually the entire city system will also lose middle-class black or Hispanic families. The large minority enrollment in the Catholic schools, for example, may well be a stepping-stone to large-scale abandonment of the city by middle-class minorities, a process that is already far advanced in Washington, Newark, St. Louis, and Cleveland.

Chicago's long-term self-interest in the school fight is not simply to oppose desegregation, but rather to assure the stability of as many well-integrated schools as possible within the city while pushing in every possible way for involvement of the suburbs in the school integration process. Schools change racial composition before neighborhoods, and racially identifiable schools become key factors in ending the migration of white families to integrated areas. The reasons for the change in the local elementary schools are simple: the new minority families tend to be younger, to have more school-age children than present residents, and to rely more strongly on public education. Very few neighborhood schools stabilize spontaneously after substantial residential desegregation begins. Unless the school district helps through policies designed to foster integration, a key element of an integrated neighborhood is very difficult to attain. Help—in such forms as special programs, magnet schools, zoning, or busing plans—is necessary. Once rapid residential integration begins, neighborhood schools may not be the bulwark of the neighborhood's stability, but one of its most vulnerable points. It is very important to move beyond neighborhood assignment policies.

At the other extreme, there is considerable evidence that metropolitan school desegregation plans produce more integrated residential areas over time, remove one of the principal factors in residential steering, and slow the racial transition process, since there is no fear of ghettoization of the local schools and no incentive to move to a whiter school elsewhere. In Wilmington, Delaware, after a metropolitan plan was implemented, white public school enrollment *rose* in twenty-five parts of the central city because the children were now entering predominantly white middle-class schools (and receiving part of their education in the suburbs), rather than a nine-tenths minority system. For school finance purposes, for school integration purposes, and for residential desegregation and integration, officials of the Chicago school system and the inner suburbs should carefully consider the possibility of metropolitan school litigation. For these basic reasons such cases have been brought by central-city school systems in cities including Wilmington, Indianapolis, St. Louis, and Kansas City. In Chicago there has been no serious discussion of this issue and no analysis of the various large metropolitan areas in the South that have been under orders to integrate on an areawide basis for more than a decade.[49]

Chicago is not helpless in the face of ghettoization. City officials contributed powerfully to the creation and maintenance of this process but they have never attempted to mobilize resources against it. They have instead engaged in denial of the problem or quixotic attacks on its symptoms. Some communities in the Chicago area, however, have achieved a good deal of success with virtually no help from the higher levels of government and sometimes despite their policies. Much could be done to move toward the only alternative the city has to the continuation of the destructive processes of the past seventy years—residential and school integration. It would not be a panacea, but it is a necessary part of any strategy for reviving the city and avoiding needless loss of additional resources. A fully developed strategy would, of course, include employment and economic development, compensatory education, adult education, and other social and economic programs addressing the accumlulated inequalities in minority communities. Though an integration policy would serve the end of racial justice, it need not be undertaken for that reason. In a society with Chicago's racial composition and social and economic patterns, it is a matter of simple self-interest.

49. Diana Pearce, "Breaking Down Barriers: New Evidence on the Impact of Metropolitan School Desegregation Housing Patterns," report to National Institute of Education, 1980; and Willis D. Hawley and associates, *Strategies for Effective School Desegregation* (Lexington, Mass.: Lexington Books, 1983), chaps. 1–4.

PART THREE

The Policy Response

KENNETH A. SMALL

Transportation and Urban Change

FOR many years transportation policymakers in the United States were accused of ignoring the basic interrelationship between transportation and land use. Evaluations of transportation projects typically failed to assess the desirability of resulting land use changes and lacked careful appraisals of how those changes would in turn influence travel projections. Furthermore, land use policy was taken as given despite its important effect on the functioning of transportation facilities. Now the pendulum has swung in the other direction. Spurred in part by influential scholarly writings, planners and officials increasingly have given the interaction of transportation and land use important consideration.[1] Indeed, land use goals are now accorded an almost reverential place among the criteria for choosing transportation strategies.

Unfortunately, the term *interaction* can be used to camouflage a con-

This paper draws from work done while I was engaged in a study of urban decline at the Brookings Institution. I am grateful to my collaborators in that study, Katharine Bradbury and Anthony Downs, for their generous supply of ideas, data, advice, and criticism; and to Charles Lave and Wilfred Owen, among others, for comments on earlier presentations of these findings.

1. A few examples are Lowdon Wingo, Jr., *Transportation and Urban Land* (Washington, D.C.: Resources for the Future, 1961); Ira S. Lowry, "A Model of Metropolis," RM-4035-RC (Santa Monica: Rand Corp., 1964); Gregory K. Ingram, John F. Kain, and J. Royce Ginn, *The Detroit Prototype of the NBER Simulation Model* (National Bureau of Economic Research, 1972); Wilfred Owen, *The Accessible City* (Brookings, 1972); Owen, *Transportation for Cities: The Role of Federal Policy* (Brookings, 1976); Stephen M. Putnam, "Urban Land Use and Transportation Models: A State-of-the-Art Summary," *Transportation Research*, vol. 9 (1975), pp. 187–202; Boris S. Pushkarev and Jeffrey M. Zupan, *Public Transportation and Land Use Policy* (Indiana University Press, 1977); and Robert L. Knight and Lisa L. Trygg, *Land Use Impacts of Rapid Transit: Implications of Recent Experience*, DOT-TPI-10-77-29, prepared for Office of the Assistant Secretary for Policy, Plans, and International Affairs, U.S. Department of Transportation (DOT, 1977).

fusion between the two directions of causality that it implies. On the one hand, the shape and developmental history of an urban area greatly influence travel patterns and, by implication, the need for transportation facilities. At the same time, the transportation system itself helps determine where households and firms locate and thereby affects urban development. This paper seeks to disentangle and examine hypotheses about the causal mechanisms behind these two generalizations.

Many policy implications depend on the strength of these links. Altshuler and his associates, noting the "axiomatic" functional relationship between travel and land use patterns, add: "There is little certainty, however, about the strength of their mutual influence relative to the many other forces that bear upon each, and particularly upon land use."[2] A major purpose of this paper is to push beyond the isolation of these mechanisms and assess their importance in quantitative terms. This focus is attained by concentrating mainly on large-scale interactions: those of an entire central city or its suburbs.

The entire question has been thrown into a new light by the recent phenomenon of widespread decline in the economic role of major cities in the United States. Having developed tools for dealing with urban growth, transportation planners must now shift gears to cope with a new terrain. One question is, should they just shift into reverse? That is, does the shrinkage of cities and entire metropolitan areas simply call for a return to transportation policies appropriate for smaller, less congested areas? More specifically, does net migration out of Frost Belt metropolitan areas imply that gross investment in their transportation infrastructure should simply stop, allowing the shrinking population to carry on its activities using those facilities already in place? Such a finding would certainly have its appeal to financially pressed states and cities, especially if existing facilities could be enjoyed at a somewhat lower level of congestion with minimal infusion of maintenance and operating funds. In contrast, if new location patterns create new transportation needs, adjustment could prove costly and difficult.

A related question arises from the many recent cases of selective revitalization of inner cities. It is widely believed that an increase in gentrified close-in neighborhoods, with their smaller, multiple-earner families, could increase the utilization of city transit systems. Similarly, renovating and expanding central business districts, even in cities that are declining in

2. Alan A. Altshuler with James P. Womack and John R. Pucher, *The Urban Transportation System: Politics and Policy Innovation* (MIT Press, 1979), p. 374.

most dimensions, are thought to encourage greater use of public transportation. Alternatively, one might argue that such revitalization has good transit as a prerequisite.

A third question is whether transportation policy can reverse the loss of economic activity in large cities, irrespective of any spontaneous revitalization. From the Westway in New York to the proposed rapid rail system for Los Angeles, transportation investments are viewed as part of an effort to make cities more attractive. Rail transit, especially, is advocated as an integral part of plans to revitalize cities experiencing loss of employment and population. How well founded are these hopes? Do transit investments compare favorably on a cost basis with other revitalization tools? What kind of system is best suited to this purpose: rail transit, bus with exclusive guideway, conventional bus, or paratransit?[3] Should it concentrate on circulation within the city or on bringing suburbanites to downtown jobs and stores?

This essay is organized around the two sides of the mutual causality between transportation and land use. I begin by discussing some broad urban development trends and their likely future course. I then consider how urban form influences travel patterns and find the effects surprisingly small. I next ask the opposite and more controversial question: How does transportation policy influence other characteristics of urban areas? Some straightforward calculations suggest that the effects, while not negligible, are again smaller than one might expect. The remaining sections discuss implications for transportation policy.

Trends Affecting Urban Development

After more than a century of dramatic urbanization in the United States and other industrial nations, many large cities and even entire metropolitan areas have begun to lose population. The extent, causes, and implications of this dramatic change formed the subject of a recent collaborative study in which I took part.[4] This section summarizes some of the main results that are pertinent to transportation policy.

---

3. Paratransit includes shared-ride taxi, jitney, car pool, van pool, demand-responsive bus, subscription bus, and other forms of transportation not falling within the usual definitions of "automobile" or "mass transit."

4. See Katharine L. Bradbury, Anthony Downs, and Kenneth A. Small, *Futures for a Declining City: Simulations for the Cleveland Area* (Academic Press, 1981); and Katharine L. Bradbury, Anthony Downs, and Kenneth A. Small, *Urban Decline and the Future of American Cities* (Brookings, 1982).

Extent and Causes of Urban Decline in the United States

The extent of recent urban decline was assessed by examining statistics on the 153 largest U.S. cities and the 121 metropolitan areas within which they were located. The total population of these cities shrank by 1.25 percent between 1970 and 1975 and by another 0.35 percent in the subsequent two years; the losses are even greater if population gained through annexation is excluded. The metropolitan areas, taken as a whole, gained in population throughout this period, even in constant boundaries. These aggregate figures, of course, mask enormous differences. Of the 121 standard metropolitan statistical areas (SMSAs), 26 lost population and so did the largest central city in each of the 26, whereas 51 of the 95 central cities located in growing SMSAs gained population, even after correcting for annexation.

In order to assess possibly related social and economic problems, our study developed indices based upon unemployment rates, violent crime rates, real per capita income, local tax rates, percentage of population in poverty, and percentage of housing more than thirty years old. These problems were found to be disproportionately concentrated within large cities that are declining in population, particularly those located in declining metropolitan areas. Furthermore, these problems were worsening in such cities more than in other cities.

Some of this urban decline has been caused by basic societywide forces, such as a sharp fall in fertility rates after the mid-1960s, lower migration from farms to cities in the 1970s, tremendous increases in the use of automobiles and trucks, vigorous suburban housing construction (encouraged in part by federal tax incentives), and increased air travel (which has made remote regions more accessible). These factors have combined to slow the overall rate of metropolitan population growth and to encourage continued suburbanization within each metropolitan area.

However, differences among cities' growth experience are due to other factors. Our study empirically tested numerous theories through a set of six simultaneous regressions analyzing changes in population, employment, and real per capita income in the 121 SMSAs and their largest central cities. Several conclusions were drawn. Central-city decline was fostered by slow employment growth in the metropolitan area as a whole, cold climate, and high city-suburban disparities in housing age, racial composition, and tax rates. Local government fragmentation and high areawide unemployment also contributed to decline. In addition, rather weak evidence was found that a high per capita level of automobile ownership in an SMSA led to somewhat greater subsequent suburbanization of its population. Highway capacity in the SMSA or the existence of a beltway did not show any consistent relationship with growth or decline.

Future Trends

Armed with these conclusions about the factors affecting recent experience, we examined their likely course in the next ten to twenty years. Metropolitan growth as a whole is strongly affected by fertility, immigration, and migration from farms. Fertility has steadily declined throughout this century with the exception of the postwar baby boom years, and this trend appears to be rooted in social changes too deep to be reversed. Nevertheless, birthrates may rise somewhat due to the temporary increase in the number of women of childbearing age. At the same time, immigration from abroad promises to more than compensate for the fact that the present farm population is too small to provide more than a trickle of farm-to-urban migration. Thus the metropolitan population may grow despite continued net migration from metropolitan areas to small towns and rural areas. Much of the growth will take place in suburbs, especially in the South and West, which will continue to be favored by climate, high real income, good highway transportation, and plentiful land. But even in the South and West some cities have grown mainly through annexation of suburban areas, and it is likely that in future years they will encounter increasing resistance as suburban residents unite to protect their fiscal independence. As a result, many of these cities will be unable to counteract falling interior densities by adding territory and will join the ranks of declining cities.

The outflow of households and jobs from large cities to their suburbs will persist, though probably more slowly. At the same time office space will continue to grow in big-city downtowns, still the beneficiaries of the economywide service-sector expansion. Revitalization in selected older city neighborhoods will continue to be a significant, though numerically small, phenomenon; but housing deterioration will continue and probably spread to adjacent neighborhoods, including some suburban ones.

One reason big-city population decline tends to persist, once begun, is that it sets in motion certain self-reinforcing forces. These include the disproportionate withdrawal from cities of high- and middle-income households, rising local taxes and deteriorating public services, further racial isolation, city-suburban disparities in age of the housing stock, losses of economies of agglomeration and scale, the tendency of physical deterioration to induce poorer maintenance by owners of surrounding properties, and the falling political power of cities in Congress and state legislatures. Moreover, these population losses are rooted in certain long-range social trends that seem likely to persist, indeed that many people regard as desirable. These include rising real incomes, greater use of cars and trucks, widespread desire for new or low-density settlements, financial advantages of homeownership, and strongly entrenched tendencies for people to segregate their neighborhoods socioeconomically and racially. Consequently, population decline in most large older U.S. cities is irreversible, at least in the near future.

One might wonder, of course, whether increases in energy prices might alter this conclusion by raising commuting and home heating costs, thereby influencing households to choose the smaller and more centrally located residences typical in cities. To test this possibility, our study analyzed the likely effects of an increase in gasoline price of $1 a gallon and in fuel oil price of 75 cents a gallon over 1977 levels (in constant dollars).[5] The technological possibilities for shale oil or liquefied coal make larger price increases unlikely to persist for very long. (By comparison, between October 1977 and October 1980 the price of gasoline rose by only 26 cents in constant 1977 dollars, and it has subsequently declined.)[6]

Even assuming no offsetting changes, the increase in travel costs resulting from the rise in gasoline prices would create relatively minor incentives for suburban commuters to move into cities. Including both commuting and other travel, the total gasoline cost differential between living in the suburbs and living in the city would rise by less than $200 a year per household, based upon national average travel patterns. The average city-suburban cost difference for home heating and cooling, given typical mixes of single and multifamily units in both areas, would rise by

5. This work is also reported in Kenneth A. Small, "Energy Scarcity and Urban Development Patterns," *International Regional Science Review*, vol. 5 (Winter 1980), pp. 97–117.

6. This was calculated as follows. First, the 1980 price of gasoline ($1.217 per gallon) was divided by the 1980:1977 ratio of the gasoline component of the consumer price index in order to determine the 1977 price of gasoline ($0.624). The 1980 price was then divided by the 1980:1977 ratio of the total CPI to express it in constant 1977 dollars ($0.884). The difference is $0.26. By July 1984 the gasoline price in 1977 dollars had declined to 71.9 cents per gallon, less than 10 cents above the October 1977 level. Data sources were: *Monthly Labor Review*, vol. 102 (January 1979), pp. 109, 113; *Monthly Labor Review*, vol. 104 (January 1981), pp. 89, 93; *Monthly Labor Review*, vol. 107 (October 1984), pp. 69, 73; and *Survey of Current Business*, vol. 60 (November 1980), p. S-32.

about $55 per year. A more detailed analysis in the Cleveland area revealed significant incentives for commuters living in far-out suburbs to move closer in, but still the overall impact upon the city's population was almost negligible. There was even a small net incentive for some employers to move *out* of the city.

Furthermore, most households would adjust through means other than changing the locations of their homes or jobs. Possibilities include making fewer trips, carpooling, shifting to more fuel-efficient vehicles, installing home insulation, changing thermostat settings, and redesigning home heating equipment for greater fuel efficiency. Such adjustments would reduce the relocation incentives to even smaller levels. Altogether, then, there seems little likelihood that higher energy prices or possible shortages will greatly alter the fate of large cities.

Revitalization Policies for One Declining City: Cleveland

To test the possible effectiveness of policies aimed at counteracting urban decline, we carried out detailed quantitative simulations of how five major policy "packages" would work if applied in the Cleveland metropolitan area. Cleveland was chosen because it is typical (except in degree) of many other declining cities and metropolitan areas, especially in the Midwest and Northeast.

The first step was a projection of what would happen with no major policy changes. This revealed that continuation of current underlying trends would produce further extensive decline in the city's population, number of households, and employment. Housing and fiscal conditions would also continue to deteriorate.

Five sets of possible revitalization policies were then defined: (1) a job stimulus package including private job incentives and an expanded Comprehensive Employment and Training Act program; (2) a housing rehabilitation package that increased new housing construction and rehabilitation within the city severalfold; (3) a fiscal equalization package that merged all municipal and county governments within Cuyahoga County and added some new intergovernmental transfers; (4) a transit improvement package with expanded daily service plus major new facilities; and (5) a suburban growth control package containing constraints that reduced suburban growth by 25 percent from what it otherwise would have been, with four-fifths of this reduction shifted into the city of Cleveland. Both direct and indirect impacts of these policy packages were quantified, including

Table 1. *The Effects of Alternative Policies in City of Cleveland,*
1980–90
Thousands

Policy	Jobs	Households	Population
Changes with no major policy change[a]	−65.7	−23.4	−104.8
Impact of major policy changes[b]			
Job stimulus	10.0	2.0	5.0
Housing rehabilitation	4.1	8.8	22.4
Fiscal equalization	9.3	9.6	24.4
Transit improvement	7.0	0.2	0.4
Suburban growth control	4.4	10.0	25.5
All-out revitalization	32.6	25.7	65.4

Source: Katharine L. Bradbury, Anthony Downs, and Kenneth A. Small, *Futures for a Declining City: Simulations for the Cleveland Area* (Academic Press, 1981), p. 162.

a. Projection of 1980–90 changes occurring under continuation of 1980 trends to 1990, starting from projected 1980 values of 300,200 jobs, 216,200 households, and 574,500 people.

b. Projection of effects relative to what would have occurred without major policy changes.

multiplier effects upon household spending, job location, and household location.

The results are summarized in table 1. Considered individually, none of the policy packages offset more than one-sixth of the loss of city jobs or more than one-half of the loss of households that would otherwise have occurred from 1980 to 1990. When all five were combined into one all-out revitalization package, they reduced the city's job loss by about 50 percent, completely offset its loss of households, and cut its population loss by about two-thirds. Because of the political opposition many of these policies would engender, this represents a generous maximum estimate of how much of the Cleveland area's future decline might be counteracted by such public policies. However, many other possible responses to decline were not tested, including improvements in public schools and other social conditions.

One important conclusion is that in severely declining cities feasible public policies could greatly reduce present rates of population, job, and household loss; but they probably could not halt such declines in the next decade or so. This reinforces my previous conclusion about irreversibility of decline.

Determinants of Urban Travel Behavior

The major trends in urban travel over the past few decades have been documented and can be summarized briefly as more trips, more of them in suburbs, and a higher proportion by automobile.[7] In many metropolitan areas, the total number of trips doubled over a fifteen-year period, far outstripping population growth. In the largest thirty-three metropolitan areas, the number of work trips beginning and ending in suburban areas rose 50 percent between 1960 and 1970, while the number wholly within central cities declined 11 percent. Automobile traffic on urban roads rose from 182 to 666 billion vehicle-miles between 1950 and 1977, while ridership on urban mass transit declined from 13.8 to 5.7 billion passengers.

It appears that low-density living, rising incomes, smaller household size, and huge federal highway subsidies all contributed to these trends. There seems little doubt that low residential density discourages transit use to some degree;[8] my own study found residential density of an entire central city strongly affects transit use, though its effect on automobile ownership is small.[9] High income definitely seems to encourage automobile use and to discourage transit use; automobile ownership per adult is also favored by small household size.[10] My study found that these three factors together accounted for one-third to one-half the observed changes in auto ownership and the use of mass transit for commuting in twenty large metropolitan areas between 1970 and 1975. The relevance of highway capacity could not be confirmed by this analysis, but this may be only because intermetropolitan differences are so small compared with the enormous highway expansion that occurred in all metropolitan areas after 1950.

What do these findings portend for the future? If real incomes resume their historical rise and suburbanization continues, automobile ownership and use will continue to rise, especially in suburban areas and on major peak-period arteries connecting suburbs with still-thriving central business districts. Transit use will continue to fall at least relatively, barring events or policies that make automobiles less desirable. The trend toward smaller

7. John R. Meyer and José A. Gómez-Ibáñez, *Auto Transit and Cities* (Harvard University Press for the Twentieth Century Fund, 1981), pp. 20–34.

8. Pushkarev and Zupan, *Public Transportation and Land Use Policy*, pp. 24–63.

9. Kenneth A. Small, "Transportation, Land Use, and Urban Decline," working paper (Brookings, February 1981). The conclusion on automobile ownership is also supported by Gary B. Fauth and José A. Gómez-Ibáñez, "Demographic Change, New Location Patterns, and U.S. Transportation Policy," Discussion Paper D78–17 (Harvard University, Department of City and Regional Planning, May 1979).

10. Small, "Transportation, Land Use, and Urban Decline"; Fauth and Gómez-Ibáñez, "Demographic Change, New Location Patterns, and U.S. Transportation Policy"; and Douglas P. Sharp, "Projections of Automobile Ownership and Use Based on Household Lifestyle Factors" (Ph.D. dissertation, University of Pittsburgh, 1978).

households will also exert a modest pressure toward increasing automobile use.

The Cleveland case study described earlier suggests that suburbanization alone, even where unusually strong, has more effect on the geographic distribution of travel than on the type of transportation used. As already noted, that study projected a case in which population and employment continue their rapid suburbanization. The implications for travel behavior were then derived on the assumption of no change in the share of work trips between any given origin and destination made by mass transit. The resulting projections indicate a substantial decrease in trips by both auto and mass transit to jobs in the city of Cleveland; a small rise in transit trips and large rise in auto trips to suburban jobs; and little change in trips by either mode to the central business district. Total transit patronage would decline by 9 percent between 1980 and 1990, while automobile work trips would increase by just over 3 percent, slightly more than the projected 2 percent rise in total SMSA employment. Transit use would become even more concentrated on peak-period radial trips to the downtown area. More surprisingly, the average work trip would become *shorter* as jobs suburbanize, so that aggregate vehicle-miles for work trips would rise only 1 percent.

In contrast to these rather bland predictions of the effects of suburbanization, anything that substantially changes the cost or convenience of driving could have a major impact on transit systems. Econometric studies have found that transit use for work trips is fairly sensitive to automobile costs, presumably because transit now has such a small share that even a modest reduction in the proportion using cars translates into a large increase in the proportion using transit. For example, the hypothetical increase in gasoline price described earlier was considered in the Cleveland study. If not offset by cost-saving measures such as more fuel-efficient cars, this increase was estimated to cause a 45 percent rise in transit use for commuting.[11] Similarly, if economically efficient tolls were to be adopted on central-city expressways, they would be large enough (on the order of 14 to 35 cents per vehicle-mile) to have a substantial impact on the choice of transportation mode.[12]

11. Bradbury, Downs, and Small, *Futures for a Declining City*, p. 191.
12. Theodore E. Keeler and Kenneth A. Small, "Optional Peak-Load Pricing, Investment, and Service Levels on Urban Expressways," *Journal of Political Economy*, vol. 85 (February 1977), p. 18.

Effects of Transportation on Urban Development

Growth of any portion of an urban area, no matter what the causal factors, requires transportation. One need only try to imagine a New York without subways or a Los Angeles without boulevards. It follows that the decision not to provide such facilities could, in principle, have prevented growth. In addition to this role, however, transportation is increasingly viewed as a tool for promoting desired growth patterns and even reversing the decline of older central cities. To evaluate this potential, it is useful to consider both a historical perspective and an analysis of likely future changes.

Most theories of urban land use predict that lowering transportation costs should *increase,* not decrease, decentralization. Transportation improvements have been implicated in the residential suburbanization characterizing U.S. urban areas since at least the late nineteenth century.[13] The electric railways brought about streetcar suburbs, later to be expanded into widespread bedroom communities based upon automobile access to the urban center. With the introduction of trucks and the construction of a ubiquitous highway network, employers loosened their ties to the rail or water terminals that previously had dominated locational considerations in many industries.[14] Other forces such as rising incomes, federal home-ownership subsidies, and technological changes in manufacturing processes supported these developments. It has subsequently been nearly impossible to separate their relative contributions in order to determine the difference made by specific transportation policies.

One particular type of highway improvement, the limited-access beltway surrounding a central city and its closer suburbs, has been studied in a number of specific cases. The weight of evidence supports the contention that this type of facility has accelerated suburbanization.[15] Whether a beltway attracts activity to a metropolitan area as a whole is not certain,

13. See Edwin S. Mills and Bruce W. Hamilton, *Urban Economics,* 3d ed. (Scott, Foresman, 1984).

14. Leon Moses and Harold F. Williamson, Jr., "The Location of Economic Activity in Cities," *American Economic Review,* vol. 57 (May 1967, *Papers and Proceedings, 1966*), pp. 211–22.

15. For a summary of studies see Florence Mills, "Effects of Beltways on the Location of Residences and Selected Workplaces," *Transportation Research Record,* no. 812 (1981), pp. 26–33.

but any such effects would tend to cancel each other as many metropolitan areas compete in this way. Thus continued support of beltway construction as a matter of national policy is likely to contribute to the decline of many central cities.

Radial expressways or transit lines linking central cities and suburbs have more ambiguous effects. On the one hand, increased accessibility to metropolitan areawide labor and customer markets makes the central business district a more attractive location to many businesses. On the other hand, the improved transportation makes it easier and cheaper for downtown workers to choose suburban residential locations.[16] In the absence of conclusive empirical evidence,[17] it seems clear that there is no hope of determining even the direction of some of these effects, much less their magnitudes, without quantification. To this end, I have attempted to make some calculations designed to assess their approximate strengths.

Before one asks what the effects might be of various transportation improvements, it is useful to know the current distribution of workers and their modes of travel (see table 2). The majority of workers in 1975 lived in the same type of area that they worked in; that is, almost 38 percent of the metropolitan work force lived in the suburbs and worked in the suburbs, and almost 35 percent lived and worked in a central city. Only 20 percent commuted from the suburbs to the city, and just 8 percent were "reverse commuters." In each possible combination of workplace and residence, the overwhelming majority of workers traveled by car; the only category demonstrating considerable use of mass transit was city dwellers who worked in the city.

I investigated four types of transportation improvements: radial freeways, beltways, radial transit, and in-city transit.[18] Starting from a set of assumed travel-time savings for each improvement and using the above data on actual travel behavior, I calculated the impact of these savings on households and firms and expressed it as an annual commuting-cost dif-

16. For a very detailed housing market analysis that verifies this even in a multinuclear area, see A. Anas, "Evaluating the Effects of Transportation–Land-Use Policies on Housing Values and Household Welfare," *Environment and Planning A*, vol. 12 (July 1980), pp. 747–64.

17. Meyer and Gómez-Ibánez, *Auto Transit and Cities*, pp. 113–20.

18. A radial freeway is a limited-access highway extending from outlying suburban areas into the central city. A beltway is one surrounding the central city some distance out. Radial transit is a high-speed rail or bus network, utilizing exclusive right-of-way for all or part of its extent, linking outlying suburbs to the central business district. An in-city transit improvement is similar, but does not extend outside the city boundaries; it also upgrades conventional transit or paratransit within the city.

Table 2. *Distribution of Metropolitan Workers, by Workplace, Place of Residence, and Travel Mode, 1975*

Workplace, residence, and travel mode	Percentage of workers using travel mode[a]
City workplace	
City resident (34.8 percent)[b]	
Travel by car	74.0
Travel by transit	16.7
Suburban resident (19.5 percent)[b]	
Travel by car	89.3
Travel by transit	9.7
Suburban workplace	
City resident (8.1 percent)[b]	
Travel by car	93.0
Travel by transit	5.6
Suburban resident (37.7 percent)[b]	
Travel by car	90.9
Travel by transit	1.8

Source: Author's calculations from U.S. Bureau of the Census, *Current Population Reports*, series P-23, no. 99, "The Journey to Work in the United States: 1975" (Government Printing Office, 1979), table F.

a. Other travel modes not shown (such as bicycling, walking) would bring total in each workplace-residence category to 100 percent.

b. Percentages shown are share of total metropolitan work force in each workplace-residence category. People working at home and people working or living outside metropolitan areas are excluded.

ferential. This determines the size of the incentive to change from one location to another, which in turn affects net migration rates.

The assumed travel-time savings are shown in table 3. They are intended to capture typical characteristics of the various transportation improvements. For example, the radial systems are assumed to provide some savings to trips within the city, but more to inbound trips from the suburbs; the beltway, in contrast, affects only trips beginning or ending in the suburbs. Both transit systems are assumed to provide some relief of highway congestion for the average automobile commuter, especially on peak-direction radial highways within the central city itself. The radial freeway is hypothesized to have a less favorable impact on downtown congestion than a radial transit improvement because of the additional traffic likely to be generated there. Note that each number given is an average for *all* trips of the specified type, not just for those actually using the new facilities; some trips would realize much greater savings, others none at all. On the whole, I have tried to make fairly generous assumptions, so as to represent major projects with genuine benefits.

Specifically, the radial freeway is assumed to provide eight minutes of

Table 3. *Projected Time Savings as a Result of Four Hypothetical Transportation Improvements, by Workplace, Place of Residence, and Travel Mode*

Minutes

Workplace, residence, and travel mode	Current travel time[a]	Time savings			
		Radial freeway	Beltway	Radial transit	In-city transit
City workplace					
City resident					
Travel by car	15.5	2	0	3	3
Travel by transit	35.9	0	0	6	8
Suburban resident					
Travel by car	23.6	8	3	6	3
Travel by transit	46.0	6	0	12	6
Suburban workplace					
City resident					
Travel by car	21.6	4	3	0	0
Travel by transit	46.5	0	0	3	3
Suburban resident					
Travel by car	15.9	2	6	0	0
Travel by transit	29.0	0	0	0	0

Source: Author's calculations and U.S. Bureau of the Census, "The Journey to Work in the United States: 1975," table 2.

a. Mean one-way travel times for all standard metropolitan statistical areas for "drive alone" and "public transportation."

time saving to the average inbound auto commute trip from the suburbs; a somewhat smaller amount to inbound transit trips (express buses); and a still smaller saving to other types of auto trips, which presumably would utilize the new highway for a shorter distance. The beltway is assumed to provide a saving of six minutes on the average suburb-to-suburb auto commute, half that on inbound or outbound auto trips, and none on transit (since few transit lines would use it). The radial transit system is assumed to provide a large saving (twelve minutes) on suburb-to-city transit trips, with smaller savings on other trips to city jobs and on reverse-flow trips by transit. The in-city transit improvement is taken to have the same effects as the radial transit system on the portions of trips within the city, plus an extra two-minute saving for transit trips wholly within the city. Needless to say, many fine points are omitted. I have chosen the simplest set of assumptions that are sufficiently detailed to capture the important differences among these alternative transportation improvements.

In order to place the time savings in perspective, they are converted to annual cost savings in 1983 dollars, assuming an average value of time of

$4.40 an hour (roughly half the average manufacturing wage in 1983).[19] The average cost savings for a worker in each combination of workplace and residence are shown in lines 1–4 of table 4. (Experimentation showed that the computations are not very sensitive to the modal shares shown in table 2, so no correction is made for changes in those shares induced by the improvements themselves.)

The average cost saving for *all* metropolitan workers and residents, using the distribution of workers among the four combinations of workplace and residence, is also shown. This may be interpreted as an indication of the benefit of the project to the average worker and thus as an indication of the increase in attractiveness of the metropolitan area as a whole (to the extent that the project is financed from outside the area). Although data are lacking from which to estimate the resulting changes in intermetropolitan migration, it may be noted that the annual cost savings shown are rather small in comparison with existing intermetropolitan differentials in wages, living costs, and taxes. Of course, additional benefits would accrue to nonwork travelers and, in the case of highways, to freight shippers.

One can, however, quantify the impacts on *intra*metropolitan location decisions.[20] First, consider a typical *firm* drawing its labor force from a metropolitan market and choosing between a city and a suburban location. The savings its workers would realize from each job location and each transportation improvement are shown in lines 5 and 6 of table 4. Next, consider a typical *household* containing 1.2 workers with an average distribution of job locations. It would realize savings in commuting costs, depending on its choice of residential location, as shown in lines 7 and 8 of table 4.

To relate these cost differentials to urban development changes, one can apply a disequilibrium view of migration. Ongoing net migration is a response to a net advantage of one location over another in the eyes of a typical household or firm, and any new cost differential is added to or subtracted from that advantage, thereby altering the migration rate.[21] The empirical evidence relating the cost differential to migration, while weak,

19. Measurements of value of travel time typically find it to be about one-half the wage rate. See Nils Bruzelius, *The Value of Travel Time: Theory and Measurement* (London: Croom Helm, 1979).

20. The methodology described here was developed by Bradbury, Downs, and Small, *Futures for a Declining City*, pp. 77–83.

21. Note that because the issue is city-suburban *differentials*, the question of incidence is irrelevant: regardless of whether the average benefit accrues to firms or households, both will respond to the differences in benefits achieved at different locations.

Table 4. *Projected Annual Cost Savings as a Result of Four Hypothetical Transportation Improvements, by Workplace and Place of Residence*

Savings in 1983 dollars

Workplace and residence	Cost savings			
	Radial freeway	Beltway	Radial transit	In-city transit
Savings per worker[a]				
City workplace				
1. City resident	52	0	113	125
2. Suburban resident	272	94	230	115
Suburban workplace				
3. City resident	131	98	6	6
4. Suburban resident	64	192	0	0
Average[b]	106	99	85	66
Savings per employee of firm[c]				
5. City workplace	178	54	180	119
6. Suburban workplace	93	152	3	3
Differential	85	−98	177	116
Savings per household[d]				
7. City residence	106	54	77	85
8. Suburban residence	212	167	150	75
Differential	−106	−113	−73	10
Cumulative ten-year impact on city (percent of initial number)				
Jobs[e]	1.0	−1.2	2.2	1.4
Households[f]	−1.4	−1.5	−1.0	0.1

Source: Author's calculations.

a. Assuming 240 round trips a year with time valued at $4.40 an hour, and distribution of travel modes shown in table 2.

b. Weighted by the distribution of workers among the four workplace-residence categories shown in table 2.

c. Weighted average savings per worker by firm location. Line 5 is the weighted average of lines 1 and 2, and line 6 is the weighted average of lines 3 and 4. The weights are the residential distribution of workers shown in table 2: 42.9 percent city, 57.1 percent suburbs.

d. Weighted average savings per household by residence location, times number of employed workers per household. Line 7 is the weighted average of lines 1 and 3, and line 8 is the weighted average of lines 2 and 4. Calculation assumes the average household has 1.2 employed workers (*Statistical Abstract of the United States, 1982–83*, table 1349, and *1981*, table 635), and is weighted by the workplace distribution shown in table 2: 54.2 percent city, 45.8 percent suburbs.

e. Assumes annual impact is 2.0 percent of city jobs for each $1,645 change in city-suburb differential in annual cost per employee.

f. Assumes annual impact is 2.4 percent of city households for each $1,810 change in city-suburb differential in annual cost per household.

was used in a previous study to derive the needed parameters (see the footnotes to table 4).[22] Applying these parameters to the cost differentials yields estimates of the resulting ten-year impact on the number of jobs or households in the city. These estimates are shown in the last part of table 4, each as a percentage of the total number of jobs or households in the city at the start of the period. No secondary relocations or muliplier effects are considered.

Several observations are in order. First, these examples illustrate the earlier point that radial improvements encourage residential suburbanization. Second, transit systems have more favorable effects on the city than do highway systems. This is because they preferentially benefit transit users, thus shifting the calculus in favor of those trips with higher transit shares. Third, a beltway provides intrametropolitan locational incentives that are unambiguously detrimental to the city. Fourth, radial systems, especially highways, tend to add more jobs than households to the city, making it more of a daytime center of activity. Fifth, the ultimate effects of *all* these transportation improvements on population and jobs in the city appear rather modest, though not inconsequential. This, of course, is a function of their overall scale.

A more detailed analysis of two transit policies comparable to those considered here was included in the case study of the Cleveland area, using a finer geographic breakdown, and using travel time savings derived from consultants' reports on a major transit improvement package actually proposed for the Cleveland area. That study included secondary effects resulting from the primary migration changes: households relocating in response to the altered job distribution and firms relocating in response to the altered spending patterns of other firms and of households. It was found that the decentralizing effect of radial transit on households was approximately offset by the secondary response to the increased centralization of jobs. Thus the net effect of radial transit on household location is

22. Bradbury, Downs, and Small, *Futures for a Declining City*, pp. 77–83. I have adjusted their household-migration parameter slightly to account for differences between the Cleveland SMSA and the U.S. averages used here and have updated their numbers to 1983 prices using the CPI. It might be thought that the incentives for location changes would be offset by capitalization of the new cost differentials into property values and rents. Eventually this will be true, but only after densities have adjusted to their new equilibrium levels; until that time, capitalization serves as the mechanism through which increased demand for favored locations calls forth an increased density of structures there, thus permitting the induced migration to occur. Since the empirical studies used to derive the needed parameters did not control for land prices, no adjustment for capitalization is warranted here.

ambiguous in direction, quantitatively as well as theoretically. In contrast, transit improvements within the city have an unambiguous positive effect on numbers of jobs *and* households in the city, since direct and secondary impacts reinforce each other. All these results, it should be reiterated, ignore the effects of any local financing mechanisms. They also ignore the possibility that better access to the central business district could allow more firms to locate outside it and still maintain needed contact with each other.

Of course, changes in the transportation system can dramatically change the relative accessibility of individual neighborhoods, thereby altering their land prices and ultimately their character. Transit lines can be expected to attract high-density development within walking distance, thereby clustering development into corridors or around stations. Highways are well known to foster development near interchanges, though it is usually less compact because it relies on auto rather than pedestrian access. These processes are not always automatic, however, and depend greatly on accompanying policies such as zoning, land assembly, or tax rebates.[23]

Past and Present Policies

The findings discussed so far, tentative as many of them are, have far-reaching policy implications. It is useful to begin with a brief critique of transportation policy as it has been practiced in recent years.

Highway Construction

Since the beginning of the interstate highway program in 1956, construction of new high-capacity roads has taken place in virtually every large metropolitan area in the nation. Since most of this construction has made surburban areas more accessible, the analysis above suggests that it would have had an adverse impact on the population growth of central cities. Thus federal encouragement of highway construction has probably contributed significantly to decentralization over the postwar period. At the same time, highways were by no means the only major factor involved: the calculations reported in table 4 indicate that large-scale construction of circumferential and radial expressways could probably account for only a fraction of the actual net migration between cities and suburbs.

23. See Knight and Trygg, *Land Use Impacts of Rapid Transit.*

It is also important to recognize the positive role that highways have played. Good roads have greatly lowered the cost of transporting people and goods within urban areas and have thereby improved their efficiency as economic units. The standard of living of the great majority of urban households has thereby been increased.

It is clear, however, that all social groups have not shared equally in these benefits. There is a further question: could most of these benefits have been achieved through some alternative transportation policy whose side effects would have been less detrimental to central cities? My analysis suggests that other transportation improvements have less decentralizing impacts; thus a program involving a more balanced mix of highway construction and other measures might well have been preferable. Yet the incentives given to state and local governments by federal subsidy programs overwhelmingly favored new highway construction. This has begun to change in recent years, and an examination of those elements receiving increased emphasis gives a clearer picture of how a better mix of transportation policies might have been chosen.

Subsidies to Conventional Transit

Beginning with the Urban Mass Transportation Act of 1964, the federal government has undertaken a large program of grants in support of urban transit systems. With the exception of a few small discretionary programs, these grants were until 1974 exclusively for capital expenditures to construct, upgrade, or expand conventional transit.[24]

This capital bias resulted in a heavy emphasis on new construction, expansion, or renovation of metropolitan rapid rail systems. The new systems in Washington, D.C., and Atlanta were the first to take advantage of the full 80 percent capital subsidy available under the act. The political imperatives of satisfying an increasingly suburban constituency have guaranteed that these very expensive systems would extend well into the suburbs. Thus the capital bias in the federal transit program has encouraged the type of transit least likely to retard decentralization.

24. For reviews of the federal program of grants see George W. Hilton, *Federal Transit Subsidies: The Urban Mass Transportation Program* (American Enterprise Institute for Public Policy Research, 1974); George M. Smerk, *Urban Mass Transportation: A Dozen Years of Federal Policy* (Indiana University Press, 1974); Owen, *Transportation for Cities*; Altshuler and others, *The Urban Transportation System*; and Meyer and Gómez-Ibáñez, *Auto Transit and Cities.* Many state and local governments have complemented this program with operating subsidies, and since 1974 they have received federal aid for this purpose.

In the last decade, a number of developments have reduced this bias somewhat: the growth of state operating subsidies, the advent of federal operating subsidies in 1974, some small demonstration and urban-oriented grant programs, and, most recently, the inability of the federal government to fund all eligible projects, which has led to a reduction in the effective cost-sharing percentage. On the other hand, current attempts to eliminate operating subsidies could further aggravate the capital bias.

Highway Renovation

A portion of federal highway funds has always been reserved to aid states in maintaining the existing highway network. Requirements for resurfacing, restoration, rehabilitation, and bridge repair have gradually increased as central-city structures, and now major portions of the interstate system itself, have aged. This has resulted in steadily increasing federal budget allocations for highway renovation. Furthermore, in 1978 the federal share for these projects was increased from 70 to 75 percent for highways and from 75 to 80 percent for bridges.

It is difficult to characterize the development effects of this shift in emphasis. Repairing highways and bridges would appear to facilitate the same types of travel as building new ones. However, since the road network in central cities is older than that in suburban areas, an emphasis on repair may preferentially improve highway travel within cities. This is especially true of the many old bridges connecting portions of cities built on rivers, for which capital requirements to overcome the effects of deferred maintenance are extremely large.[25] Thus, aside from its obvious appeal as sound management of the existing highway capital stock, the emphasis on renovation should have a more positive impact on central cities than the massive construction of the past.

Transportation Systems Management

Since 1975 local governments requesting federal transportation grants have been required to develop transportation systems management plans for optimal use of existing capital structures, including both highway and

25. These have recently been documented in a series of studies published by the Urban Institute as *America's Capital Stock Series*, George E. Peterson, general editor (1979–81). See also Pat Choate and Susan Walter, *America in Ruins: Beyond the Public Works Pork Barrel* (Washington, D.C.: Council of State Planning Agencies, 1981).

transit rights of way. Such plans have obvious appeal on efficiency grounds. In addition, many management measures increase use of public transit, which in turn has a beneficial effect on the attractiveness of locations within the city. On the other hand, such measures as carpooling, vanpooling, and demand-responsive transit facilitate travel mainly among dispersed origins and destinations.

Future Policies

With these points in mind, I now turn to a systematic discussion of policies to deal with the future trends identified in the earlier discussion.

Dealing with Growth and Congestion

Many metropolitan areas, and parts of others, are now growing and will continue to grow at a rapid rate. Most trends point toward a continuing increase in the automobile's share for nearly all types of trips. Even a severe energy shortage would reduce auto use by no more than 10 to 20 percent, well under a decade's growth in many of the faster-growing parts of metropolitan areas. Thus there will be a continuing demand for new or upgraded highways to accommodate this traffic. A few cities will also experience growing demand for transit service.

Growth in automobile traffic will almost certainly be accompanied by growth in the extent, severity, and duration of congestion. In growing cities, the associated problems can be severe and if unsolved will eventually limit the growth and economic productivity of these areas. In declining cities, there will be a noticeable shift in the locations experiencing congestion, from the city itself to major suburban arterials. Even in these cities, however, downtown employment is likely to hold its own or increase, and the proportion of downtown jobs filled by automobile commuters from outlying areas will also increase, at least in the absence of major transit innovations. Thus, the traditional problem of peak-period congestion on radial highways will remain in most of these cities, as will congestion on downtown streets.

Increased congestion does not necessarily signify a failure of transportation policy. It is often more efficient to tolerate some congestion than to carry out expensive construction or expansion. Furthermore, it is not congestion per se that determines the economic viability of an area, but rather the entire complex of factors affecting its relative desirability as a place to work or live. For these reasons, and because the large-scale effects of transportation improvements are so modest, the decision of whether to relieve congestion, and if so by what means, should be based first on the criterion of efficiency. Proper application of traditional cost-benefit analysis is still the safest guide. Among the requirements of a proper application, I emphatically include the systematic comparison of options that include doing nothing, altering legal or regulatory constraints, and undertaking low-cost modifications of existing facilities.

The pursuit of developmental goals should be a secondary consideration in choosing among transportation policies. At a systemwide level, these goals should normally be the determining factor only when two policies rank closely on a cost-benefit test. Proponents of particular developmental goals should not be permitted to inject vague and unsubstantiated arguments into decisions that would otherwise be clear-cut, as has frequently been the case in comparisons between bus and rapid rail transit systems. This is all the more true because developmental goals can be attained through zoning, land assembly assistance, and old-fashioned boosterism— all cheaper than building an overly capital-intensive transportation network.

One reason for taking this position is that an extensive transportation network is already in place. Thirty years ago, basic decisions about transportation should have been made with more attention to their ultimate effects on central cities. Now, for better or worse, those decisions have largely been made in favor of ubiquitous limited-access highways. The remaining options are mostly either incremental, with relatively small land use effects, or involve adding an expensive new basic infrastructure to that already in place. One of the chief advantages of buses as mass transportation vehicles is that they can utilize, at little or no extra cost, an existing capital plant. Where that capital plant is already fully utilized, congestion pricing (such as higher bridge tolls during rush hours) and bus priority measures (such as diamond lanes) offer inexpensive means of increasing its passenger-carrying capacity.

Where downtown congestion is particularly severe, direct restraint on automobile use should be considered. Many studies have found pricing solutions to be highly effective;[26] though none have yet been tried in the

26. See William Vickrey, "Some Implications of Marginal Cost Pricing for Public Utilities," *American Economic Review*, vol. 45 (May 1955, *Papers and Proceedings, 1954*), pp. 605–20; A. A. Walters, "The Theory and Measurement of Private and Social Cost of Highway

United States, they deserve far more serious attention than they usually receive. Parking restrictions or fees, while ineffective against through traffic, have some advantages. Outright prohibition of auto traffic in certain zones can also be highly beneficial.

Automobile restraint is often thought to be automatically detrimental to a city's employment growth, but this is untrue. It can actually be viewed as a way of transferring roadway capacity from general use to specific uses such as transit lanes or pedestrian walkways. If travel to or within the area is thereby made more efficient or enjoyable, its viability as a business center will be increased, not jeopardized. This is true even of pricing schemes if revenues are used to increase the affected area's attractiveness, for example by improving public services or reducing taxes.

Future Highway Needs

In many cases, the preferred solution to problems of growing automobile traffic will be the traditional one of expanding the highway network. Despite recent ill repute, the nation's highway program has in most areas succeeded in its primary goal of providing mobility to large numbers of people. Like other policies that encouraged new suburban housing, highway building benefited the majority of citizens by providing something they greatly desired. It has unfortunately had the effect of still further isolating the less-affluent minority who are not well served by the highway system or who disproportionately suffer from the adverse side effects of noise, air pollution, and disruption of neighborhoods. In this way transportation policy has compounded problems arising from the racial factors discussed throughout this volume.

This leads to two conclusions. First, the federal and state organizational structure that has carried out the remarkable engineering achievements of the postwar highway program must be kept in good working order, for there is much yet to be done. Among other things, this requires a reform of state highway financing so as to remove its dependence on possibly shrinking gasoline consumption. Second, alternative means of achieving goals should be given more systematic consideration and adverse side effects more fairly dealt with. This process has already begun, with the extension of Federal Highway Administration responsibility to such areas

Congestion," *Econometrica*, vol. 29 (October 1961), pp. 676–99; Keeler and Small, "Optional Peak-Load Pricing," pp. 1–25; and Kiran V. Bhatt, "What Can We Do About Traffic Congestion? A Pricing Approach," Paper 5032-03-1 (Washington, D.C.: Urban Institute, 1976).

as ridesharing and bus priority, with increased funding for highway maintenance and renovation, and with greater attention to residential displacement.

Transit in a More Decentralized World

As most metropolitan areas continue to decentralize, the need for public
transit will continue, but it will change in character. In order to meet
diverse needs successfully, public transit must adapt.

First, an increasingly large proportion of trips will take place from
dispersed origins to dispersed destinations, either inside or outside cities.
While the majority of these trips will be best served by private automobile,
experience has shown that selected transit markets remain. A diverse group
of systems known as "paratransit" is aimed at providing this kind of service
economically. Experimentation with these modes should continue, along
with removal of inhibiting institutional or legal barriers.[27] There is also
need for more thorough testing of high-priced transit service (such as dial-
a-ride) aimed at the higher-income segment of the market.[28]

A second problem posed by decentralization is how to serve poor inner-
city residents holding or seeking suburban jobs.[29] Furnishing regular transit
service appropriate to their needs would be extremely expensive if, as is
likely, it were only lightly used. Yet special transportation services or
automobile-ownership subsidies, even if cheaper, would be highly visible
and probably unpopular with the middle-class majority. In some areas,

27. For a thorough review of experience with these modes and the various legal barriers
to their adoption, see Ronald F. Kirby and others, *Para-transit: Neglected Options for Urban
Mobility* (Washington, D.C.: Urban Institute, 1975); and Multisystems Inc., *Paratransit
Assessment and Directions for the Future* (Cambridge, Mass.: Multisystems Inc., 1980). For
a review of experience with recent demonstrations, see any of the annual reports of the Urban
Mass Transportation Administration's Service and Methods Demonstration Program, issued
by the Transportation Systems Center, U.S. Department of Transportation.

28. See Philip A. Viton, "The Possibility of Profitable Bus Service," *Journal of Transport
Economics and Policy*, vol. 14 (September 1980), pp. 295–314; and Viton, "On Competition
and Product Differentiation in Urban Transportation: The San Francisco Bay Area," *Bell
Journal of Economics*, vol. 12 (Autumn 1981), pp. 362–79.

29. See Anthony Downs, "Alternative Futures for the American Ghetto," *Daedalus*, vol.
97 (Fall 1968), pp. 1331–78; John F. Kain and Joseph J. Persky, "Alternatives to the Gilded
Ghetto," *Public Interest*, no. 14 (Winter 1969), pp. 74–87; Bennett Harrison, "Ghetto
Economic Development: A Survey," *Journal of Economic Literature*, vol. 12 (March 1974),
pp. 1–37; and William G. Grigsby and others, *Rethinking Housing and Community Development Policy* (University of Pennsylvania, Department of City and Regional Planning, 1977),
pp. 62–76.

this dilemma may be bypassed simply by removing existing obstacles to jitneys, shared-ride taxis, and other private forms of paratransit. Most cities limit the number of licensed taxicabs far below the free-market level, keeping fares correspondingly high; jitney service is usually prohibited altogether. Since taxi service is already used disproportionately by low-income central-city residents,[30] lowering its cost by reducing entry limitations and encouraging shared rides could provide substantial benefits to this group.

Third, continued strength of downtown employment combined with population decentralization will result in further growth of peak-period trips from dispersed suburban residences to the central business district. The prohibitive expense of providing enough highway capacity dictates a continued or even expanded mass transit role. Here, the choice of the most desirable type of transit is important and has been highly controversial. Where densities are sufficiently high, rapid rail systems become contenders as the lowest-cost mode. These require a very long-term commitment and thus considerable confidence that the anticipated travel will in fact take place.[31] For smaller areas or those with less-concentrated corridors, it appears from a number of studies that an integrated express bus system (a single bus with a residential collection phase and an express line-haul phase) can offer equal or better service at lower cost.[32] Not only is the capital cost usually far less, but fewer users need include an automobile trip and a transfer in their daily itinerary.

However, the success of bus rapid transit is crucially dependent on the degree of highway congestion. In evaluating its potential, therefore, it is

30. Kirby and others, *Para-transit*, pp. 117–20.

31. This can be ameliorated somewhat by starting with "light rail" (streetcar), with optional upgrading later to exclusive right-of-way.

32. For example, see J. R. Meyer, J. F. Kain, and M. Wohl, *The Urban Transportation Problem* (Harvard University Press, 1965); U.S. Department of Transportation, "Special Analytic Study," in Subcommittee on Economy in Government of the Joint Economic Committee, *The Analysis and Evaluation of Public Expenditures: The PBB System*, 91 Cong. 1 sess. (Government Printing Office, 1969), vol. 2, pp. 698–733; J. Hayden Boyd, Norman J. Asher, and Elliot S. Wetzler, *Evaluation of Rail Rapid Transit and Express Bus Service in the Urban Commuter Market*, DOT P 6520.1, prepared for U.S. Department of Transportation, Assistant Secretary for Policy and International Affairs, Office of Transportation Planning (GPO, 1973); Theodore E. Keeler and Kenneth A. Small with others, *The Full Costs of Urban Transport, Part III: Automobile Costs and Final Intermodal Cost Comparisons*, Monograph 21 (University of California, Berkeley, Institute of Urban and Regional Development, 1975); and D. N. Dewees, "Urban Express Bus and Railroad Performance: Some Toronto Simulations," *Journal of Transport Economics and Policy*, vol. 10 (January 1976), pp. 16–25.

important to consider measures that reduce congestion or provide preferential bus treatment. More than one potential rail system has been justified by comparison with an unnecessarily congestion-prone hypothetical rapid bus network.[33]

Conclusion

This paper has argued that the relationship between transportation planning and central-city decline is less close than commonly believed. True, transportation needs depend on the future patterns of urban development, but the most likely changes in these patterns have relatively modest and not very surprising effects: continued growth of automobile traffic, especially in the suburbs; a strong transit market serving economically healthy central business districts; and declining transit use elsewhere. Successful revitalization policies would retard somewhat the overall transit decline, and further increase transit's importance for commuting trips to the central business district.

Although technological improvements in transportation have greatly influenced historical development of the present urban structure, it does not appear that the developmental effects of foreseeable transportation policies are as great as those of other influences. Transportation policies are not likely to reverse existing trends. Nor are they any more effective at fostering revitalization than employment, housing, or fiscal policies. In the majority of cases, the choice among alternative transportation policies at the systemwide level should be based primarily on considerations of costs and user benefits.

A dominant factor in such considerations is the existence of the transportation infrastructure now in place. The decision to build the interstate highway system largely exhausted the nation's capacity to fund expensive transportation initiatives, and it now even threatens to exhaust the ability

33. On January 20, 1978, the city of Honolulu "tested" the adequacy of the city's street system to handle projected transit patronage by suddenly dispatching more than twice the usual number of buses down Hotel Street, a busy shopping street and major bus route. No traffic controls or alternative bus routings were applied, nor were such measures considered in the less dramatic consultant's report that rejected an all-bus system as unviable. See Daniel, Mann, Johnson, and Mendenhall, Inc., "Analysis of Transit Project Preliminary Engineering and Evaluation Program Phase II," prepared for the city of Honolulu, April 1976. For other examples see Andrew Marshall Hamer, *The Selling of Rail Rapid Transit: A Critical Look at Urban Transportation Planning* (Heath, 1976).

to maintain what is built. Remaining feasible actions are much more incremental in nature.

Practically the only transportation policies that unambiguously favor central-city revitalization are those that improve mobility within the city: upgrading intracity transit, improving traffic flow on city streets, providing for residential parking, and restraining automobile traffic where congestion is severe. Such policies have several advantages. The central business district is made more attractive for firms, but without the offsetting decentralizing tendencies of radial improvements extending to the suburbs. Firms located in the central city outside the central business district are also helped to the extent that their accessibility is improved. At least some of the benefits are likely to accrue to city residents and therefore to lower-income groups. At the same time, the city's attractiveness to upper-income households is increased, thereby reinforcing tendencies for selected neighborhoods to undergo spontaneous renewal.

A concern with the welfare of central cities, then, can justify only a very cautious and narrow recommendation regarding transportation policy: namely, some preference for projects that focus their improvements almost entirely within those cities. Beyond that, transportation plans should be designed primarily to serve the demand for transport.

HERBERT JACOB

Policy Responses to Crime

ANY consideration of the future of the city must take into account the perceived safety of its inhabitants. Few people want to live in constant danger; most consider neighborhoods that are dangerous to themselves or to their property a substantial detraction to their enjoyment of life. While some city services might be considered amenities, the provision of safety is a necessity.

Yet many American cities are pockmarked with unsafe neighborhoods. In the early 1970s, when the last detailed citywide surveys of perceptions about crime were taken, almost two-thirds of the respondents in eight major cities said that the chances of being attacked or robbed had gone up. While half of the people still thought their neighborhood was "very" or "reasonably" safe during the day, half also thought it "somewhat" or "very" unsafe during the night.[1]

This essay examines some of the ways in which ten U.S. cities attempted to cope with their crime problems during a thirty-one-year period after World War II. The period begins in 1948, when the United States had put the war behind it and new leadership had taken control in many cities. It

The research reported here was conducted at Northwestern University as part of the Governmental Responses to Crime Project, of which Herbert Jacob was principal investigator, Robert L. Lineberry was coprincipal investigator, and Anne M. Heinze was project manager. This paper draws on working papers and analyses prepared under our direction by Janice A. Beecher, Michael J. Rich, and Duane H. Swank. The research was funded by grant 78-NI-AX-0096 from the National Institute of Justice, U.S. Department of Justice.

1. James Garofalo, *Public Opinion about Crime: The Attitudes of Victims and Nonvictims in Selected Cities*, U.S. Department of Justice, Law Enforcement Assistance Administration/National Criminal Justice Information and Statistics Service (Government Printing Office, 1977), pp. 44, 58. The cities were Atlanta, Baltimore, Cleveland, Dallas, Denver, Newark, St. Louis, and Portland, Oregon.

ends in 1978 after a decade of substantial intervention by the federal
government in law enforcement activities at the local level through the
largesse of the Law Enforcement Assistance Administration (LEAA). The
ten cities are Philadelphia, Newark, and Boston in the East; Atlanta in the
south; Indianapolis and Minneapolis in the Midwest; Houston and Phoenix
in the Southwest; and Oakland and San Jose in the West. Among them
are some of the neediest American cities (such as Newark) and some of the
most affluent larger cities (such as Phoenix and San Jose).[2] They include a
city with a highly privatized political style (Houston), where few problems
are considered appropriate for public action, and some with public styles
(Boston and Philadelphia), where it is considered proper for many common
problems to be addressed through governmental action. Some are declining
cities (Newark, Philadelphia, Boston, Minneapolis, and Oakland), while
others have grown rapidly (Houston, Phoenix, and San Jose). Although
these ten cities are not a cross section of the United States (for instance,
none of them typifies the small satellite suburb), they represent many of
the circumstances that urbanologists have in mind when they speak and
write about the urban condition in the United States.

Crime and Response in American Cities

How cities respond to crime is part of the more general problem of how
governments react to challenges that confront them. My conceptualization
of this is quite standard.[3] One usually thinks that governments take action
when a problem (or a performance gap) is perceived and plausible solutions
are known and available to decisionmakers. Of course, not all problems
receive governmental attention; moreover, only a few solutions among the
many suggested can be selected and the timing of their adoption and

2. For rankings according to several indicators, see Mark Schneider, "The Quality of Life
in Large American Cities: Objective and Subjective Social Indicators," *Social Indicators
Research*, vol. 1 (March 1975), pp. 495–509; Arthur M. Louis, "The Worst American City:
A Scientific Study to Confirm or Deny Your Prejudices," *Harper's Magazine* (January 1975),
pp. 67–71; Richard P. Nathan and Charles Adams, "Understanding Central City Hardship,"
Political Science Quarterly, vol. 91 (Spring 1976), pp. 47–62; and Harold L. Bunce and
Norman J. Glickman, "The Spatial Dimensions of the Community Development Block Grant
Program: Targeting and Urban Impacts," in Norman J. Glickman, ed., *The Urban Impacts
of Federal Policies* (Johns Hopkins University Press, 1980), pp. 515–41.

3. Compare Robert L. Lineberry, *American Public Policy* (Harper and Row, 1977), pp.
61–65; and Thomas R. Dye, *Understanding Public Policy* (Prentice-Hall, 1972), pp. 17–36.

implementation must be chosen. All these choices are the result of political processes.

In this instance, there was a recognizable problem, although its dimensions were in some dispute and only incompletely recognized. In addition, many conventional and presumably effective responses were available, some of which were adopted. The question is whether there were real connections between the problem and the responses and which elements of the political process and general environment affected those responses.

Crime

Everyone knows that crime became a bigger problem in American cities during the generation in question. While criminologists dispute the precise dimensions of the growth of crime, policymakers had to confront ever-growing rates that alarmed the media and their constituents.

The exact extent of crime in any place at any time will never be known. There is always some dispute about what behavior is criminal, and many incidents that involve criminal behavior remain undiscovered or unreported. Exact crime counts, however, are unimportant for this analysis; perceptions about the amount of crime are more important. Such perceptions are both reflected in and affected by official reports of crime by police departments. Those reports are the only ones available for individual cities on an annual basis. The Federal Bureau of Investigation and individual police departments use seven offenses to construct their index of serious crime. I have relied on those data, although rape (a relatively rarely reported offense) is omitted because information for it was available only after 1958. I have generally combined the offenses into two broad categories, violent and property offenses. These broad categories are preferable to the individual offenses because it is easy for police departments to classify an incident as one kind of crime at one time or in only one city and then use another category elsewhere or at a subsequent time. Using aggregate categories reduces these problems somewhat.[4]

Figures 1 and 2 show the reported rates for violent and property crime for all U.S. cities with over 50,000 inhabitants, categorized by their population growth or decline. The ten cities analyzed in greater detail below

---

4. I count homicide, assault, and robbery as violent crimes and burglary, theft, and auto theft as property crimes. Robbers, of course, also take property but they do so by personal confrontation and force; consequently, this offense is often considered a violent crime.

Figure 1. *Mean Violent Crime Rate for Cities, by Population Change,*
1948–78

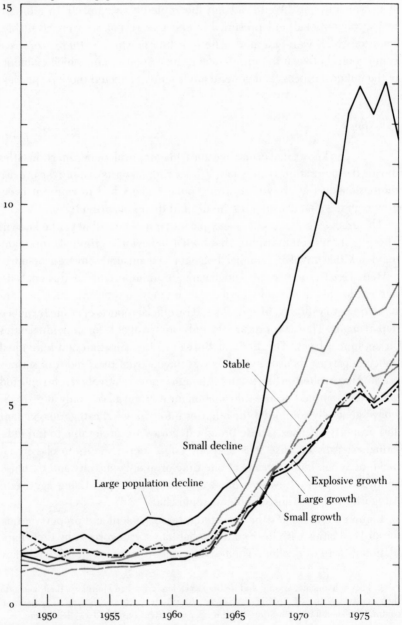

Crime rate per 1,000 population

Source: Herbert Jacob, "The Rise of Crime in American Cities," in Herbert Jacob and Robert L. Lineberry, eds.,
Governmental Responses to Crime: Crime and Governmental Responses in American Cities (U.S. Department of Justice,
National Institute of Justice, 1982).

Figure 2. *Mean Property Crime Rate for Cities, by Population Change, 1948–78*

Crime rate per 1,000 population

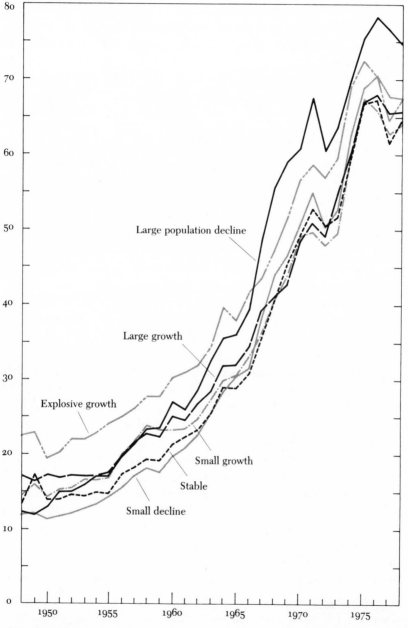

followed similar trends. The data show several important characteristics about crime.

1. Violent and property crime rates rose at different rates. The violent crime rate increased relatively little until the mid-1960s, when it increased markedly. The property crime rate, on the other hand, began its ascent in the late 1950s and continued with only two interruptions at a relatively uniform rate.

2. Regardless of whether cities were growing rapidly, remaining stable, or declining in population, all experienced approximately the same rate of growth in both property and violent crime rates. The levels of the crime rates are somewhat different, but their growth rates are quite similar. The only exception (for part of the period) is for violent crime in those cities with the largest population declines. After 1967 those cities experienced a swifter increase in the violent crime rate than did other cities.

3. Cities' reported violent crime rates had the association with growth that popular lore would suggest. The declining cities experienced the highest rates of violent crime; cities that were growing reflected lower rates.

4. Population growth, however, had a different relationship with property crime rates. Change by itself, whether explosive growth or substantial decline, was related to the highest levels of property crime during most of the period. Cities with relatively stable populations (moderate growth or decline) had lower reported property crime rates.

These trends are subject to quite different interpretations. Because property crimes are much more numerous than violent offenses, city officials who watched only the total crime rates would have seen crime rising sharply from the late 1950s until the mid-1970s. On the other hand, those who distinguished between property and violent crime would have become concerned with each at different times. The rise in property crime rates would have troubled them as early as the late 1950s; violent crime would not spur them into action until the mid-1960s.

In addition, the consistent growth of reported crime in both declining and expanding cities suggests another significant characteristic of the growth of crime that to my knowledge went generally unnoticed. The rise of crime was at least as much a national as a local phenomenon. That conclusion is buttressed by additional comparisons and analyses, which I have reported elsewhere.[5] Whether cities are compared by size, ethnic composition,

5. Herbert Jacob, "The Rise of Crime in American Cities," in Herbert Jacob and Robert L. Lineberry, eds., *Governmental Responses to Crime: Crime and Governmental Responses in American Cities* (U.S. Department of Justice, National Institute of Justice, 1982).

POLICY RESPONSES TO CRIME 231

Table 1. *Relationship between Demographic Variables and Reported Crime Rates for Cities in 185 Standard Metropolitan Statistical Areas, 1970 and Changes, 1950–70*

Variable and summary statistic	Violent crime rate, 1970	Property crime rate, 1970	Change in violent crime rate, 1950–70	Change in property crime rate, 1950–70
Population[a]	0.19†	*	*	−0.24‡
Race[b]	0.72†	0.44‡	0.29‡	0.21‡
Youthful population[c]	*	0.26‡	*	*
Poverty[d]	*	*	−0.15†	*
Inequality[e]	*	0.19‡	*	*
Constant	−3.69	−46.82	8.55	2.98
R^2	0.63	0.29	0.11	0.12
F	104.49	24.80	9.02	16.30
Significance	0.00	0.00	0.00	0.00

Source: Herbert Jacob, "The Rise of Crime in American Cities," in Herbert Jacob and Robert L. Lineberry, eds., *Governmental Responses to Crime: Crime and Governmental Responses in American Cities* (U.S. Department of Justice, National Institute of Justice, 1982), pp. 24, 26.

* Not significant.
† Significant at less than 5 percent level.
‡ Significant at less than 1 percent level.
a. From decennial census.
b. Nonwhite population as percentage of total city population.
c. Population between ages of 15 and 25.
d. Percentage of families under the poverty line as defined and reported in decennial census.
e. As measured by Sheldon Danziger, "Trends in the Level and Distribution of Income in Metropolitan Areas, 1959–69" (University of Wisconsin–Madison, Institute for Research on Poverty, 1977).

region, or population growth, the rate of change in reported crime is similar. Moreover, the amount of variability in reported crime rates across cities diminished considerably between the 1950s and the 1970s.[6] This suggests that the rise of crime is to a considerable extent the result of forces that lie beyond the boundaries of individual cities.

It is especially important to keep in mind that I have been analyzing changes in crime rates rather than their levels. An examination of levels may lead to substantially different conclusions. That is apparent, for instance, when one examines the association between the percentage of blacks in a city and its reported crime rates. Table 1 shows the association between race (and other demographic variables) and violent and property crime rates for 185 U.S. cities. The table makes apparent the substantial association between the presence of blacks and crime, especially for violent crime. Moreover, in the case of violent crime nearly two-thirds of the variation is accounted for by this analysis. However, when one examines the association between those same variables and *changes* in crime rates,

6. Ibid., p. 27.

the association between changes in racial composition and changes in crime rates is much smaller. Likewise, the amount of variation accounted for by all factors in the analysis is minute. While all the analyses in the table present statistically discernible associations, those focusing on levels of crime rates are much more substantial than those focusing on changes in crime rates. Consequently, quite contrary conclusions can be reached, depending on whether one is focusing on the level of crime or changes in crime rates. The presence of blacks is closely associated with crime levels, particularly violent crime. However, the association between changes in racial composition and changes in reported crime is quite weak. While the level of crime may well reflect some current and past traits of cities, crime rates seem to change in waves that cover the whole nation at the same time in the same way.

Thus crime is similar to many other national problems that manifest themselves on the local scene. Like unemployment during a recession, it cannot be substantially reduced by local actions. While crime is generally perceived in spatial terms that suggest local responses, it is not clear that such initiatives will have a substantial effect on changes in the crime rate.

Consequently, the "need" for action in this arena is far from clear. The measures of crime have been subject to severe criticism by criminologists, and the causes of the problem are incompletely understood. While most people perceive the problem to be a local one because that is where crime takes place and because there is a strong tradition of localism in law enforcement, my analysis suggests that it is more a national problem than a local one.

Policy Responses

City officials generated numerous responses to the crime problem as they perceived it. These responses often consisted of brief forays against specific categories of offenders such as narcotics dealers, gamblers, or loitering youth. Underlying such responses, however, were more fundamental policy decisions about the allocation and uses of resources. Money had to be made available to the police. That money was then used to provide additional officers or equipment, which were then supposed to enable the police to deal with crime more effectively.

Each of the ten cities engaged in these kinds of apparent policy responses. Their scope should be examined, however, before an analysis of their link to the apparent need for action or to political processes.

EXPENDITURES. For all cities over 50,000 population police expenditures increased greatly during the thirty-one years studied. In constant dollars, the per capita expenditure increased from $7.50 in 1948 to $25.00 in 1978. Outlays for policing also rose threefold or more in the ten cities studied. Figure 3 shows the rise in per capita police expenditures in constant dollars for each of the cities. The figure suggests two sets of cities. The first, composed of Indianapolis, San Jose, Houston, Phoenix, Minneapolis, Oakland, and Atlanta, generally had relatively low levels of outlays throughout the entire period. The second cluster—Philadelphia, Boston, and Newark—displayed much higher outlays, which in some instances increased more than those in cities of the first cluster. Another important characteristic of this second cluster of cities was that they were the older, northeastern cities with a high incidence of need and relatively scarce resources. Figure 3 clearly demonstrates that all ten cities increased their expenditures for policing considerably. Almost every mayor could tell his or her constituents that large additional funds had been allocated to the police department the past year.

POLICE STAFFING. The second major response by cities was to increase the size of their police force. In part this was done through the process of civilianization—replacing officers assigned to clerical duties with civilians. However, there was also a significant attempt to increase the number of police officers and to improve the quality of the force by expanding the role of the police academy for recruits and by formalizing in-service training.

Since policing is a labor-intensive activity, most of the expenditures went to salaries and wages. There are two components of this personnel budget: the number of officers and the level of their pay. Both increased in all of the ten cities during the years studied. In all cities over 50,000 the number of police officers increased from 1.33 per 1,000 inhabitants in 1948 to 1.96 per 1,000 in 1978. The number of police officers similarly increased in each of the ten cities. As figure 4 shows, however, the increase was not constant throughout the period nor was it identical in all the cities. In some (Phoenix and San Jose are good examples) the number of officers per 1,000 population remained relatively constant during the entire period, although the police forces grew immensely along with the populations of those cities. In Boston, Philadelphia, and Newark, the police departments grew relative to their cities' declining population; Atlanta shows a very steep rise in its police per 1,000 for 1970–75.

Much of the expenditures, however, did not go to hiring additional officers but rather toward raising the pay of those already on the force. In

Figure 3. *Per Capita Police Expenditures, Ten U.S. Cities, 1948–78*
Constant dollars

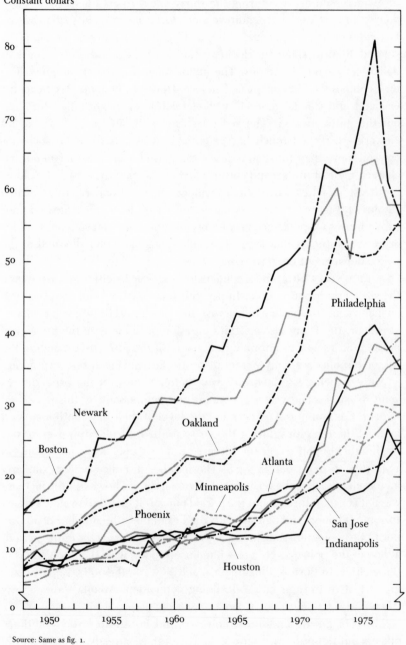

Figure 4. *Police Officers per 1,000 Population, Ten U.S. Cities, 1948–78*

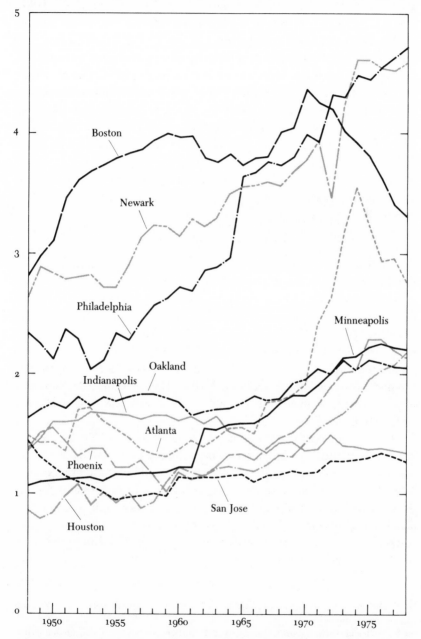

part that is reflected in the entry-level salaries (in constant dollars), displayed in figure 5. Police salaries increased faster than the inflation rate in most of the cities until the late 1960s. During the 1970s entrance salaries remained level with the inflation rate or fell somewhat behind.[7] There is no distinct clustering of cities by entrance salaries, as there was for the size of the police force. The cities with the largest number of officers per capita did not pay the highest entrance salaries or increase them the most. Those cities with large police forces relative to their population are clustered in the middle of this group of cities according to level of entrance salary, bounded consistently by Oakland at the top and Atlanta at the bottom.

Of course, entrance salaries do not reflect all of the personnel costs of a police department. Some departments had larger numbers of their officers beyond the entrance level and increased wages relatively quickly; others supplemented salaries with large amounts of overtime pay. Nevertheless, entrance salaries provide a reasonable estimate of another component of these cities' response to crime. Their police forces were not only increased but their officers received substantially higher pay.

Entrance-level requirements for the police force in these cities did not rise much during this period.[8] However, recruit training increased considerably. In 1948 three of the cities had no formal recruit training and none had more than an eight-week course. By 1978 all the cities had formal recruit training, and none lasted less than ten weeks. In Indianapolis the training period extended to a full half year. Thus considerable effort was expended in these cities to put not only more but also better-trained officers on the street.

ACTIVITY RESPONSES TO CRIME. An emphasis on the allocation of resources, both fiscal and human, may be faulted on two grounds. First, the police engage in many important activities in addition to fighting crime. Thus the relationship between crime, politics, and resource allocation is likely to be a good deal more complex than portrayed thus far. Second, allocation of resources is only one of many potential responses. Most responses require some additional resources, but additional resources alone would be conceded by most observers to be a meaningless response to the crime problem.

7. Of course, in current dollars (which is what cities spent), salaries continued to rise even during those years.
8. Michael J. Rich, Robert L. Lineberry, and Herbert Jacob, "Police Policies and Urban Crime," in Jacob and Lineberry, eds., *Governmental Responses to Crime*, pp. 75–79.

Figure 5. *Entry-Level Salary for Police, Nine U.S. Cities, 1948–78*[a]

Constant dollars

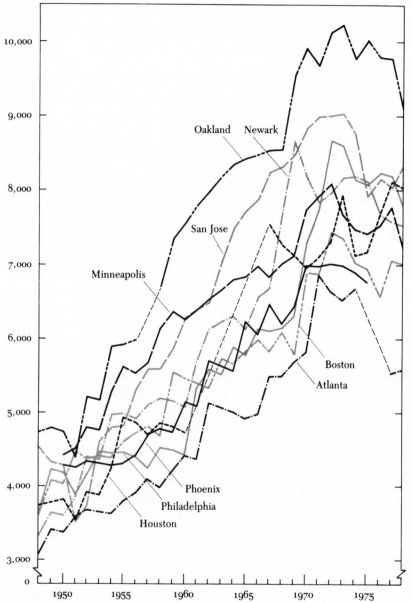

Source: Same as fig. 1.

a. Annual data not available for 1957 for Oakland, 1975 and 1976 for Atlanta, and 1961–66 for Houston. Thin dashed lines have been drawn to connect years for which data are available.

Both of these objections may be met in part by examining measures of some of the activities in which police engage. The analysis will be quite limited because it is difficult to locate consistent indicators for such activities over even the brief thirty-one-year period in question.[9] For example, it is not possible to examine the average number of police officers assigned to various duties or various areas of the city, to produce a reliable count of calls for service in most cities over an extended period of time, or to classify those calls by the type of service requested or the kind of response made. My analysis, therefore, cannot be as definitive as I would like.

One important police activity not directed against crime is the regulation of traffic flows in the city. It is just as vital to the safety of residents as the fight against crime and just as important to the economic viability of the city. During the thirty-one years studied, the number of cars increased markedly and all of the cities examined became crisscrossed by expressways. In all likelihood opportunities for enforcement of traffic ordinances did not decline; the larger number of officers, their improved training, and their enhanced equipment might arguably be expected to have resulted in a more intense effort at traffic enforcement. Figure 6, however, shows that such a secular increase did not take place in the eight cities for which there are adequate data. In some cities, like Newark, the number of citations for moving violations per officer remained relatively constant at a low level; in Oakland this number remained relatively constant at a much higher level. In Atlanta it rose to a peak around 1962 and then dropped to its 1950s level at the end of the period. The figure shows many ups and downs of a minor sort but no long-run trend. It provides no support for the hypothesis that the additional resources described above were committed to more intensive traffic enforcement.

Since the additional resources did not produce more intensive traffic enforcement (at least as measured by citations per officer), it is reasonable to expect that one will find substantial effects in the activities of police officers against serious crime. However, as figures 7 and 8 show, that is not the case. Figure 7 shows that arrests generally did not keep up with reported serious crimes in these ten cities. The drop is not precipitous

9. The most imaginative analyses of police activities, done at the University of Indiana and by the Police Foundation in Kansas City, exchange the power of a longer time perspective for the opportunity to design their own data collection instruments or to utilize recent innovations in departmental record keeping. See Roger B. Parks, "Complementary Measures of Police Performance," in Kenneth M. Dolbeare, ed., *Public Policy Evaluation* (Sage, 1975); and George M. Kelling and others, *The Kansas City Preventive Patrol Experiment: A Technical Report* (Washington, D.C.: Police Foundation, 1974).

Figure 6. *Citations Made for Moving Violations, per Police Officer, Eight U.S. Cities, 1948–78*

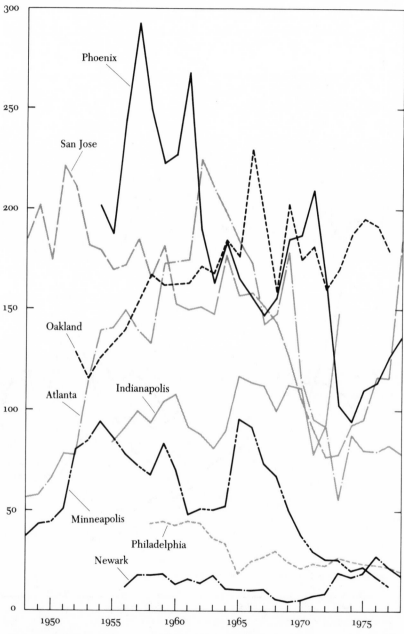

Source: Same as fig. 1.

Figure 7. *Arrest-Offense Ratio, Ten U.S. Cities, 1958–78*

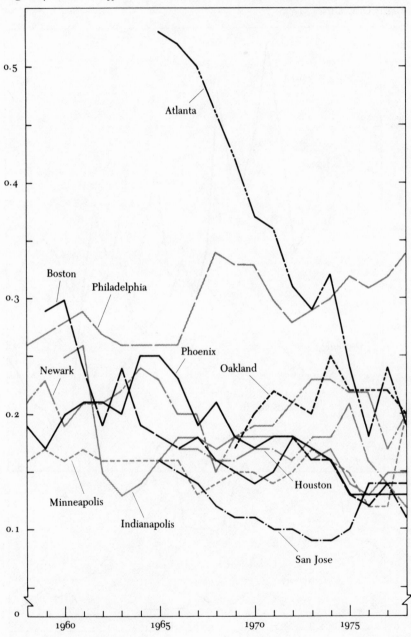

Source: Same as fig. 1.

Figure 8. *Arrests per Police Officer, Ten U.S. Cities, 1958–78*

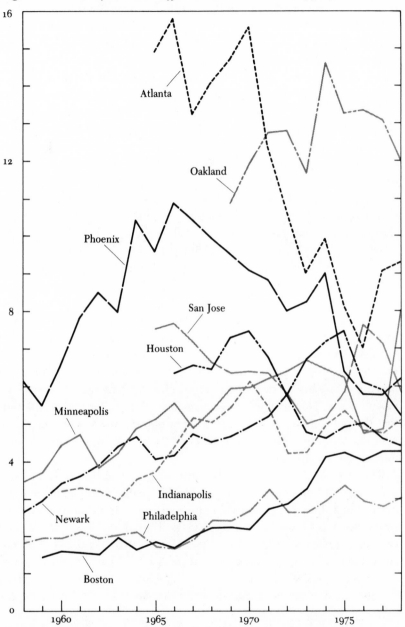

except in Atlanta, where the police made an exceptionally large number of arrests per reported crime in the middle 1960s and then fell toward the norm for these cities by the late 1970s. Philadelphia, on the other hand, shows a modest rise in its arrest-offense ratio, indicating somewhat more arrests per offense in the 1970s than in the 1950s.

Figure 8 provides information about the number of arrests for serious offenses per police officer. This figure counts all police officers wherever they are assigned; of course, some departments have more officers assigned to clerical tasks than others, and the ratio of assignment to clerical tasks also changes over time. Nevertheless, the figure provides a rough estimate of the arresting activity of police officers. Two facts stand out in this figure. The first is that the *level* of arresting activity is quite low.[10] Only in Oakland did officers make an average of one arrest a month for serious offenses. One arrest for a serious crime *every three months* is the norm for four of these cities during much of this period. Second, although some cities showed a slight rise and others exhibited rather large fluctuations, none displayed a dramatic long-term trend toward increased arrests.

Still another indicator of a city's possible response to serious crime is the proportion of arresting activity directed against violent crime rather than property crime. One might hypothesize that as violent crime became a greater concern to the citizenry, the police would attempt to make more violent crime arrests than property crime arrests. Figure 9 shows this measure for the ten cities. It shows a remarkable stability in this indicator for all but San Jose, where there was a substantial *decrease* in arrests for violent crime. The change in San Jose belies one objection to this indicator: that the police must respond to whatever opportunities exist and cannot alter that structure markedly. Apparently, they could but did not do so in nine of the ten cities examined.

The analysis thus far has shown that indicators of the need for some action against crime existed and were highly visible to city policymakers, even though they could be easily misinterpreted. It has also shown that cities allocated substantial funds toward policing, hired more officers, and gave their police more initial training. On the other hand, the evidence about the activity of the police is quite ambiguous. The additional, better-trained police officers did not produce visibly different patterns of activity directed against serious crime. Nor did they increase the one noncrime

10. My measure of arrests does not include arrests for less serious offenses, those not counted as Part I crimes by the FBI. Such arrests are much more common but are not reported as fully or accurately as Part I arrests.

Figure 9. *Ratio of Arrests for Violent Crime to Arrests for Property Crime, Ten U.S. Cities, 1958–78*

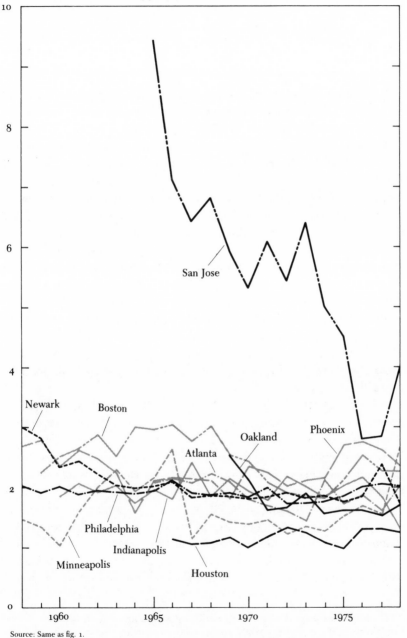

Source: Same as fig. 1.

activity for which there are good measures, the issuance of citations for traffic offenses. It is therefore necessary to examine the linkages between the apparent need and these apparent responses.

Linkages

Police expenditures and the crime rate moved in lockstep during much of the period in most of the ten cities. However, a reasonable model of the relationship would not posit a simultaneous connection between crime and spending but rather a lag of a year or two between a change in the crime rate and a similar change in the expenditure of public funds. The most reasonable lag is two years.[11] This is because a year's crime statistics are generally not compiled and released until several months into the following year, and it then takes time for these data to be registered in the budgetary decisions that lead to expenditures in the second year following the incidence of the crimes. This lag structure is demonstrated in table 2, which shows a very strong relationship between crime two years ago and police expenditures for the current year. However, the previous year's expenditures also have a very strong relationship to current expenditures.

These relationships provide potential support for two alternative hypotheses. The first is that expenditures are a response to prior crime rates. The second is essentially the incremental hypothesis, which posits that expenditures are to a large degree the product of inertia from previous expenditure decisions.

Table 2 shows that both hypotheses are equally plausible at the bivariate level since the relationship between lagged crime rates and current expenditures is almost as high as that between lagged expenditures and current expenditures. Indeed, because of the very high covariation of these two "independent" variables in the model, one cannot distinguish statistically between the two effects.

Another way of looking at the cities' budgets, however, enables one to make a tentative choice between the two hypotheses. If cities were responding to need rather than to simple budgetary inertia, one would expect that the share of their budget commanded by a high-priority program would consistently increase. Thus, if cities were responding to a perception

11. James Alan Fox, "Crime Trends and Police Expenditures: An Investigation of the Lag Structure," *Evaluation Quarterly*, vol. 3 (February 1979), pp. 41–55.

Table 2. *Correlation between Police Expenditures and the Crime Rate in Ten U.S. Cities*

	Correlation		
City	Crime rate, lagged two years, with current expenditures	Current expenditures with expenditures, lagged one year	Crime rate, lagged two years, with expenditures, lagged one year
Atlanta	0.98	0.98	0.98
Boston	0.93	0.96	0.94
Houston	0.93	0.98	0.98
Indianapolis	0.77	0.91	0.71
Minneapolis	0.96	0.98	0.95
Newark	0.93	0.96	0.93
Oakland	0.93	0.99	0.92
Philadelphia	0.95	0.99	0.95
Phoenix	0.95	0.97	0.94
San Jose	0.96	0.97	0.96

that policing now required greater effort due to the rising crime rate, the police share of the budget would increase. There is, however, little evidence of that. The share of the cities' budgets that went to policing varied considerably from city to city and over time. It was lowest in Minneapolis, where the share ranged between 6 and 13 percent; Phoenix devoted the highest budget share to the police, ranging from 13 to 22 percent. However, the relationship between share of city expenditures and the lagged crime rate is at best an ambiguous one. As table 3 shows, the relationship is statistically discernible in only seven of the ten cities, but in two of these seven it is opposite to the hypothesized direction. Thus in half of the ten cities one cannot detect a positive relationship between the crime rate and the proportion of city expenditures devoted to policing.

Thus the tentative conclusion must be that the perception of need was not by itself the driving force for the increase in police resources. It would be foolish to deny that perceptions of crime played a role, but that role was shared by many other factors, chief among which probably were the inertial forces of incremental budget making.

The incremental explanation is not an economic interpretation but a political one. It demonstrates the power of the bureaucracy and of organizational decision modes in resource allocation. It suggests that the rise in police expenditures was largely an illusory response to crime. Rather, police expenditures rose mostly because all other city expenditures rose. Some added support for this interpretation may be found by examining

Table 3. *Relationship between Share of City Budget Allocated to Policing and Two-Year Lagged Crime Rate in Ten U.S. Cities*

City	Correlation
Atlanta	0.12*
Boston	0.09*
Houston	0.67‡
Indianapolis	−0.34†
Minneapolis	0.34†
Newark	−0.07*
Oakland	−0.81‡
Philadelphia	0.82‡
Phoenix	0.75‡
San Jose	0.39†

* Not significant.
† Significant at less than 5 percent level.
‡ Significant at less than 0.1 percent level.

police expenditures per crime for this period. In 1948 cities over 50,000 population spent fifteen cents per violent crime, but thirty-one years later they spent only six cents (in constant dollars). A similar decline occurred for property crimes. Thus, far from responding to rising crime, cities were in fact spending *less* on crime in 1978 than in 1948. Bureaucratic inertia led to increased expenditures but constrained the increase below the amount one might have expected if cities had been responding to crime by committing expenditures in proportion to the rise in reported crime.

A third set of alternative hypotheses is that police expenditures responded to other indicators of need: especially, the incidence of civil disorders in particular cities might have triggered increased outlays for policing. The events of Watts, Detroit, and Newark drew wide public attention, as did the disorders associated with the Democratic National Convention in Chicago in 1968. Each of the ten cities except San Jose experienced some disorders of their own during this period. They were probably most severe in the form of black rioting in Newark and of antiwar demonstrations in Oakland.

However, when a riot-nonriot variable is entered into a regression equation that attempts to predict annual changes in police expenditures, this variable has no statistically discernible impact in any of the ten cities. The analysis (not displayed here) indicates that a riot in the preceding year is not reflected in higher (or lower) police expenditures in a current year. That statistical finding is supported by an inspection of the plots of expenditure change with the years of civil disorder demarcated. Thus the upswing in police expenditures apparently took place without being distinctively affected by civil disorders.

It is also commonplace to hypothesize that political characteristics of cities might affect the ways in which they respond to a policy need. I have measured three characteristics. One pertains to the cities' power structure. The second notes the degree of black political penetration, indicated by the election of a black as mayor. The third taps local concerns for law and order by whether a "law and order" candidate was elected as mayor.

For the first, my research team interviewed knowledgeable observers for their evaluation of the power structure of their city.[12] We sought an evaluation of the degree to which the city was dominated during a particular mayoral incumbency by the business elite, the political elite, the bureaucracy, or a pluralistic system of interest group brokerage. None of the cities can be described as falling simply into one of the four categories; the politics of each was characterized by some instances of political elitism, some of bureaucratic domination, some of business power, and some of pluralism. However, there was a considerable range in the rankings of these cities. For instance, Boston ranked first among the ten as a city governed by a political elite; Oakland ranked ninth. On bureaucratic power, Oakland ranked first and Boston tenth. In a city like Boston where the political elite was dominant, one would expect a greater response to crime in the form of increased expenditures than in Oakland, where the elite was relatively weak and the bureaucracy strong. The independent effect of this political factor would be especially apparent in a comparison of Boston with Oakland since both were relatively declining, needy cities. Indeed, the level of expenditures in the two cities is consistent with the hypothesis. Yet the ratio of expenditures to crime changes in the same way for both. Thus differences in the power structure of the cities seem not to have affected changes in police expenditures.

The second political characteristic is the rise of blacks to positions of power. Newark elected Kenneth Gibson as mayor in 1970, and Atlanta elected Maynard Jackson in 1973.[13] Once more, one cannot discern an effect of these events on police expenditures. Indeed, it is unclear whether one should expect a rise in expenditures (reflecting the fact that criminal victimization falls especially hard on the black community) or a decline in expenditures because of the hostility between the black community and the police. The data, however, show quite clearly that police budgets did

12. See Janice A. Beecher, Robert L. Lineberry, and Michael J. Rich, "Community Power, the Urban Agenda, and Crime Policy," *Social Science Quarterly*, vol. 62 (December 1981), pp. 630–43,

13. Oakland elected a black, Lionel Wilson, in 1977; however, that was too late in the period of the study to show any effect.

not fare differently in cities with black mayors nor did the budgets show a distinctive change after a black was elected to the mayor's post.

Third, this period was marked by the rise to prominence of politicians who made law and order the centerpiece of their campaigns and administrations. This was most true in Philadelphia, where Frank Rizzo moved from the police department to the mayor's office in 1972. Another police officer to make that move was Charles Stenvig in Minneapolis in 1969 (with a second term, after an intervening defeat, beginning in 1975). Returning to figure 3, one can examine the fate of the police budgets in those two cities in those particular years from two perspectives: a comparison with what was happening in the immediately preceding years and a comparison of their experience with that of the other cities in the same time period. In both instances, one cannot discern any impact of these law-and-order candidates. Philadelphia's police expenditures had risen sharply in the term of Rizzo's predecessor; they leveled off during Rizzo's term. In Minneapolis, Stenvig's terms came during a rise in police expenditures that both preceded his inauguration and continued after his departure. One cannot discern a distinctive impact of a law-and-order mayoralty.

These analyses further reinforce the conclusion reached in the analysis of the effect of crime rates and incrementalism. As was the case for those factors, neither a measure of need nor indicators of the political process appear to have had a discernible effect on police expenditures.

The data, however, suggest that one external event may have had a significant effect: the availability of funds from the federal government through the various activities of the Law Enforcement Assistance Administration. That impact, however, is not in the form of consistent increases in the police budgets during the ten years that the LEAA operated. Rather, in more than half of the ten cities, the *volatility* of police budgets (the annual percentage change in constant dollars) was markedly greater after 1968 than before. Moreover, where one cannot discern an increase in volatility after 1968, it is because police budgets had already become quite volatile. In no city did police budgets become less volatile after the funds from the LEAA became available.

One possible inference of this finding is that federal funds made police budgeting somewhat less dependent on local resources and also less subject to the entrenched local controls that kept them in equilibrium in earlier years. Police departments could expand their budgets by seizing opportunities in federal programs, but they were also subject to cutoff. No city could sustain the rate of change that was created with the infusion of federal funds.

The increasing volatility of police expenditures as a result of LEAA grants shows an indirect effect of riots and civil disorders. As noted earlier, one could not find such an effect looking at city-level data. These events, however, had an impact in Washington. They were directly responsible for passage of the Safe Streets Act of 1967, which established the LEAA. This is another indication of the significance of the nationalization of crime. Civil disorders were able to influence city police expenditures through their effect on Washington when they were unable to do so locally.

One final irony lurks in these data. Expenditures for policing rose rapidly during the 1960s, only to level off or fall (in constant dollars) during the late 1970s. Those changes were clearly not in response to the prominence of crime on the agenda of election campaigns or on the perceived list of problems facing the cities in the late 1970s. My research team analyzed the contents of newspaper reports of mayoral elections and conducted interviews with knowledgeable respondents who tried to report for each mayoral incumbency the major issues facing the city. Crime was almost a constant issue in election campaigns, lagging behind only one other issue— the amorphous concern about "leadership." When we asked about possible problems facing these ten cities and gave respondents a list of thirteen issues to choose from, crime rose steadily from the middle of the list in the early years to the most prominent problem in the late 1970s. That means that as crime achieved the top position on the agendas of these cities, allocation of resources to the police was already declining. Electoral and populist political power obviously played second fiddle to the constraints imposed by bureaucratic decision rules affecting police expenditures.

Conclusion

Appearances are often deceptive, and such is certainly the case with respect to city responses to crime. Looking at surface manifestations, one readily comes to the conclusion that crime became a much more serious problem during the period studied than it had been and that cities responded with a generous allocation of monetary and personnel resources. However, closer inspection raises doubts about each element of that analysis. First, the true dimensions of the rise of crime are not clear, although it seems reasonable to think that it rose, and certainly all the indicators available to policymakers would have led them to believe that. The allocation of funds, however, poses many problems. While more money was spent on policing than before even in constant dollars, the police share of the city budget did not rise in lockstep with the crime rate; it sometimes rose and sometimes fell. Moreover, the amount of money spent on crime did not keep up with the crime rate, so that far fewer dollars per serious crime were spent in 1978 than in 1948. Finally, the rise in expenditures (and manpower) was probably more a response to inertial bureaucratic pressures (incrementalism) than a response to crime rates or changes in the crime rates. There was little evidence that expenditure increases were due to civil disorders, the crime rate, the advent of black mayors, the election of law-and-order candidates as mayors, or the prominence of crime on the political agenda. Indeed, when each of these is entered into a multivariate regression model, none consistently shows a discernible effect on police expenditures. Only one force other than sheer bureaucratic inertia had a discernible effect—the presence of federal funds from the LEAA. Its effect, however, was not necessarily to enhance police resources but to increase the volatility of police budgets. For some years, expenditures were increased; in others, they declined by larger amounts than before the advent of federal funds.

It is difficult to tell whether incrementalism was a constraint, rather than a driving upward force, in the case of city police expenditures. One cannot be certain that expenditures would have risen more rapidly without processes that limit change to small increments. However, had cities simply spent the same amount per reported crime in 1978 as they had thirty-one years earlier, the calculations suggest that police expenditures would have been higher.

There is little room in the results of this analysis for the effect of political forces on the basic decisions about allocating resources to law enforcement in the city. One comes to the conclusion that campaign talk about crime and becoming tough on criminals is meaningless rhetoric. Crime is a staple issue that many candidates feel compelled to address while running for office, but they experience paralysis when they reach city hall.

That apparent paralysis may be the result of another illusion. I began by proposing that governments take action when perceived problems and plausible solutions coincide. The indicators of police activities suggest that the police had difficulty in transforming their additional resources into effective activity. More officers who were better trained and better equipped nevertheless lacked the means by which to combat serious crime. The title of a recent conference on what to do about crime captures this lack of technology. It was "What To Do When Nothing Works."

In addition to the policies described here, cities also tried a large array of more focused actions against crime not examined in this analysis. Cities changed patrol practices, altered the assignment of officers over time and space, or shifted their priorities with respect to serious crime and from one kind of serious crime to another. New bureaus were established in police departments to deal with special kinds of problems such as rape, burglary, gambling, or narcotics; after some years many such divisions were abolished. In the ten cities there was constant activity of this sort. However, its most distinctive trait was that it was almost always short-lived and left little or no trace in the larger picture. For example, Minneapolis experienced more change in police chiefs than most cities; every mayor appointed his own chief and sometimes they lasted less than the two years of the mayor's term. However, Minneapolis cannot be seen as more responsive to major crime than the other cities; it is scarcely distinguishable on *any* of the indicators examined. By contrast, San Jose had only five chiefs during the thirty-one years; none of the differences examined can reasonably be laid to this stability of leadership in the department. The campaigns against one kind of offense or another or changes in departmental structure or policy seem to be mostly froth riding above a fundamental stability of activity. Given what is known about how police officers do their work,[14] such stability of practice amidst a constant background of superficial change ought not to be surprising. Work habits die slowly, and when the workers are under relatively loose supervision such habits are even more resistant to change.

It is fair, therefore, to conclude that crime was not effectively addressed by these cities during the period examined. They did not harness extraordinary resources to the task. Those resources that were committed did not alter existing police activities in any fundamental way. It may also be fair to conclude that crime *cannot* be effectively addressed by the customary local policies. If I am correct in concluding that change in the crime rate is a national phenomenon that is the product of macrosocial forces beyond the control of local government policy, local policing will be doomed to failure. What is required is to consider the crime problem in a different way.

14. Contrast Jonathan Rubinstein, *City Police* (Farrar, Straus and Giroux, 1973); Michael K. Brown, *Working the Street: Police Discretion and the Dilemmas of Reform* (Russell Sage Foundation, 1981); William A. Westley, *Violence and the Police: A Sociological Study of Law, Custom, and Morality* (MIT Press, 1970); and Jerome H. Skolnick, *Justice without Trial: Law Enforcement in Democratic Society* (Wiley, 1967).

One alternative is to seek greater federal intervention through more fiscal assistance or more direct administration of police forces. Such a course seems quite unpromising to me. My data suggest that lack of resources is not the problem. Rather, what is lacking is the knowledge of how to reduce crime. The national government does not possess any superiority in this regard. More federal funds are likely to produce the same results as before—volatility in police spending but few concrete results. More direct federal action is more likely to reduce the liberties of Americans than it is to secure their safety.

A different course of action would rely on a mix of both private and governmental action to enable Americans to adapt themselves better to the consequences of crime. One kind of private activity that has already occurred is the expansion of private police forces. However, they protect only the wealthy and corporate property. Other private initiatives are required. People need to exhibit more concern for their safety in strange neighborhoods and for their empty homes while they are at work in order to reduce the opportunity for crime. More adequate compensation for injuries and losses suffered by the victims of crime may reduce the fear associated with crime and make it a less compelling (although not less prevalent) problem. The private initiatives required by such an approach involve neighborhood activities and personal reorientation. It requires that people keep an eye on their neighbors' houses. It also demands that they stay out of neighborhoods where they do not "belong," that is, out of neighborhoods that are dominated by groups hostile to them. Such circumspection may seem to be a surrender to the balkanization of big cities. I believe, however, that it simply maintains a degree of separateness that has long characterized large cities in the United States. On the public side, compensation programs may well be the kind of redistributive activity that the national government more logically engages in than do the cities. That would leave to the cities their ongoing policing activities that may serve to maintain a semblance of law and order and to help the community use the law not just for protection but for sustaining the norms that underlie the social system.

TERRY NICHOLS CLARK

Fiscal Strain: How Different Are Snow Belt and Sun Belt Cities?

SINCE the fiscal crises suffered by cities such as New York, Cleveland, and Chicago, many observers have sought the causes. A common answer is that the crises are caused by economic decline, and that urban fiscal problems can be solved by strengthening the local economy. As Jane Jacobs observed during New York's 1975 crisis, "I don't know that New York can recover now. A city can't let its skills, manufacturing plants and suppliers' plants wither away and then not suffer the consequences."[1] A few years later Felix Rohatyn stated, "It is no coincidence that our cities under the greatest strain are tied to our industries in most severe difficulty. An arc of industrial and social crisis extends today from Baltimore to St. Louis."[2] He suggested addressing the problem with a federally supported recon-struction finance corporation to help troubled industries in the Northeast. A similar emphasis on the economic base was at the heart of President Jimmy Carter's national urban policy, which targeted federal funds to distressed cities through programs that sought to build a "new partnership" between the private and public sectors.

The Sources of Fiscal Strain

This essay argues that such identification of the problem is largely incorrect, and thus attempted solutions are misplaced. My analysis shows that large, old cities in the Northeast do not spend or borrow distinctly

1. *New York Times*, July 30, 1975.
2. *Chicago Tribune*, July 20, 1981.

more or less than other cities. Political processes better explain the fiscal policies of city governments, although these processes differ by city and time period. The public and private sectors often operate separately. Their dynamics are sufficiently distinct and local that any global assessments of problems or solutions are likely to fail. Urban fiscal problems have been overly defined as emerging from private-sector responses to national economic trends. A more informed local and public-sector orientation would help correct the balance. Many solutions are available, but to succeed they must be addressed to the right problem. For attacking urban fiscal problems, public officials deserve more attention and assistance than they have received.

Is There a "Northeast Syndrome"?

In the mid-1970s population grew in the South and West and declined in the Northeast. Although these trends had been under way for decades, they received special attention in debates on federal aid to New York City, federal grant formulas, and the Carter administration's national urban policy. Regional voting blocs occasionally emerged in Congress. Despite much debate, there has been limited serious research to determine if northeastern cities are actually more fiscally strained.

To compare cities, Thomas Muller and George Peterson have used population change as a measure of a declining-city syndrome.[3] Richard Nathan, Paul Dommel, and their associates have developed indices including population change, income, and old housing.[4] I have used a "Northeast syndrome" measure combining northeastern region, city age, and population change.[5] Does such a composite measure predict the fiscal well-being of cities? It might if most large northeastern cities were losing population, densely populated, had many poor and black residents, and were in fiscal difficulty—and Sun Belt cities were the opposite in these respects. Casual accounts often imply as much. Few such discussions have been informed by a systematic conception; rather a diffuse idea of "distress"

3. Thomas Muller, *Growing and Declining Urban Areas: A Fiscal Comparison* (Washington, D.C.: Urban Institute, 1975); and George E. Peterson, "Finance," in William Gorham and Nathan Glazer, eds., *The Urban Predicament* (Washington, D.C.: Urban Institute, 1976), pp. 35–118.

4. Richard P. Nathan and Paul R. Dommel, "Issues and Techniques for Federal Grants-in-Aid Allocation to Distressed Cities," *Urban Affairs Papers*, vol. 3 (1981), pp. 21–34.

5. Terry Nichols Clark, "Fiscal Management of American Cities: Funds Flow Indicators," *Journal of Accounting Research*, vol. 15 (1977 Supplement), pp. 54–106.

often leads to interchangeable use of various Northeast syndrome indicators. This may follow logically if one assumes fiscal strain is simply a function of economic decline, but neither more casual discussions nor systematic research have addressed the question of how closely connected are the fiscal stress of local governments and the underlying economic well-being of cities.

One instructive approach consists of simply correlating the variables often discussed as defining distressed or growing cities, such as northeastern and north central region, population change, and similar socioeconomic measures. Table 1 shows that when this is done most correlations are strikingly low. The characteristics do not "go together" as neatly as popular accounts suggest. There is some, but limited, clustering. No correlations with the northeastern region measure exceed 0.5 except another regional measure, which overlaps with it conceptually. While several of the correlations in table 1 are statistically significant, no single dimension emerges.[6]

Is There a Link between Socioeconomic Characteristics and Fiscal Policy?

If social and economic characteristics like those analyzed in table 1 were major sources of fiscal difficulties, one would expect large, older cities in

6. My colleagues and I experimented with several procedures to construct a composite measure including many of these variables, but decided against using one because of difficulties of interpretation. We conducted correlational and factor analyses of the variables in this section and others and analyzed unweighted indexes, factor-weighted indexes, and several individual demographic variables in regressions to explain fiscal strain indicators. See Clark, "Fiscal Management of American Cities"; Erwin Zimmerman, "Memoranda on Modeling" (University of Chicago, 1976); and Terry N. Clark, Irene S. Rubin, Lynne C. Pettler, and Erwin Zimmerman, *How Many New Yorks? The New York Fiscal Crisis in Comparative Perspective*, Comparative Study of Community Decision-Making, Research Report no. 76 (University of Chicago, 1976). Inspection of table 1 can reveal what more elaborate analyses show; there is no clear single cluster. Several clusters can be extracted depending on the criteria applied. But difficulties in interpreting composite variables are such that results are usually clearer with individual variables, as used here.

We analyzed the sixty-two permanent community sample (PCS) cities using data collected by the National Opinion Research Center (NORC). The cities were selected for NORC citizen surveys and are thus representative of the places of residence of the American population down to 50,000 in population. Over the past eighteen years the PCS has become the largest data file in existence concerning local political processes and fiscal policy in American cities. The sample, data, and other issues considered briefly here are elaborated in Terry Nichols Clark and Lorna C. Ferguson, *City Money: Political Processes, Fiscal Strain, and Retrenchment* (Columbia University Press, 1983).

Table 1. *Relationships among Socioeconomic Characteristics of Sixty-two U.S. Cities*[a]

Characteristic	Northeast region[b]	East central region[b]	Population size	Population change, 1960–75	Population density	Age of city	Percentage of old housing	Percentage black	Percentage of families below federal poverty level	Median family income	Market value of taxable property	City wealth index[c]
Northeast region[b]	1.00											
East central region[b]	0.50	1.00										
Population size	0.04	−0.06	1.00									
Population change, 1960–75	−0.28	−0.39	−0.06	1.00								
Population density	0.45	0.40	0.41	−0.39	1.00							
Age of city	0.46	0.23	0.57	−0.58	0.48	1.00						
Percentage of old housing	0.43	0.40	0.15	−0.86	0.53	0.78	1.00					
Percentage black	−0.03	−0.15	0.53	−0.39	0.33	0.54	0.54	1.00				
Percentage of families below federal poverty level	0.13	−0.18	0.47	−0.40	0.21	0.70	0.41	0.75	1.00			
Median family income	−0.21	0.05	−0.24	0.46	−0.08	−0.63	−0.51	−0.49	−0.89	1.00		
Market value of taxable property	−0.31	−0.28	0.05	0.34	−0.07	−0.37	−0.41	−0.19	−0.41	0.61	1.00	
City wealth index[c]	−0.34	−0.20	0.03	0.43	−0.08	−0.46	−0.49	−0.24	−0.54	0.74	0.95	1.00
Change in median family income, 1960–70	−0.09	−0.07	−0.07	0.59	−0.30	−0.42	−0.60	−0.28	−0.37	0.39	0.27	0.39

Source: Author's calculations based on data from U.S. Census Bureau and National Opinion Research Center.

a. These are simple r's (Pearson correlation coefficients) for the sixty-two permanent community sample (PCS) cities. If $r \geq 0.21$, $p \leq 0.10$; if $r \geq 0.32$, $p \leq 0.01$.

b. 1 = in region; 0 = not in region.

c. Median family income and equalized taxable property value, weighted by city's percentage of reliance on property taxes for own revenues.

the Northeast to spend more than others. But they do not. As shown in table 2, few of the socioeconomic characteristics were significantly related to any measures of fiscal policy; this is true whether one is trying to explain either overall levels of expenditure and debt or changes from one period to the next.[7] This suggests that socioeconomic characteristics do not completely determine local governments' fiscal policies; rather the two are often distinct. Some cities that are large, old, and in the Northeast spend at high levels, but not all such cities do. Some city officials adapt to social changes; others do not.

This point is illustrated by an examination of expenditure levels for basic services in nineteen cities (table 3). Thirteen are in the Northeast, large in population, old, and densely populated. Yet their expenditures differ markedly; Boston spent almost twice as much per capita as Pittsburgh. Similarly, outside the Northeast there are cities like Atlanta and San Francisco, which share many socioeconomic characteristics and fiscal problems with cities like New York and Philadelphia. The presence of so many "exceptions" to the stereotype generates the low correlations in the previous tables. Social and economic characteristics of cities provide resources that their city governments may or may not draw upon; one cannot explain fiscal policy outputs by these resources alone.[8]

7. Empirical analyses in this section are deliberately kept simple. We present bivariate relationships, but instead of using contingency tables we use correlations that make the low relationships clearer. The weak results were a surprise. Our concern here is not to refute any single theory, only to show that relations are weak enough that further variables are important to consider. These simple correlations are further weakened when variables from this table are included individually in multiple regression analyses with the core variables discussed below. While many of the variables have significant effects on fiscal measures, they do not suppress the significance of the political variables included in the core model. More recent data are not used due to the time necessary for the Census Bureau to collect fiscal and other data from individual cities and then for completion of the sort of analysis in this paper. While the numbers obviously change over time for individual cities, they are unlikely to affect major relationships among variables.

8. The distinction between private resources and public expenditures was stressed in Terry N. Clark and others, *How Many New Yorks?*; and Terry N. Clark, ed., "A Symposium Issue: Community Development," *Urban Affairs Papers*, vol. 3 (1981); and it has been elaborated by Peggy L. Cuciti, *City Need and the Responsiveness of Federal Grants Programs* (Congressional Budget Office, 1978); Touche Ross and Company and The First National Bank of Boston, *Urban Fiscal Stress* (Lexington Books, 1979); U.S. Department of the Treasury, Office of State and Local Finance, *Report on the Fiscal Impact of the Economic Stimulus Package on Urban Governments* (Government Printing Office, 1978); and John P. Ross and James Greenfield, "Measuring the Health of Cities," in Charles H. Levine and Irene Rubin, eds., *Fiscal Stress and Public Policy* (Beverly Hills: Sage Books, 1981), pp. 89–112.

Table 2. *Relationships between Selected Characteristics of Cities and Measures of Their Fiscal Policy*[a]

Characteristic	Total tax burden	Change in long-term debt 1960–70	1970–74	1974–77	Change in common functions 1960–70	1970–74	1974–77	Change in own revenues 1960–70	1970–74	1974–77	Change in general expenditures 1960–70	1970–74	1974–77	General expenditures, 1977[b]	Long-term debt, 1977[b]	Own revenues, 1977[b]	Common functions, 1977
Northeast region[c]	0.07	0.23	0.13	0.22	0.19	−0.35	−0.20	0.02	−0.09	0.00	0.28	−0.02	−0.01	−0.16	−0.26	0.09	0.09
East central region[c]	0.07	−0.08	0.22	0.05	0.09	−0.02	−0.21	0.06	0.04	−0.37	0.05	0.19	−0.30	−0.11	−0.16	0.11	0.01
Population size	0.04	0.05	0.18	0.22	0.02	0.24	0.00	0.06	0.10	0.04	0.21	0.10	0.08	0.12	0.32	−0.12	0.39
Population change, 1960–75	−0.09	−0.19	−0.20	−0.24	−0.42	0.16	0.16	−0.42	−0.14	0.25	−0.47	−0.14	0.14	−0.13	0.00	−0.04	−0.36
Population density	0.43	0.00	0.09	0.12	0.30	−0.28	−0.20	0.06	0.00	−0.16	0.29	−0.02	−0.02	0.11	−0.16	0.00	0.44
Age of city	−0.03	0.44	0.23	0.48	0.16	0.03	−0.13	0.32	0.07	−0.07	0.58	0.06	0.03	0.09	0.18	−0.14	0.38
Percentage of old housing	0.05	0.28	0.19	0.38	0.17	−0.15	−0.22	0.39	0.09	−0.24	0.62	0.11	−0.09	0.03	−0.05	−0.02	0.33
Percentage black	0.09	0.21	0.00	0.04	0.06	0.17	−0.24	0.24	0.16	−0.27	0.43	0.03	−0.16	0.21	0.30	−0.19	0.29
Percentage of families below poverty level	−0.10	0.42	0.05	0.30	0.00	0.05	−0.09	0.26	0.00	−0.08	0.44	0.07	0.02	0.23	0.34	−0.18	0.18
Median family income	0.20	−0.43	−0.18	−0.38	0.00	0.06	−0.05	−0.23	0.06	0.00	−0.34	−0.14	−0.09	−0.14	−0.25	0.15	−0.03
Market value of taxable property	0.11	−0.16	−0.14	−0.17	0.10	0.10	−0.07	−0.04	0.17	0.12	−0.18	−0.02	−0.05	0.04	−0.04	0.38	−0.09
City wealth index[d]	0.13	−0.25	−0.14	−0.25	0.11	0.11	−0.07	−0.07	0.19	0.09	−0.24	−0.02	−0.05	0.00	−0.09	0.34	0.06
Change in median family income, 1960–70	−0.13	−0.28	−0.01	−0.04	0.05	0.10	0.06	−0.13	0.12	0.03	−0.39	0.01	−0.01	−0.13	0.14	0.05	−0.18

Source: Author's calculations based on data from U.S. Census Bureau and National Opinion Research Center.

a. See note a, table 1. The measures of fiscal policy output (revenue, expenditure, or debt) presented here can be deflated by resource measures to generate fiscal strain indicators. They are undeflated here to assess the degree of interrelation between socioeconomic characteristics and fiscal policy measures.

b. The three noncommon function level measures are regressed on the index of functional performance, which measures the range of functions performed by the city government.

c. 1 = in region; 0 = not in region.

d. See note c, table 1.

Table 3. *Expenditures on Basic Municipal Services, Nineteen U.S. Cities, 1977*
Dollars

City	Per capita expenditure[a]
Northeast	
Boston	280
Baltimore	258
Newark	252
Philadelphia	244
Cleveland	240
Minneapolis	239
New York	224
Detroit	223
St. Paul	207
St. Louis	201
Chicago	188
Milwaukee	178
Pittsburgh	144
South and West	
Atlanta	201
Long Beach	289
Palo Alto	294
Pasadena	236
San Francisco	262
Seattle	270

Source: Author's calculations from U.S. Census Bureau data. These are two subsets of the sixty-two PCS cities, selected to illustrate diversity among northeastern cities and high spending by some in the South and West.

a. On common functions, which include police, fire, highways, sewerage, sanitation, general buildings, parks and recreation, general control, and financial administration.

Is Population Loss a Source of Strain?

Population decline is a widely used measure of urban distress.[9] Some even see population loss as a direct cause of fiscal strain.[10] Indeed, the idea

9. Richard P. Nathan and Paul R. Dommel, "The Cities," in Joseph A. Pechman, ed., *Setting National Priorities: The 1978 Budget* (Brookings, 1977), pp. 283–316.

10. Thomas Muller asked, "What is the relationship between local fiscal solvency and good economic health?" and answered, "There is little doubt that the most important prerequisite to fiscal well-being is a sound local private-sector economy," using population change data as documentation. See "Is the Urban Crisis Over?" Hearings before the Subcommittee on Fiscal and Intergovernmental Policy of the Joint Economic Committee, 96 Cong. 1 sess. (GPO, 1979), p. 91. See also George Sternlieb and James W. Hughes, eds., *Post-Industrial America: Metropolitan Decline and Inter-Regional Job Shifts* (Rutgers University, Center for Urban Policy Research, 1975). These authors have expressed more qualified views in other writings. See also Muller, *Growing and Declining Urban Areas;* and Peterson, "Finance."

that population loss causes fiscal strain was emphasized in the background report for President Carter's national urban policy to help justify the urban development action grants and aim them toward the "neediest cities" and to incorporate population change in the 1978 dual formula for community development block grants.[11]

What is the evidence that population loss is actually related to the fiscal policies of city governments? If population declines, and spending does too, the city will not suffer fiscal strain. Per capita spending then will not increase with population declines. But the inertia of policymakers and expectations of citizens and organized groups, especially city employees, can make it hard to adjust expenditures downward as population shrinks. New York City is a common example of the long lag between population decline and fiscal policy adjustment. In such cases population decline does have unhappy fiscal consequences.

Closer analysis indicates that relations between population change and expenditure vary over time (table 4). From 1960 to 1965 changes in per capita general expenditures and population were unrelated. But from 1965 to 1972 and 1970 to 1974 the relationship was negative; that is, cities losing population increased expenditures faster than cities gaining population. In 1974–77, however, this relationship reversed itself: cities decreasing in population also decreased expenditures. The same pattern holds for revenues raised from a city's own tax base, indicating that intergovernmental revenues did not change these relationships.[12] If these were the only available data, one might conclude that fiscal adaptations to population

11. For the background report, see Urban Regional Policy Group, *A New Partnership to Conserve America's Communities: A National Urban Policy*, HUD-S-297, U.S. Department of Housing and Urban Development (GPO, 1978). The politics of the national urban policy and the three "distress standards" (pre-1939 housing, poverty, and below-average population growth) did not escape one Texas observer, who said this "discriminatory urban package . . . [is] clear evidence that the Administration has associated itself with Massachusetts Speaker Tip O'Neill, New York Senator Jacob Javits and other members of the frostbelt coalition [which] has been hard at work pushing through discriminatory legislation deliberately designed to let the Northeast raid the federal treasury at our expense." R. J. Hoyer, "President Carter's Urban Policy: Some Second Thoughts," *Texas Town and City*, vol. 65 (October 1978), pp. 5–12. See also George Vernez, Roger J. Vaughan, and Robert K. Yin, *Federal Activities in Urban Economic Development*, Report R-2372-EDA (Santa Monica: Rand Corp., 1979), pp. 72–73.

12. The dates on the two axes of the table do not exactly match. We could have added additional shorter periods for population change, but decided not to for several reasons. The population figures between the decennial censuses (unlike the fiscal data) are only estimates, so it is better not to overinterpret them. Rankings across cities would also differ little if we used population change for 1960–65 instead of 1960–70, and would complicate presentation.

Table 4. *Relationships between Changes in Municipal Expenditures and Revenues and Population Changes, 1960–77*[a]

Expenditure and revenue change[b]	Population changes[b]	
	1960–70	1970–75
Changes in per capita general expenditures		
1960–65	0.038	. . .
1965–72	− 0.396	. . .
1970–74	. . .	− 0.207
1974–77	. . .	0.195
Changes in own per capita revenue		
1960–70	− 0.441	. . .
1970–74	. . .	− 0.241
1974–77	. . .	0.315

a. See note a, table 1.
b. Percentage changes.

declines are slow and uneven, thereby generating at least temporary fiscal crises.

But this interpretation should not be applied mechanically. For population loss to generate fiscal problems city government revenues must (1) decrease with population declines, and (2) decrease more than any decline in the level of expenditures that might also occur. Neither of these two linkages appears to be necessarily true. Population loss does not inevitably decrease revenue. The link must go through specific revenue sources, the most important being the property tax. Does population loss diminish property values and in turn property tax revenues? No doubt it can do so eventually, but in the short run population losses have not generated such effects.

As for expenditures, population loss could increase per capita costs if economies of scale were significant. Research to date, however, suggests diseconomies of scale for services like police and fire.[13] There are expenditures that could increase if the remaining population were older, poorer, and more costly to local government. Cities losing population do have slightly more poor and black residents (table 1). Still, these relationships

13. Elinor Ostrom, "Metropolitan Reform: Propositions Derived from Two Traditions," *Social Science Quarterly*, vol. 53 (December 1972), pp. 474–93; and Elinor Ostrom and others, *Community Organization and the Provision of Police Services* (Sage Papers in Administrative and Policy Studies, 1973). Some costs like fixed equipment maintenance are, of course, less susceptible to short-term reductions when population declines. Peterson, "Finance," p. 44.

are not overwhelming.[14] The evidence is weak that population loss inherently increases service costs; many other variables complicate the relationship.

The effects of population loss are weakened by other factors. One is the increase in illegal aliens, which results in an undocumented population increase.[15] Another is the size of urban households, which has declined for several decades as a result of longer life spans, later marriages, fewer children, and more singles.[16] These factors generate more demand for housing and increase property values. Property values are still high and increasing in many "declining" cities.[17]

Concern about population decline often reflects a projection of what might occur if it continues. Decline was a new public issue in the mid-1970s, and initial reactions were often exaggerated. Yet local officials in Pittsburgh, for example, point out that population decline helped eliminate slums and crowding, permitted construction of more spacious parks, and allowed for more desirable land use. Public debates emerged in the mid-1970s on such themes as "urban conservation," "small is beautiful," and "gentrification." The opposite arguments from those of population decline were even applied to gentrification: more rich residents are bad. But the extent of gentrification has been exaggerated in many discussions.[18] The idea that any population decline is undesirable seems less widespread than just a few years ago. Still, for city government staff, adapting to declining resources is usually more difficult than adapting to growth. When decline is rapid, and unions and civil service boards are strong, it is especially hard for leaders to adapt. But many cities still do.

In brief, population changes and other economic and social character-

14. William H. Frey, "Central City White Flight: Racial and Non-racial Causes," *American Sociological Review*, vol. 44 (June 1979), pp. 425–48.

15. Data are crude because illegal aliens avoid census takers. U.S. government estimates of illegal aliens vary from 5 to 12 million, although a Mexican government study puts the numbers of Mexicans at only 1 million. *New York Times*, October 13, 1980.

16. William Alonso, "The Current Halt in the Metropolitan Phenomenon," in Charles L. Leven, ed., *The Mature Metropolis* (Lexington, Mass.: Heath-Lexington Books, 1978), pp. 30–45.

17. The less acute decline in households than in total population and the persistent growth of the market value of property in many cities declining in population appear in a table from George A. Reigeluth, "The Economic Base," in George E. Peterson, ed., *Urban Economic and Fiscal Indicators* (Washington D.C.: Urban Institute, 1978), p. 8a. It shows, for example, that Boston lost more households than other cities from 1970 to 1975, yet its property values increased more than San Diego's.

18. Shirley B. Laska and Daphne Spain, eds., *Back to the City: Issues in Neighborhood Renovation* (Pergamon, 1980).

istics can indicate problems to which local officials must adapt. But whether and how they adapt is not determined by the economic and social context, as is clear from large differences in fiscal policies across cities confronting similar social and economic circumstances. Social and economic characteristics are important resources; they do not by themselves decide fiscal policies.

Fiscal strain is a lack of adaptation by a city government to declines in its socioeconomic base and can be measured by a ratio of city government spending or debt to indicators of a city's economic resources. Fiscal strain can be reduced by either trimming expenditures and debt or increasing the economic resources of the community. While some local officials may seek to increase their economic base, this is much harder in the short term than changing expenditures, debt, and other government policies, which over time may encourage private development.[19] Addressing growth and productivity is an important national issue, and one to which city governments may contribute.[20] But it is naive for local public officials to expect to have major effects on the community's wealth in the short terms during which most of them hold office. Fiscal balance can be achieved much more readily by attending to the expenditure policies of the city government itself than by encouraging economic growth in the private sector.

Modeling Fiscal Policymaking

If social and economic factors by themselves do not explain fiscal strain, what does? My interpretation incorporates four theoretical perspectives: economic base, citizen preference, organized groups, and political leaders.[21]

1. Economic and population base. Some theories, as reviewed above, look to the city's economic strength for an explanation of the fiscal well-being of its public sector. Drawing on this perspective, I include local income and equalized taxable property value as wealth measures, but I

19. Clark, "Fiscal Management of American Cities"; and Terry N. Clark, ed., *Urban Affairs Annual Reviews*, vol. 21: *Urban Policy Analysis* (Sage, 1981).

20. John D. Kasarda, "The Implications of Contemporary Distribution Trends for National Urban Policy," *Social Science Quarterly*, vol. 61 (December 1980), pp. 369–400.

21. The theory of urban fiscal strain summarized here is elaborated in Terry N. Clark and Lorna C. Ferguson, "Fiscal Strain and Fiscal Health in American Cities: Six Basic Processes," in Kenneth Newton, ed., *Urban Political Economy* (St. Martin's, 1981), pp. 135–55; and Clark and Ferguson, *City Money*.

conceive of them more as resources facilitating implementation of preferences than as direct causes of decisions.

2. Citizen preferences. Analyses that interpret public policies as largely the response of political leaders to the preferences of voters identify citizen preferences as the key force behind public policies.[22] In drawing upon this body of research, I find it convenient to introduce the concept of a bloc or sector to refer to citizens sharing preferences concerning local fiscal policy. I explored potential blocs of citizens by using survey data, and retained three for most analyses: black citizens, middle-class citizens (defined by income), and municipal employees. The poor were initially included in the analysis, but the effects of this sector were seldom statistically significant.

3. Organized groups. The group theory tradition emphasizes organized groups as the mechanism by which interests are translated into public policy.[23] Citizens are seen as too poorly informed to be influential; instead, leaders respond to organized groups that emerge in areas where policy preferences are intense. Some advocates even make the claim that public policies are simply a reflection of the balance of interests among major groups. But if groups reflect all relevant interests that citizens have, and if policies in turn reflect group activities, then group theory can be reduced to a citizen preference theory. Group theory can be stretched in this way, but I prefer instead to treat organized groups as something different from the opinions of large blocs of voters. I have thus included measures of the activities and influence of the principal organized groups affecting urban fiscal policy and have assessed their effects empirically. Two groups were retained for the core model: the percentage of municipal employees organized for collective bargaining and the political activity level of black groups. Other measures that were analyzed but found to be insignificant included the power of business groups, civic groups, neighborhood groups, and poor groups.

4. Political leaders. According to elite theories of Pareto, Mosca, and Schumpeter, and selected studies of American cities,[24] leaders have their

22. Preference aggregation problems, as identified by Arrow, have many solutions and are handled by Downs largely by assuming a two-party system and single-peaked, unidimensional citizen preferences. See Anthony Downs, *An Economic Theory of Democracy* (Harper and Row, 1957); Kenneth J. Arrow, *Social Choice and Individual Values*, 2d ed. (Wiley, 1963); and Amartya K. Sen, *Collective Choice and Social Welfare* (Holden-Day, 1970).

23. David B. Truman, *The Governmental Process* (Alfred A. Knopf, 1951); and Robert A. Dahl, *Who Governs?* (Yale University Press, 1961).

24. Dahl, *Who Governs?*

own independent policy impact. These writers reject the claim (made by proponents of the citizen preference theory) that leaders simply translate public opinion into policy decisions. In my analysis, I am able to determine whether leaders are only brokers who carry out the preferences of others or are dynamic leaders who impart their own preferences in formulating public policy. As the major policies of interest here are related to city government spending, leaders' preferences were measured either by coding campaign statements of mayoral candidates or by asking mayors and council members about their preferences for spending levels in each of eleven policy areas. Since more powerful leaders should have more impact, the leaders' preferences were weighted by their power, as measured by interviews with other local leaders or by legal characteristics such as appointment powers.

The factors identified by these four theories—economic base, blocs of citizens, organized interests, and political leaders—do not necessarily influence fiscal policy the same way under all circumstances. For example, the importance of the economic base can be seen especially when one looks at cities over a long time period or in connection with a major outlay of funds. The impact of citizens is especially great when their fiscal policy preferences are more homogeneous, because this allows political leaders to better discern what the public wants. Citizens are more important when leaders have more information about citizen preferences. Similarly, citizens are more important in cities where there are fewer political disturbances (strikes, riots, newly active organized groups). These last three characteristics reinforce one another to heighten the importance of citizen preferences and reduce that of organized groups and political leaders. For example, in a small, homogeneous town, leaders can be reasonably well informed of citizen preferences, as there is a broad consensus on many issues. Thus political leaders act primarily as brokers who implement the well-defined views of their community, and they do not appear to have any independent effect on fiscal policy. But in large, heterogeneous, conflictual cities, many voting combinations are possible and organized groups are more active. Leaders can play a dynamic role in forming governing coalitions; thus their own policy views appear as a decisive factor affecting fiscal policy.

A Model to Test the Factors Affecting Urban Fiscal Policy

A core model of seven variables was specified, including measures of the size of the middle-class and black blocs, organized activity of municipal employees, political leaders' spending preferences, and an index of city wealth. The range of functions for which the city government was responsible was measured with an index of functional performance, permitting analysis of noncommon functions like general expenditures and debt as well as the functions common to most cities. Building on past work, the percentage of Irish residents was included to indicate citizen support for organized groups and a more traditional patronage style of politics.[25]

Two broad fiscal policy measures were used as dependent variables. These included fiscal policy outputs and fiscal strain indicators. Fiscal policy outputs were general expenditures, the city's own revenues, common functions, and long-term debt, both per capita in 1977 and as percentages for three periods from 1960 to 1977. Fiscal strain indicators were computed by dividing each fiscal policy output by one of three measures of economic

25. The core model was specified as:

$$(1)\ FS_i\ =\ \gamma PSR_k^a L^b OM^c IR^d MC^e FP^f BL^g W^h \epsilon$$

and

$$(2)\ FPO_j\ =\ \gamma L^a OM^b IR^c MC^d FP^e BL^f W^g \epsilon,$$

where

FS_i = fiscal strain indicator i;
FPO_j = fiscal policy output j;
PSR_k = private-sector resource k;
L = leadership interaction term (leader's preferences times leader's power);
OM = organization of municipal employees;
IR = percentage of Irish stock residents (legitimating separable goods);
MC = percentage middle-class families ($\$10,000–\$15,000$ median family income in 1969);
FP = index of functional performance;
BL = percentage of black residents (used for all fiscal policy outputs except 1970–74 changes, when black political activities used);
W = index of city wealth (median family income and equalized taxable property value, weighted by city's percentage of reliance on property taxes for own revenues);
a to h = coefficients to be estimated;
γ = constant;
ϵ = error term.

The above equations show only direct effects. Total (direct plus indirect) effects are generally similar for the major fiscal policy outputs and fiscal strain indicators, especially general expenditures, within each time period and are summarized in table 5.

Twenty-five other variables were added to the core model one at a time to assess possible effects on fiscal policies, including population size and change, percentage poor, change in percentage poor and percentage black, cost of living, opportunity wages in services, intergovernmental revenues, percentage of own revenues from property taxes, and reform government (city manager, at-large elections, and nonpartisanship). Several had significant direct effects, but none suppressed below significance more than 7 percent of the core model coefficients.

Table 5. *A Summary of Regression Analyses of the Determinants of Fiscal Policy and Fiscal Strain*

| Independent variable | Measure of fiscal policy or fiscal strain[a] | | | |
	Change, 1960–70	Change, 1970–74	Change, 1974–77	Per capita level, 1977
Size of middle-class bloc	Minus	Zero	Minus	Minus
Size of black bloc	Plus	Zero	Zero	Zero
Index of functional performance[b]	Zero	Zero	Zero	Plus
Organized activity of municipal employees	Zero	Zero	Zero	Zero
Ethnic political culture	Zero	Zero	Zero	Plus
Political leaders' spending preference multiplied by their power	Zero	Plus	Zero	Plus
Index of city wealth[c]	Zero	Zero	Zero	Plus

a. See text for definition of measures of fiscal policy and fiscal strain.
b. See note b, table 2.
c. See note c, table 1.

resources: population change, median family income change, or a city wealth index combining equalized taxable property value and median family income. Sixteen fiscal policy outputs and twenty-two fiscal strain indicators were each analyzed separately with the core model. The basic results are summarized in table 5.

The comprehensive approach exemplifed in this model resolves many apparent conflicts from the past. For example, debates over the relative importance of voting blocs, organized groups, and elites are resolved by indicating how each is important to different types of cities and time periods. There are striking differences among the three periods and the 1977 level (table 5).

Growth in the 1960s: The Importance of Bloc Size

The 1960s was a decade of general growth in fiscal expenditures. Cities with large middle classes increased expenditures less between 1960 and 1970, while those with more black residents increased expenditures more. Both findings illustrate the importance of voting blocs since the larger a bloc is in a city, the more responsive fiscal policies are to it. Organized groups and political leaders had fewer effects. These patterns did not hold for every city; scatterplots indicate that some cities like New York, Boston, and San Francisco were well above the regression line, which suggests that they were increasing spending more than the size of their middle class or black blocs predicted. By the end of the decade they were joined by enough other cities to shift the national pattern. Exact timing varies by city, but from the late 1960s until about 1974 new patterns of decisionmaking emerged.

The Late 1960s and Early 1970s:
The Dynamic Political Leader Emerges

In this second period the influence of voting blocs falls and that of political leadership rises in importance. Cities with powerful leaders who favored more spending increased expenditures from 1970 to 1974. What led mayors to campaign for more expenditures? We correlated mayors' campaign statements with many plausible sources, but most seemed to have no effect. Neither size nor change in black and poor blocs, nor median family income, nor unionization had any measurable effects (table 6). The only three variables that turned out to be of significance were three that measured black political activity. Mayors campaigned for more spending: (1) if their cities had suffered severe racial disorders; (2) if "ethnic and religious groups" were powerful supporters of the mayor; and (3) if blacks were active supporters of the mayor. Of course, only cities with numerous black citizens experienced such activities; and the larger the bloc, the more likely were these three activities. The causal ordering thus runs from numerous black citizens to black political activities, which in turn persuaded leaders to campaign on, and then implement, higher spending programs (see figure 1).[26] Surprisingly, black political activities had no effect on fiscal policy independent of mayoral commitments. Thus it seems that a sizable black community and organized group activities were important as background factors, but a dynamic political leader was essential to implement their spending preferences into actual fiscal policies.

These results recall the urban turmoil of the late 1960s, punctuated by riots, arson, and militant black groups. The mass disorders that marked this period were concentrated in the late 1960s. Municipal employee strikes showed a similar upsurge in these years.[27] While these trends are part of

26. This sequence was estimated using a recursive system of regression equations, which interestingly indicate zero direct effects on fiscal policy from size and political activity of the black sector.

27. Clark and Ferguson, *City Money*.

Table 6. *Relationship between Selected Economic and Political Factors and Mayoral Campaign Statements concerning Municipal Spending*[a]

Economic and political factor	Mayoral campaign statements
Percentage of families below federal poverty level, 1969	−0.038
Change in percentage of poor families (below $3,000), 1959–69	−0.037
Percentage of black families, 1970	−0.042
Change in percentage of blacks, 1960–70	0.140
Black families as percentage of all families below federal poverty level, 1969	0.187
Percentage of middle-class families ($10,000–$15,000 median family income), 1969	−0.189
Index of severity of racial disorders	0.306*
Power of ethnic and religious groups supporting mayor, 1967	0.290*
Importance of blacks supporting mayor, 1967	0.227*
Index of agreement between mayor and business groups	0.038
Business power factor	0.038
Unionization	−0.110
Median family income	−0.021
Importance of neighborhood groups supporting mayor, 1967	0.059
Percentage of Irish residents	−0.118
Index of city wealth	−0.008

* Significant at 10 percent level.
a. These are simple correlations (r's) between the mayor's campaign statements and each of the other variables.

the common wisdom, it was surprising to see how powerful an effect they had on urban fiscal policy.

The distinctiveness of the late 1960s and early 1970s is clear in several related developments. The civil rights movement, anti–Vietnam war rallies, and political campaigns of McCarthy and McGovern helped focus these activities. The Johnson administration supported black claims of racial injustice and sought changes through Great Society programs. An analysis of the political participation of young adults and their parents from 1956 to 1976 found the late 1960s and early 1970s deviant, in that the young were substantially more politically active, as were Americans young and old on the ideological left.[28] At the same time, mayors were being

28. Paul Allen Beck and M. Kent Jennings, "Political Periods and Political Participation," *American Political Science Review*, vol. 73 (September 1979), pp. 737–50.

Figure 1. *Effect of Black Political Activity and Responsive Mayors*
on Increased Municipal Spending, 1970–74[a]

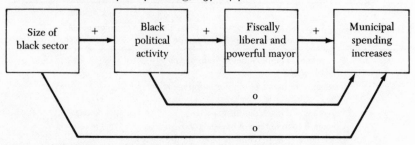

Source: Author's calculations based on data from U.S. Census Bureau and National Opinion Research Center.
a. + = clear positive relationship; o = no relationship.

urged by many policy advisers to be more dynamic.[29] Two comparative
studies found mayors in the 1960s to have significant effects on public
policy; one of these found that organized groups reinforced mayoral initiatives.[30] A sympathetic national climate and specific political and fiscal
incentives encouraged cities to undertake more ambitious social programs.
It is consistent with the above propositions that in cities and time periods
characterized by greater political instability and mobilization of new sectors,
organized groups and political leaders emerge as more important determinants of public policy.[31]

Figure 2 elaborates the above results. Its horizontal axis is the leadership
measure used in the regression analysis: the mayor's support for government
spending as indicated by his campaign statements, multiplied by his power.
Cities on the far right, such as Gary, Indiana, had powerful mayors who
favored spending.

Gary is a valuable case, as it shows the dynamics behind the statistical
results and is a striking illustration of national trends. From the Depression
until the mid-1960s a strong Democratic party organization dominated
Gary politics. As whites' prosperity increased, they became less attached

29. Leonard I. Ruchelman, ed., *Big City Mayors* (Indiana University Press, 1970); and
John P. Kotter and Paul R. Lawrence, *Mayors in Action* (Wiley, 1974).

30. Wen H. Kuo, "Mayoral Influence in Urban Policy Making," *American Journal of
Sociology*, vol. 79 (November 1973), pp. 620–38; and Gerald R. Salanick and Jeffrey Pfeffer,
"Constraints on Administration Discretion: The Limited Influence of Mayors on City Budgets,"
Urban Affairs Quarterly, vol. 12 (1977), pp. 475–98.

31. Mark C. Eckel, "Political Instability and Policy Responsiveness in Fifty-one American
Cities" (M.A. essay, University of Chicago, 1980). His analysis of PCS cities using city-specific
disturbance measures finds political leaders more important in cities with more riots and
strikes.

to the machine and its patronage politics. Simultaneously, blacks grew to almost half the city's population and provided the machine's principal base. In 1963 the party's mayoral candidate, Martin Katz, lost every white precinct but won because of party loyalty in black precincts. Richard Hatcher was elected to the council the same year and was expected to cooperate with the machine, as had all previous black council members. But he soon made it clear that he represented a new black politics. In 1967 he was elected mayor, defeating Katz. In the late 1960s, when he controlled neither the party nor the council, he built up a coalition of supporters generously funded by the Ford Foundation, other private foundations, and federal grants. His opponents initially kept down expenditures, but after 1971 Hatcher controlled the council and had a freer hand in implementing fiscal policies. Manpower programs, housing, and social services increased dramatically. General expenditures grew by 112 percent from 1970 to 1974, more than in all but two of the sixty-two cities. Hatcher showed considerable talent in obtaining outside funds: intergovernmental revenues increased 307 percent from 1970 to 1974, and the city's own revenues, mostly property taxes, went up just 60 percent. Richard Hatcher exemplifies the dynamic political leader discussed above. He mobilized a new electoral base, raised substantial resources, and gradually consolidated his leadership. But this pattern of growth ended for Gary in 1974.

Fiscal Retrenchment in 1974–77

Retrenchment began in about half the sample cities in 1974. However, it was only after Proposition 13 passed in California in 1978 that many Americans realized the importance of this development for the future of the welfare state.

SOURCES OF RETRENCHMENT. The role of government has been seriously questioned; continuing debates are illuminated by examining the most common interpretations of the sources of retrenchment.

1. Early assessments of Proposition 13 saw retrenchment as specific to California—linked to the state's surplus, real estate boom, or peculiar politics. This is undercut by the city-level data, which show retrenchment starting in 1974, thus preceding Proposition 13 in half the cities.

2. Two interpretations stress economic resources. One is that recession constrained resources and hence government. Widely argued as an explanation for the New York fiscal crisis, this does not account for the increasing

Figure 2. *Relationship between Mayoral Support for Municipal Spending and Increase in General Expenditures in Forty-two U.S. Cities, 1970–74*

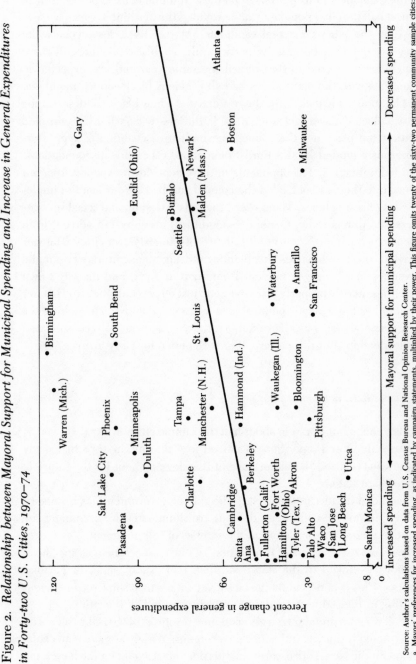

Source: Author's calculations based on data from U.S. Census Bureau and National Opinion Research Center.
a. Mayors' preferences for increased spending, as indicated by campaign statements, multiplied by their power. This figure omits twenty of the sixty-two permanent community sample cities: Albany, Baltimore, Chicago, Cleveland, Clifton (N.J.), Dallas, Detroit, Houston, Indianapolis, Irvington (N.J.), Jacksonville, Los Angeles, Memphis, New York, Philadelphia, St. Paul, St. Petersburg, San Antonio, San Diego, and Schenectady.

retrenchment over the later 1970s, even after the mid-1970s recession had come to an end.[32]

3. Next is the declining Northeast syndrome argument, which I have already shown to be weak. City wealth and changes in wealth and population were similarly unrelated to spending changes, as shown in the core model.

4. Another resource interpretation is that cutbacks in federal aid drove cities into difficulty. But I find that retrenchment began locally and before most federal cutbacks. When intergovernmental revenue is added as another variable to the core model, either as a percentage change for each of the three periods or for the 1977 level, it does not suppress core variable coefficients. This deflates the Washington-centered conception of cities. Even though cities like Gary used considerable outside funds, they had a strong local commitment to such programs. In the same period some cities, like Dallas, refused to apply for many federal programs. When the Comprehensive Employment and Training Act (CETA) ended, New York continued many employees with local funds, while Chicago terminated CETA-supported programs, and Dallas, having never participated, had nothing to change. All illustrate the dynamics of using intergovernmental revenues to achieve local priorities.

5. Neo-Marxists have accused banks and business elites of generating urban fiscal crisis by encouraging the uneven development of capital across cities and regions.[33] One version of this argument leads to a Northeast syndrome interpretation, as considered above. Another version stresses business elites as a conservative interest group seeking reduced government spending. This has, for example, been a popular explanation for expenditure cuts in New York City. I too expected powerful business leadership to suppress spending, but an analysis of many different types and combinations of financial and business leaders did not show this to be the case. This is not because business leaders are unimportant—they are the most important type of organized group in many American cities—but because they are often not fiscally conservative. In about half the PCS cities they supported spending on the model cities program and similar redistributive programs, yet in the other half they opposed such programs. In California most

32. Modest effects of inflation and recession are also suggested in Clark and Ferguson, *City Money*; and Advisory Commission on Intergovernmental Relations, *State-Local Finances in Recession and Inflation*, Report A-70 (GPO, 1979).

33. Roger E. Alcahy and David Mermelstein, eds., *The Fiscal Crisis of American Cities: Essays on the Political Economy of Urban America* (Random House–Vintage Books, 1977); and James R. O'Connor, *The Fiscal Crisis of the State* (St. Martin's, 1973).

business groups opposed Proposition 13, as did most organized groups of every sort. In selected cities business groups forcefully promoted retrenchment in the late 1970s, but across the PCS cities business leaders appear to have had no effects.

6. Municipal employees are also an important organized group, but again I find that they had no significant impact on increasing expenditures over the period from 1960 to 1977 or in preventing retrenchment at the end of the period. This counterintuitive result comes from the fact that where strong unions increase compensation, numbers of employees also decrease, offsetting the fiscal effects of the increased compensation. Gary, where unions are weak, expanded its work force in the late 1970s while New York, where unions are powerful, trimmed its back, so that by 1977 New York paid over $17,000 per average employee while Gary paid $6,208.

7. What of political leaders? Certainly Edward Koch has been blamed for retrenchment by many New Yorkers, as have Peter Flaherty in Pittsburgh and Pete Wilson in San Diego. But while these mayors were more fiscally conservative than many of their predecessors, were political leaders independently important or just brokers, reflecting broader currents of opinion? Leaders were independently influential in shaping fiscal policy in the early 1970s, but they did not have any effect independent of other factors shaping policy during the retrenchment of the late 1970s. This in no way denies that political leaders in many cities had forceful confrontations with employees and service recipients who resisted cutbacks. But it suggests that they acted with conviction because they were not alone. They had citizen support behind them.

8. The influence of citizens emerges as the fundamental explanation of retrenchment in my analysis. Retrenchment resulted in large part from a taxpayers' revolt. As I have discussed in more detail elsewhere, the great majority of Americans favor lower taxes.[34] The poor and blacks are less conservative, but they too came to favor reduced spending on items like welfare over the 1970s. Catalysts like Howard Jarvis, author of Proposition 13, helped, but Jarvis had placed tax reduction referenda on the California ballot for years. Proposition 13 succeeded because of a ground swell of support. Mayors and city council members across the country have similarly

34. Clark and Ferguson, *City Money*. Some people have suggested recession and inflation as causes of fiscal conservatism among citizens. Many such factors may have led cities toward fiscal conservatism, but they are insufficient in themselves to explain retrenchment in the late 1970s.

adopted more fiscally conservative policies, some reluctantly, others campaigning vigorously and winning elections on these issues. They have succeeded where and when voters supported them.

EXAMPLES OF RETRENCHMENT. These general patterns are illustrated by considering how selected cities achieved retrenchment. Which cities illustrate the national downtrend in spending? Some that had seen only moderate increases since 1960 still cut back. For example, Hamilton, Ohio; Hammond, Indiana; and Fullerton, California, are cities with large middle-class populations, few minorities, and citizens who consistently seemed to favor Republican leaders and less government spending. These cities' leaders generally held down spending, apparently reflecting their constituents' preferences. Given continued political stability, voter preferences suffice to explain low spending in such cities.

San Diego also illustrates consistent low spending. From 1960 to 1974 it increased expenditures just modestly. Although a larger and more heterogeneous city than those mentioned above, San Diego has few blacks; the principal minority group is Mexican-Americans, who were less mobilized than blacks in the 1960s. San Diego's dominant political culture comes from its large middle- and upper-class population, including a large military and retired segment, and for years Republican mayors and council members fared well on low-spending platforms. Under Mayor Pete Wilson, the property tax rate was cut in the early 1970s (facilitated by the real estate boom). The press is editorially conservative, but plays down local politics; beaches, parks, and recreation are the salient issues. Political parties and ethnic organizations are weak. The Chamber of Commerce and the Taxpayers' Association work closely with the city government to promote tourism and controlled development. A respected Board of Fiscal Overseers is used by the city council to review important policies. The municipal staff has considerable autonomy, is paid well, and has earned a national reputation for innovation in areas like productivity and financial management. The taxpayers' revolt was championed not by leading organized groups, but by four new council members who ran in a vigorous populist manner on antispending issues in 1977. They found enough support from more senior council members to begin trimming the budget by almost 20 percent one year before Proposition 13. In San Diego, as in many already low-spending cities, retrenchment in the mid-1970s simply reinforced traditional policies of fiscal conservatism. As Howard Jarvis remarked, "If all cities were like San Diego, we would not have needed Proposition 13."

But retrenchment was a revolutionary concept in other cities, like New York. Even though John Lindsay warned of bankruptcy in his 1964 campaign for mayor, once in office he and his successor Abraham Beame usually defined New York's problem as too little revenues, not too high expenditures. This changed only after the fiscal crisis of 1975 and considerable pressure from federal and state governments. Taxpayers too seemed to grow more visible. New York often illustrates disparities between the activities of organized groups and the less prominent views of unorganized voters. Apparently no one has surveyed New York citizens on their fiscal policy preferences in the last decade or so (an interesting reflection of its political culture), but most mayoral candidates after the early 1960s ran successfully on programs of fiscal conservatism, at least relative to their predecessors. John Lindsay campaigned as a low-spending Republican in his first term and in his second term won by a plurality only when two conservative opponents split the anti-Lindsay vote. Beame ran initially as the former comptroller who "knows the buck," and the little-known Edward Koch surprised political knowledgeables when, as the most fiscally conservative candidate, he defeated Bella Abzug and the incumbent Beame for the Democratic nomination. Yet once in office all these mayors increased expenditures; some argue they were capitulating to organized group pressures.[35] New York's heterogeneity and political instability strengthened the role of organized groups and political leaders who favored continued high spending. By contrast, when Chicago launched major social programs in the 1960s and 1970s, Mayor Richard Daley kept firm control of them and segregated the funds so that when federal support ended they could be terminated. In New York groups who benefited from these programs often lobbied successfully to continue the programs at local expense.[36]

New York and Chicago are similar in being large and heterogeneous, qualities that encourage activity by organized groups. But until recent years, political leadership was far more stable in Chicago, which reduced uncertainty for political leaders and facilitated responsiveness to the concerns of middle-class citizens about high taxes. The many competing organized groups in New York led political leaders to compromise by letting

35. Ken Auletta, *The Streets Were Paved With Gold* (Random House, 1979); David Rogers, *The Management of Big Cities: Interest Groups and Social Change Strategies* (Sage, 1971); and Donald H. Haider, "Fiscal Scarcity: A New Urban Perspective," in Louis H. Masotti and Robert L. Lineberry, eds., *The New Urban Politics* (Ballinger, 1976), p. 187.

36. Ester Fuchs, "New York and Chicago Fiscal Policies" (Ph.D. dissertation, University of Chicago, 1981); and Charles J. Orlebeke, *Federal Aid to Chicago* (Brookings, 1983).

each group have more, while Chicago's centralized Democratic party under Daley was able to restrain spending on more separable or private goods, like public housing or neighborhood projects. Patronage in Chicago was controlled and allocated through the party to individuals, while in New York organized groups received blocks of jobs and the mayor had little control. After its 1975 fiscal crisis New York did acquire a measure of centralized financial control by establishing the Emergency Financial Control Board. Other cities have adopted varying procedures to centralize control for retrenchment, such as San Diego's Board of Fiscal Overseers or a special committee reporting to the mayor (as in Boston) to make the hard decisions. Centralization in these cases is largely to shield an executive from interest group pressures for more spending on specific projects. The intent is to respond instead to the unorganized citizens who favor lower taxes.

Expenditure and Debt Levels in 1977

Thus far I have discussed changes in fiscal policy from one period to another. This section examines the overall level that expenditures reached in 1977 not only as a result of the changes in the three time periods discussed above but also as a consequence of the accumulated decisions taken by public officials throughout the cities' entire political history. Whenever one examines overall levels of expenditure, as distinct from changes from one period to the next, two findings generally emerge: (1) the role of the economic base of a city becomes more apparent, and (2) the accumulated impact of all the factors identified in separate periods (such as those already discussed) can be discerned. Thus it is not surprising that most of the factors that influenced changes in expenditure in one or more of the three earlier periods also influenced the overall levels of expenditure in 1977. Most findings in table 5 have already been interpreted, but a few are worth emphasizing again in this context.

The city wealth index proved to be an important determinant of the overall level of expenditure, although it had no effect on changes from one period to the next. Wealthier cities spent at higher levels in 1977 as the result of a long, gradual process, much of which predates 1960. Middle-class residents generally favor less spending, but wealthier cities still spend more for reasons analogous to those that lead affluent individuals to consume more private goods. These results illustrate the opposing effects of wealth and the size of the middle class.[37] Thus cities with large middle classes spent less in 1977. However, the size of the black sector was insignificant in determining the level of expenditure. Many cities with large black populations are in the South, which traditionally spent less. Cities performing more functions naturally spent more.[38]

Another long-term process involves white ethnic politics, which is captured in the model by the percentage of Irish residents. After the late nineteenth century cities with numerous immigrant residents, especially the Irish, developed political organizations that expanded local government by providing jobs to needy persons.[39] Overt patronage by Irish political leaders dropped off by the late 1970s, but the cumulative effects of past policies were still clear in 1977.

Powerful mayors who campaigned for more spending in 1967 increased spending in the late 1960s and early 1970s. Their effects were still visible in the 1977 levels, indicating that their legacy, like that of the Irish, lives on in the fiscal record. By contrast, the 1976 leadership measure was unrelated to either changes in expenditures from period to period or to 1977 levels, again documenting 1974–77 as a period with political leaders who acted as brokers rather than as dynamic individuals.

Summary and Conclusion

Municipal fiscal policies and socioeconomic characteristics are distinct. Conceptions like "declining Northeast cities" and "Sun Belt cities" should be used cautiously. Such characteristics as region, population size, population change, and city age are only loosely correlated. Population change in particular has been used as an urban distress indicator; it is better treated as one more socioeconomic resource. Population decline became salient only in the mid-1970s, and it was sufficiently new that some reactions were

37. Most past studies have confused effects of the two variables. See Roy Bahl, Marvin Johnson, and Michael Wasylenko, "State and Local Government Expenditure Determinants: The Traditional View and a New Approach," in Roy Bahl, Jesse Burkhead, and Bernard Jump, Jr., eds., *Public Employment and State and Local Government Finance* (Ballinger, 1980), pp. 65–119. Our findings more generally underline the importance of distinguishing fiscal capacity from taste measures, sometimes recognized but not always respected in this research tradition.

38. This is not per se substantively meaningful, but including the functional performance index helps remove its effects from other variables in the model.

39. Terry N. Clark, "The Irish Ethic and the Spirit of Patronage," *Ethnicity*, vol. 2 (1975), pp. 305–59.

extreme, often based on projections of untoward effects if decline continued too far (like the title of a talk show, "Is Chicago Dying?"). The view that population loss is bad has since lost ground; it is neither inherently good nor bad, but offers opportunities to do things differently. City governments have substantially differed in their reactions to population loss and changes in other social and economic resources. Widespread beliefs to the contrary, fiscal policy changes by city governments over the 1960s and 1970s were only weakly related to most socioeconomic resources.

Such resources are just one of four elements important to explain fiscal strain. The others are preferences of citizens, organized group activities, and policy preferences of political leaders. The processes differ among three time periods. In 1960–70 preferences of citizen voting blocs explained fiscal policy changes for many cities. But in the late 1960s and early 1970s, organized groups and dynamic political leaders were driving forces behind spending increases, while voting bloc preferences became a negligible factor. In 1974–77, a time of retrenchment, cuts in expenditure levels were not explained by declining socioeconomic resources, poverty, intergovernmental grant cutbacks, conservative business leaders, municipal employees, or political leaders. Instead, voters were the driving force; the taxpayers' revolt was just that. New, fiscally conservative leaders were elected in cities as diverse as San Diego and New York. Such leaders reduced spending and debt in many cities. Finally, in considering 1977 per capita levels of spending and debt, longer-term patterns grow more important. In particular, private wealth becomes significant: wealthy cities spend more.

Over a long period private resources like wealth do affect the level of spending and debt of city governments. But in the important period from 1960 to 1977, a multicausal analysis shows that such resources had no significant effects on fiscal policy changes. My results differ from many earlier studies that suggest that socioeconomic resources explain urban fiscal problems. The differences derive from my inclusion of measures of important political processes and my analysis of both levels and changes in separate time periods.

In the short term, political leaders are primarily affected by other leaders and organized groups who monitor policies closely. Over a period of four years or so, however, preferences of voting blocs can shift leaders' policies substantially. It is often longer still before constraints of population, income, and taxable property affect fiscal policy. These are overall patterns for the sample cities from 1960 to 1977. Some cities clearly adapted rapidly to various constraints, as may others in the future. Social and economic resources constrain options, but the direct sources of policy, good or bad, are leaders themselves.

There are numerous policies that cities can adopt to ease fiscal strain without total reliance on federal assistance. Certainly cities would benefit from a strengthened national economy and from simplification of federal and state regulations and grant programs, but the best way to satisfy the demands of local citizens for both low taxes and good services is to improve productivity in city government. Many city governments are seriously pursuing productivity options by means of performance indicators, data about the cost of services, productivity teams, and applied common sense. Inefficient and overstaffed city governments are particularly open to improvement, but cities of all sorts have found ways to improve productivity.[40]

40. My recommendations for addressing urban fiscal problems in specific contexts are found in U.S. Conference of Mayors, *Issues in Financial Management of Local Governments* (Washington, D.C.: U.S. Conference of Mayors, 1981), and *A Mayor's Financial Management Handbook* (Washington, D.C.: U.S. Conference of Mayors, 1982), both developed for use in workshops with mayors.

ANTHONY DOWNS

The Future of Industrial Cities

ONE of America's most perplexing but important urban problems concerns the future of large, older U.S. cities containing sizable minority populations, especially blacks. The total populations of nearly all such cities have been falling for decades, although the minority populations of most have steadily risen. Of the twenty-five largest U.S. cities in 1980, fourteen lost population between 1970 and 1980. In those fourteen cities, the average share of blacks was 34.4 percent, compared with 22.5 percent in all central cities combined. These cities also have relatively high unemployment rates, partly because so many minority residents are unskilled. Yet the economies of these and other central cities are undergoing major technical transformations that may make them even less able to employ unskilled residents.

This essay examines certain key aspects of the future of such cities, using Chicago as an example. In it, I try to confront the implications for that future raised by the other essays in this volume.

Recent Trends Concerning All Large American Cities

The future of these cities will be heavily influenced by the major trends affecting *all* large U.S. cities. My colleagues and I have analyzed the key factors associated with both the growth and decline of population, employment, and real incomes in the 121 largest cities and their standard metropolitan statistical areas (SMSAs).[1] We also analyzed the factors that

1. Katharine L. Bradbury, Anthony Downs, and Kenneth A. Small, *Urban Decline and the Future of American Cities* (Brookings, 1982).

caused these cities to grow or decline relative to their suburbs. The data in that study were taken from the two periods 1960–70 and 1970–75, though Katharine Bradbury has also updated some of the findings with data from the 1980 census.[2]

Of the 121 cities that were the largest in their respective SMSAs in 1970, 44 grew in population and number of households from 1970 to 1975, 43 lost population but gained in number of households (a condition we called stagnation), and 34 lost both population and households (severe decline). Over the entire decade from 1970 to 1980, of 153 cities with over 100,000 population in 1980, 63 gained in population and 90 lost; so the dominance of losers over gainers was continued in the second half of the decade. Yet these numbers illustrate the tremendous diversity of conditions prevalent in America's large cities. Such diversity makes it difficult to generalize about their futures. Nevertheless, we drew some major conclusions.

Our statistical analysis of past city population growth showed significant relationships between faster growth and (1) SMSA population growth, (2) SMSA employment growth, (3) mean January temperature (warmer weather was associated with faster growth), (4) a small number of separate suburban jurisdictions, (5) a high percentage of Hispanics in the city or SMSA, and (6) a city public school district extending out beyond the city's boundaries. Cities also grew faster in relation to their suburbs if city-suburban differences were small concerning (1) the percentage of older housing in each area, (2) the percentage of blacks, and (3) local property tax rates. In all cases, opposite conditions caused slow city growth or actual decline.

Our analysis revealed that several basic societywide forces had long been contributing to declining population in nearly all large U.S. cities, though those forces were offset by other factors in growing cities. The forces involved included rising real incomes, widespread preferences for low-density living, increased use of automobiles, massive construction of new housing in the suburbs (as Brian Berry shows in his essay), falling fertility rates, lower migration from farms to cities, and new technologies of production and distribution requiring low densities. Most people consider most of these factors either quite desirable or unalterable. Thus big-city population losses were the obverse side of a process that upgraded living conditions for the vast majority of urban households.

Also associated with urban decline were past biases in federal policies

2. Katharine L. Bradbury, "Urban Decline and Distress: An Update," *New England Economic Review* (July–August 1984), pp. 39–55.

that favored new suburbs over older cities (although those biases were not sufficient to fully account for urban decline). A final factor of importance was the desire of a majority of urban citizens to segregate themselves from other people who were either socioeconomically or racially different from themselves. This desire helps explain why so many poor urban households became concentrated in older inner-city neighborhoods, distant from most middle- and upper-income urban households.

Is Severe Decline Reversible in the Near Future?

My colleagues and I concluded that severe urban decline, which occurs mainly in cities in the northeast and north central regions, is probably irreversible in the near future. To test this conclusion, we simulated adoption of several large-scale antidecline programs in the Cleveland SMSA.[3] These included creating more jobs, rehabilitating housing, improving transportation, merging the city and county governments fiscally, and deliberately restraining suburban growth. We also tested large-scale expansion of federal welfare payments. These tactics slowed but did not halt the losses of jobs and people that the city of Cleveland would otherwise have experienced. However, actual adoption of such strong antidecline policies is not likely because of their high costs and powerful political resistance to some of them.

Moreover, higher energy costs will also not reverse or even stop urban decline, as Kenneth Small proves in his essay. In fact, higher energy costs increase the regional advantage of energy-exporting areas like Texas and Louisiana, because such areas can use revenues from taxes on energy to reduce their other taxes. This might accelerate the already-strong migration into the South and West. Higher capital costs of new housing may actually exert a stronger impact in slowing decline, because they make new suburban housing more expensive relative to older inner-city housing. But even that impact will not stop further declines in population, households, and jobs in many severely declining cities.[4]

In spite of this seemingly pessimistic conclusion, there are also many

3. Katharine L. Bradbury, Anthony Downs, and Kenneth A. Small, *Futures for a Declining City: Simulations for the Cleveland Area* (Academic Press, 1981).

4. The many effects of higher energy costs upon future urban development, housing, and regional growth disparities are explored in Anthony Downs and Katharine L. Bradbury, eds., *Energy Costs, Urban Development, and Housing* (Brookings, 1983).

positive elements in the futures of large U.S. cities, including those in
severe decline. Office space and service jobs will grow, especially in
downtown areas. Many more older residential neighborhoods will be
renovated than in the past. Slowed in-migration of the poor will also provide
greater chances for neighborhood stability to develop.

Unfortunately, the conservative belief that more vigorous private economic growth can solve city problems is false. City unemployment and
poverty rates were very high in the late 1960s, especially among minorities,
even when overall unemployment rates were as low as 3 percent. Most of
the reduction in urban poverty populations since 1959 has resulted from
larger government transfer payments and in-kind services, not from greater
private prosperity.

Also, improving city economies in general and hoping the benefits will
"trickle down" to those people who are presently destitute or unemployed
will not work. To aid such people, policies and programs must aim benefits
directly at them. We believe such aids should consist of directly empowering
individuals and households in something like voucher programs for jobs,
schools, transportation, and housing. That would be better than using
traditional bureaucratic channels.

This conclusion is supported by Terry Clark's analysis of city fiscal
problems. He showed that city governments get into fiscal difficulties
mainly because of their own spending and taxing policies, not because
their cities contain unusually high percentages of poor households. Hence
public policy should not reward those city governments for their fiscal
profligacy, but focus benefits directly upon the citizens who need them
most.

The Double Transformation of Big Cities with Large
Minority Populations

Another set of implications about the futures of big cities with large
minority populations can be derived from several of the essays in this
volume by looking at those essays with a perspective slightly different
from the viewpoints of their authors. The total populations of such cities
are falling, but their minority populations are growing and often form a
majority of their citizens. Among the large U.S. cities that probably have
minority populations as a majority of their residents as of 1984 are Chicago,
Philadelphia, Detroit, Baltimore, Atlanta, Washington, New Orleans,

Birmingham, Gary, Newark, Richmond, Oakland, St. Louis, San Antonio, Memphis, Miami, and Savannah. Most of these cities are undergoing two simultaneous transformations, as described by John Kasarda. These transformations are creating a serious mismatch between the job opportunities available in these cities and the capabilities of many of their residents. This mismatch is likely to increase future economic dependency among big-city populations, thereby weakening their economies.

The first transformation is a technical and functional one from production and distribution activities, including manufacturing, to information industries, research, administration, and other services, many highly technological in nature. Many of the new jobs created by these activities require much greater skills than older ones did. In fact, the number of low-skill jobs in these cities is falling. This transformation also creates many jobs that could easily be decentralized to sites outside the cities through electronic means. But there may be a growing need for continued face-to-face contacts to permit discourses among specialists. An example is the contacts between lawyers and accountants and their clients. Both lawyers and accountants use languages that are largely incomprehensible to mere humans—including their clients. To make communication possible, it is of great value to be able to have in-person discussions where facial expressions, hand gestures, and other supplementary means of communication are used. If such contacts are still necessary on a large scale, cities—especially their downtowns—will have growing economic functions.

The second transformation these cities are experiencing is a demographic one from white to minority group populations, mainly poor and unskilled. Whites are leaving many big cities in massive numbers, Hispanics are entering in large numbers, and the number of blacks already there is expanding through high birthrates. This transformation is occurring in part because of the white majority's deliberate policy of segregating itself from both poor and nonpoor minority group members. Such segregation is most evident in housing and schools, where it operates by excluding nearly all poor households and most minority households from new suburban areas. Segregation is less evident in workplaces, although residential segregation also produces massive racial separation of jobs.

As a result, many minority group members live in areas that provide a much lower quality of life in every respect than that enjoyed by most whites. Confronted by a triple handicap of shrinking job opportunities, poor education, and low-quality neighborhoods, these minority citizens are caught in a situation from which there appears to be no escape. They are increasingly driven to being supported by public welfare programs. As a result, much of the social structure of the black community is disintegrating, and a permanent underclass appears to be developing.

This same undesirable result could happen to many city Hispanics in the future, according to William Julius Wilson's analysis. He believes this social disruption has been caused mainly by the sheer size of both the absolute increase in young minority group members in cities and the sustained minority in-migration into them. Constant inflows of poor newcomers undercut the entire community's ability to upgrade itself. Since black in-migration into big cities has stopped, family structures and other capabilities may improve for blacks in the near future. But Hispanic migration is growing, so these conditions may worsen for Hispanics.

I am rather skeptical concerning the importance Wilson attaches to the end of in-migration as a source of future stability in the black community. After all, black inflows into most U.S. cities essentially stopped around 1965. Yet many adverse social conditions among blacks, such as crime and illegitimacy rates, have greatly intensified in the twenty years since then.

The growing mismatch between jobs and capabilities in these cities means they will need increasing amounts of federal transfer payments to keep up elementary public services, as well as to cope with greater dependency. This is true in spite of widespread national sentiment for reducing the role of both the federal government and local governments in social programs.

The Role of Political Forces in the Transformation

Another key point emerging from the papers in this volume is that the double transformation occurring in large cities is not solely economic in nature. It also has major political causes. Attributing basic urban changes largely to the "natural" operation of "free market forces" is popular today, but it is not realistic. True, the loss of jobs and the shift of most new investments in plant and equipment from cities to suburbs and nonmetropolitan areas was caused by a combination of technological and basic economic forces that probably would have been strong in any event. But public policies also encouraged that shift. The decisionmaking process dominating economic policies was a centralized one in which national policies overrode local forces, partly to enhance the influence of business.

When many big cities began to suffer losses of jobs and taxable resources, political pressure arose for some type of compensating aid. It could have consisted of attempts to redirect jobs back into cities. But that would have been swimming against the tide of dominant major technological and social forces. So this aid instead took the form of redistributing financial resources to cities from elsewhere and within cities from more to less affluent citizens.

But city and local governments themselves cannot engage in effectively redistributing incomes. If they try, the businesses and affluent citizens taxed at high rates in order to aid the poor will move elsewhere, as New York City discovered to its sorrow. Hence it was necessary for funding of these compensatory programs to be at the federal level, even though their administration was often local (as in block grant programs). Such arrangements reached their peak in the 1960s and early 1970s, when hundreds of federal programs put money directly into cities, partly in response to the racial riots of the late 1960s. Over 40 percent of the expenditures of large cities were financed by intergovernmental transfer payments.[5]

This compensatory arrangement was developed by the Democratic party, which needed the votes of big-city residents. But migration shifting more people south and west, the aging of the baby boom generation, and slower economic growth all led to greater conservatism in the nation generally. When Ronald Reagan was first elected president, one of his central goals was dismantling these mechanisms for redistributing income to the poor and the big cities. He proposed to do so both by cutting domestic spending generally and by restructuring many programs so their financing would be transferred to the state and local levels. If these programs were to be so restructured, they could no longer effectively redistribute incomes, as explained above. Also, regional resource inequalities would be perpetuated. If these structural changes were to pass, big cities would have to reduce their services. Their ability to cope with the poor people society has concentrated within their borders would therefore fall as well.

Possible Remedies for the Adverse Effects

What remedies to these rather staggering problems have been proposed by the authors of the essays in this volume? Gary Orfield advocates greater racial integration of society as the best basic strategy. He proposes met-

5. U.S. Bureau of the Census, *Statistical Abstract of the United States, 1978* (Government Printing Office, 1978), p. 311.

ropolitan-area school desegregation and aggressive fair housing enforcement in suburban areas. This strategy would require a concerted effort by all metropolitan-area leaders aimed explicitly at such integration.

William Wilson proposes a massive program of public spending aimed at creating jobs and improving conditions generally in big-city ghettos. He admits that prevailing sentiments are against government spending. But he denies that those sentiments are grounded in an accurate analysis of the causes of the nation's economic problems. This enrichment strategy essentially declares that the nation must politically defeat the current program of urban austerity. Such a strategy advocates continuing major federal spending in cities to compensate them for declining jobs and resources.

John Kasarda proposes both suburban integration like that espoused by Orfield and building a dynamic core area of housing, electronically "wired" office space, tourist and convention attractions, and other elements in and around big-city downtowns. I call this a strategy of suburban and core-area integration and development. It is designed in part to take advantage of the big-city technical transformation described above by creating more jobs using the emerging technologies and urban relationships.

In 1968 the National Advisory Commission on Civil Disorders (the Kerner Commission) analyzed these problems in a similar way as part of its study of the causes of racial riots in major U.S. cities. It also proposed similar remedies. Its final report advanced three possible strategies: a "present policies" strategy of continued segregation and poverty for minorities, a strategy of "ghetto enrichment" through major federal spending but with no basic change in racial segregation, and a strategy of "combined racial integration and ghetto enrichment." It castigated the first approach as likely to perpetuate two racially separate and unequal societies. It thought the second approach was better, but rejected it too. The commission believed that even ghetto enrichment could not produce true equality of opportunity so long as blacks were spatially segregated from whites. Hence its members unanimously recommended the third approach combining integration and ghetto enrichment.[6]

But in the seventeen years since 1968, American society instead has followed a strategy of mild ghetto enrichment. That strategy has consisted of bigger government transfers and subsidies to both individuals and city governments, plus continued racial segregation. The Reagan administration

6. National Advisory Commission on Civil Disorders, *Report* (GPO, March 1968), pp. 215–26.

has proposed cutting expenditures on enrichment. Hence it is essentially recommending a return to the first strategy of continuing both segregation and serious poverty for minorities. In fact, the number of poor persons in U.S. cities has risen significantly in the past few years, especially in households headed by black females. Yet this strategy of both segregation and continued poverty was the one that the Kerner Commission unanimously rejected as the worst possible alternative for America.

Some Realistic Conclusions

Upon considering the foregoing description of big-city problems and proposed remedies, what conclusions can be drawn if one is willing to confront the facts honestly? The first conclusion is that the white-dominated U.S. society has clearly chosen to create and maintain two racially separate and unequal societies, as the Kerner Commission feared it might. In spite of all pious statements to the contrary, the leaders and citizens of nearly all parts of U.S. society have no intention whatever of changing that deliberate policy.

This strategy is based upon two principles espoused by the white majority. One is: "Don't let minority groups live near us or go to our schools." That means spatial segregation. True, individual black households and other minority households can much more easily move into all-white suburban areas than ever before, if they have high enough incomes. But once any large number enter any suburban area, it begins to become segregated too, mainly because additional whites stop moving in to replace those that leave through normal turnover. The second principle is: "Don't waste public funds on social programs that don't work." That means society should not try to help those now isolated in low-quality communities to improve the inferior opportunities they now receive.

This principle is not accompanied by any strong proof that specific social and economic programs are not effective. Instead, repeated declarations by Reagan administration officials and other critics that "government social programs have failed" are taken as sufficient proof to justify major program cutbacks. Of course, many cutbacks are legitimate, either because the programs concerned are indeed ineffective or because general budgetary pressures require spending reductions on programs of relatively low priority, even if they work. Yet such "proof by assertion" is certainly not scientifically valid and is even dead wrong concerning many social programs that were quite successful. But this blanket condemnation has achieved great political persuasiveness because most white Americans want to believe it.

The net result is a social policy that preserves the inequality of opportunities that so blatantly marks most U.S. minority group communities across the nation. The success of this policy in keeping the quality of education in big-city public schools dramatically inferior to that in most suburban schools is the greatest social scandal in America. It is in the economic interests of many white suburban workers to keep city minority groups poorly educated, because that reduces competition for new high-technology jobs. Few people would put this fact so bluntly, even in their own minds. But certainly this factor weakens suburbanites' willingness to tax themselves to help improve big-city public schools or other aspects of life in ghetto areas.

If this conclusion is correct, there is no point in advocating racial integration as the central social strategy for coping with big-city problems. I have argued in favor of racial and economic integration for many years.[7] I still believe this is the best approach in theory, and perhaps marginal progress can be made in pursuing it. But the political leaders of all large metropolitan areas do not have the slightest interest in pursuing this strategy in any meaningful way. This is true both of most white leaders, who want to maintain their basically segregated neighborhoods, and most black leaders, who want to preserve the political power that comes from concentrating minorities within the central city. So devoting scarce political energy and resources to integration must be considered a marginal activity.

Gary Orfield disputes this conclusion. He points out that the Chicago suburbs of Oak Park and Park Forest and the city neighborhood of Hyde Park all made racial integration work. But he does not mention that they did so only when threatened with black inundation and only because they could deflect major black growth somewhere else. There is no chance whatever of getting the vast majority of all-white neighborhoods in the cities or the suburbs truly interested in achieving racial or ethnic integration. These neighborhoods are not now suffering from the worst problems of the big cities. Moreover, their residents do not want to take any chance of starting to do so through integration.

---

7. See Anthony Downs, *Opening Up the Suburbs: An Urban Strategy for America* (Yale University Press, 1973), and Downs, *Racism in America* (U.S. Commission on Civil Rights, 1970).

Future Strategies That Might Benefit Big-City Minorities

If integration is not going to work as a central policy, what strategies should be pursued? First one must ask: for whose benefit? The idea that a metropolitan area, or even a city, is a single entity with clear and unified interests is a myth. There are many different groups in a city and its suburbs, often with interests that directly conflict. The rest of this analysis adopts the viewpoint of Chicago's major minority communities, since they have the biggest problems and the greatest need for government assistance.

Presumably the key goals of minority citizens are to get more jobs, much better schooling, and better neighborhood conditions. They cannot hope to attain equality of either conditions or opportunities with the white majority in the near future. But they can seek to reduce the degree of inequality of opportunity within a segregated context. However, that implies a continuation of government transfer payments from outside the city.

The most obvious strategy for a sizable minority in any big city is to gain political control of the city's government. In early 1983 a black mayor was elected in Chicago. Although he has had difficulty in gaining full control of the city's government, he has been able to provide more city government jobs to minority-group members than they have ever had before. This has also happened in other cities where black or Hispanic mayors have been elected. Minority control of big-city governments also greatly increases the bargaining power of minorities in relation to major property owners who pay taxes, and increases their political power in Congress and the state legislatures. The total political power of cities is falling as they lose population and taxable resources. Nevertheless, the political and economic prize of controlling big-city governments is still a notable one well worth winning for minorities. After all, the Irish and other ethnic groups used city government to advance their welfare for decades in many big cities. So why shouldn't blacks and Hispanics follow the same route?

True, a majority of a big city's population is not the same as a majority of its eligible voters. So blacks and Hispanics need to win the support of many white voters, or split the latter's vote, before they can control the governments of big cities in which they constitute bare majorities of the total population. That is what happened in Chicago, where the presence of two popular white candidates on the ticket split the white vote and allowed Mayor Harold Washington to win. In many big cities key minorities need to overcome their own fragmentation into conflicting groups and their deliberate cooptation by the white politicians who have long dominated local politics before they can fully control their local governments.

This raises a key point that any white person hesitates to mention. Big-city minority communities need to exercise a lot more internal leadership and discipline than most of them have shown up to now, both politically and socially. This is not to downplay the role of external forces in creating minority group deprivation. But elements of any solution must come from within minority communities themselves, just as happened with other ethnic groups in the past. In particular, the frequent characterization of blacks and Hispanics as victims of larger social forces must not lull them into abandoning vigorous efforts to help themselves advance. However accurate that characterization may be, it must be accompanied by recognition that self-help efforts can make a huge difference in the welfare of both groups and individuals in a relatively open society. This fact has been strikingly demonstrated by many recent immigrants from Southeast Asia.

Politically, minority groups need allies within the city to improve their situation. The best natural allies are those who stand to lose most if the minority community cannot produce competent workers. That means businesses locked into the city itself, such as downtown property owners, nonbranching banks, or newspapers. They might support more ghetto enrichment as a quid pro quo for further integrated core development benefiting them.

The minority community should consider three other tactics. One is constantly emphasizing that spending more on educating minority group children is investing in the city's future, not just aiding the poor. Non-minority voters may be willing to support such investments for economic reasons, even if they are opposed to any increases in what they regard as welfare programs. A second tactic would be launching a series of nonviolent demonstrations in white areas and schools about the poor quality of minority schools. These demonstrations would resemble the civil rights protests of the 1960s. A third tactic is trying to shake up the public school bureaucracy itself. This might be through limited use of vouchers on an experimental basis to support competition with existing public schools. There must be radical change within big-city public school systems if they are effectively to meet even the minimal needs of urban blacks and Hispanics.

Moreover, it would be enlightening for the white leadership of metropolitan areas, including most of the lawyers and business leaders, to think long and hard about a city's future from the viewpoint of the city's minority community. Chicago's former mayor, Jane Byrne, did so symbolically when she moved into the Cabrini-Green public housing project for a short while. But the private-sector leadership of Chicago needs to do so in a more sustained and meaningful way. Perhaps the election of a black mayor will stimulate their considering such a perspective more seriously. For these leaders to do this is especially crucial because major social changes in this democracy almost always start with initiatives either from the citizens or from private-sector leaders. Such changes are almost never begun by government officials or politicians, who in the U.S. system are essentially reactors.

Conclusions

The policy of white Americans of sustaining separate but unequal societies for blacks, Hispanics, and certain other minorities exists throughout the nation, but especially in its big cities. Yet America's overall future will to a surprising degree be determined by the future of its minority citizens. In 1980 one out of every four American children under the age of 15 was black or Hispanic, even though the total population consisted of only about 18 percent blacks and Hispanics. In the bellwether state of California, more than 40 percent of the total population in 1980 consisted of blacks, Hispanics, Orientals, and members of other minority groups. If current rates of population growth for specific ethnic groups are unchanged, within two generations, or about sixty years, most U.S. children could be black, Hispanic, or Oriental. And when the U.S. celebrates its tricentennial in 2076, non-Hispanic whites may be a minority.

My conclusion that prospects for true equality of opportunity for Americans of all ethnic backgrounds are bad and will probably not improve much in the near future may seem terribly pessimistic. However, these are the realities that have existed in this country for over 300 years. After all, the goal of racial equality under law has been an official, legally recognized social aspiration for less than three decades. During that period, this society has almost certainly moved closer to true equality of opportunity among all racial and ethnic groups than ever before—even though it is still tremendously distant from achieving that goal.

True, the double transformation of many large cities described in this volume is moving those cities in the wrong direction. But the big inflow of poor blacks to those cities has stopped, and perhaps William Wilson is right in hoping that cessation will create better conditions in black urban communities.

In any event, I do not believe in pessimism. Instead I believe in continuing to try to improve conditions, no matter what the odds. The pursuit of that belief is what created this country, what brought it to adopt the concept of racial equality under law as its standard, and what will eventually make that concept a reality—perhaps in an America where minorities have become the majority. That is a hopeful conclusion, because hope is a great virtue. But hope is a virtue precisely when it goes beyond a purely rational response to the visible facts. Realism in assessing the situation, but hope surpassing realism when trying to influence policy and launch remedial actions: that is where the best future for America's large cities lies.

Index